STRICTLY
ENGLISH

STRICTLY ENGLISH

The correct way to write ...
and why it matters

Simon Heffer

BOOKS

Published by Random House Books 2010
10 9

Copyright © Simon Heffer 2010

Simon Heffer has asserted his right under the Copyright, Designs
and Patents Act, 1988, to be identified as the author of this work

First published in Great Britain in 2010 by
Random House Books
Random House, 20 Vauxhall Bridge Road,
London SW1V 2SA

www.rbooks.co.uk

Addresses for companies within The Random House Group Limited can be found at: www.
randomhouse.co.uk/offices.htm

The Random House Group Limited Reg. No. 954009

A CIP catalogue record for this book
is available from the British Library

ISBN 9781847946300 (Hardback edition)

The Random House Group Limited supports The Forest Stewardship
Council (FSC), the leading international forest certification organisation. All our
titles that are printed on Greenpeace approved FSC certified paper carry the FSC logo. Our paper
procurement policy can be found at www.rbooks.co.uk/environment

Mixed Sources
Product group from well-managed
forests and other controlled sources
www.fsc.org   Cert no. TT-COC-2139
© 1996 Forest Stewardship Council

Designed and typeset by
Dinah Drazin

Printed and bound in Great Britain by
Clays Ltd, St Ives PLC

Excerpt from *No Fond Return of Love* © Barbara Pym 1961, reproduced by kind permission of
Virago Press, an imprint of Little, Brown Book Group.
Excerpt from *Such, Such Were the Joys* by George Orwell (copyright © George Orwell), reprinted by
permission of Bill Hamilton as the Literary Executor of the Estate of the
Late Sonia Brownell Orwell and Secker & Warburg Ltd.

Contents

Moi, je crois que la grammaire, c'est une voie d'accès à la beauté. Quand on parle, quand on lit ou quand on écrit, on sent bien si on a fait une belle phrase ou si on est en train d'en lire une. On est capable de reconnaître une belle tournure ou un beau style. Mais quand on fait de la grammaire, on a accès à une autre dimension de la beauté de la langue.

Muriel Barbery, *L'élégance du hérisson* (2006)

And lay my prayer book at my head,
And my grammar at my feet,
That all my school fellows as they pass by
May read them for my sake.

Little Sir Hugh, from *Jamieson's Popular Ballads* (1783)

The science of speaking correctly; the art which teaches the relations of words to each other.

Definition of "Grammar", from *A Dictionary of the English Language*, by Dr Samuel Johnson (1785)

To Bryony, Nessyah, Harry, Lizzie and Jim,
my Godchildren

Acknowledgements

This book was the idea of Nigel Wilcockson, my publisher at Random House, who had been shown one of the regular emails I send to colleagues at *The Daily Telegraph* pointing out errors in the use of English in the paper. I thank him not merely for his initiative, but for his thoughtful and perceptive support during the process of my writing this book and preparing it for publication. In particular, he suggested a restructuring of my original manuscript that has greatly improved the comprehensibility of my argument. Richard Brookes thought of the title.

I am especially grateful too to Murdoch MacLennan, Chief Executive of Telegraph Media Group Ltd, for granting me the sabbatical from my duties as Associate Editor of *The Daily Telegraph* in which I was able to complete this book; and to the Master and Fellows of Corpus Christi College, Cambridge, my *alma mater*, who very generously agreed to my becoming a Fellow Commoner of the College for a year and provided me with the warm hospitality and stimulation without which my sabbatical would have been infinitely less attractive and productive. I must also thank Lord Howard of Rising, the chairman of the trustees of the Literary Trust of the late J Enoch Powell, for giving me permission to quote in full one of Powell's articles.

Having been given responsibility for editorial standards at a great newspaper, and charged with undertaking the whole-sale revision of its style book, I found my mind being focused intently on the question of how we use English today. My colleague Emma Hartley, who assisted me in that revision, helped shape my thinking: as did Richard Preston, Christopher Howse, Jeff Randall and Bob Williams. Robert Colvile did me the invaluable service of reading the manuscript and detected errors and ambiguities from which he has saved me; Sally Chatterton read the proofs and found more errors; those that remain are my fault alone. The manuscript was copy-edited superbly by Ros Fergusson, who improved it greatly.

Sarah Cain and Sir Alistair Horne both provided material to me that was useful in the preparation of this book. I must also pay sincere tribute to the great grammarians of the last century or so – H W and F G Fowler, Otto Jespersen, C T Onions and Eric Partridge principal among them – to whose works I refer throughout my own book, and who, I hope, would concede that certain developments have taken place in our language that require a book such as this to be written today to supplement their own endeavours. I have a similar debt to the editors of the *Oxford English Dictionary*, without which no sensible book on the use of English would be possible.

My agent, Georgina Capel, has overseen this process with her customary professionalism, commitment and enthusiasm, for which I thank her. The greatest thanks of all must go to my beloved wife and children, who not only provided the life-support system essential to an author, but also endured with fortitude and cheerfulness their widowhood and orphandom while I was writing this book. My wife also read the proofs with an alarming level of scrutiny that put my own abilities in the shade, for which I especially thank her.

Simon Heffer
Great Leighs
15 June 2010

Preliminary notes

A word about sex

I have no desire to complicate what follows any more than may be necessary. One inevitable complication, however, is gender. I am an equal opportunity writer. This book is for everyone: women, men, girls and boys. As I discuss later, though, one of the glaring deficiencies of the English tongue is that we have no single pronoun to cover the phrases *he-or-she*, *him-or-her* and *his-or-her*. An attempt has been made in the last century or so to fill this void with *they*, *them* and *their*. I regard that as abominable and want no part of it. I know why it happens: we live in an age of equality and it is natural for writers not to wish to cause offence to one gender or the other by using a specific pronoun that excludes one half of the human race. So one reads sentences such as "every writer likes to ensure that their command of the language is of the highest order". One will not, however, read them in this book. I adopt the old rule that "the masculine will be taken to include the feminine wherever necessary". This implies no offence to my women readers. It implies my desire to avoid the tedious verbosity of sentences such as "every writer likes to ensure that his or her command of the language…", and also to avoid the solecism already outlined. So when you read "every writer likes to ensure that his command of the language…" please be assured that I am thinking of Jane Austen, George Eliot, Virginia Woolf and Barbara Pym as much as I am of anyone else.

xiii

Getting technical

Occasionally in this book I shall use terms that describe rhetorical devices that one uses in everyday speech or writing, often without realising one is using them, but usually being conscious of their effects. Many readers will know some of them; others may be glad to find what a certain device or form of usage is properly called. I do not wish to give the impression that what follows in the next nine chapters is especially technical or recondite: it is not. However, people who wish to use the language to a reasonable degree of sophistication may come across these terms in other writings on language or usage as well as in this book. Therefore I have thought it prudent to include a glossary detailing exactly what they mean. It will be found on pages 302–306.

Prologue
Can English be good?

The question is not rhetorical. Those who study language scientifically often believe that language is what it is. There are no rights and wrongs: all departures from a generally-accepted norm are interesting and viable in themselves. The idea of a "norm" is itself sometimes viewed as artificial. The weight of custom and practice makes it no more "normal" than any other form of usage. With the ease of mass communication in the early 21st century, not least because of the internet, a global language such as English will mutate more rapidly than ever before, with various forms of it demanding recognition as legitimate. Beauty is no longer even in the eye of the beholder; as such people see it, "good" and "bad" are not judgements that any of us has the right to make about the use of English.

There is, however, a non-academic view of this question that is concerned with the use of English in everyday life. Whether the linguistics experts like it or not, there remains an idea of "standard English" as it is spoken in Britain; there are different but related standards in other countries where English is the principal or a principal language, notably in America, but also in Australia, India and the Far East. These standards are set by an educated class within those communities: and those who wish to be included, or to consider themselves included, in that class must subscribe to the rules. In Britain, most serious newspapers and editors who work for book publishers continue to conform to the national, educated standard. So, at least in its serious programming, does the BBC, the state broadcaster; and other networks in their news and documentary output make an attempt to do so. Conformity with the local standard is usual in other Anglophone countries in their publications and in mainstream broadcasting. In some cases this standard is quite unlike British English: in an Australian newspaper one will often read, in a report of an assault, that the victim has been "bashed"; a slang word in British English, but normal usage in Australian. The reverse is seen in educated speech in India: the standard of writing on a newspaper such as *The Times of India* is of a strictness and formality hardly seen in the British quality press since the 1950s or 1960s, and is intensely refreshing in its conservatism and purity.

Standard English (however, sometimes, inexactly understood) is also a measure that certain of us impose upon others – those applying for a job, for example, or seeking other favours. It is a fact that people are judged by how they speak and write, however offensive or unfair that may seem to some. This is partly the legacy of a popular grammatical movement in the late 19th and early 20th centuries whose textbooks remain on the shelves of many professional writers to this day. It is also because of the British trait of looking down upon people whom we consider less educated than we are: for a grammatically precise command of English and an ability to choose words correctly have long been considered by many to be the mark of an educated person. Millions of English speakers believe there is such a thing as good English, and aspire to write it and speak it. That you agree with this contention, or feel you might be persuaded to agree, is perhaps why you are reading this book. Few Britons in recent decades will have learned the standard in schools. As a result, they cannot use the precision tool of our language to its full capabilities. This book should help its readers develop, or refresh, the skills required to write and speak grammatically correct English and to make the right choice of words when doing so.

Setting a standard

There have been concerted attempts to codify grammar and to agree definitions of words in the last 150 years or so. Thanks to this, a rulebook has been seen to exist by which we may measure something called standard English. The advent of compulsory education in 1870 enabled, in theory, such a standard to be taught. Indeed before that, when only a small proportion of the population had an education, and most Britons were illiterate, there was little need for advice on how to write English properly. Those who could write had been to the old public or grammar schools, in which Latin and Greek dominated the curriculum. They therefore grew up understanding (in some degree or other) the mechanics of language: for there is no better way of doing so than by studying one that is not one's mother tongue; and, having had the rudiments of classical grammar thrashed into them from the age of seven or eight, they supposedly knew how to apply them to English. "Grammar", wrote Professor Otto Jespersen (1860–1943), the Danish expert on English, "deals with the structure of languages."[1] However, like all structures, this one may be weakened or even collapse if not formed correctly. If undermined, it may not serve the purpose for which it was intended, or at any rate may not serve it so well as it should.

This book seeks to describe something that may be regarded as "good English" by those who hanker after such a notion. Good English will be seen to require logical grammar and a thoughtful choice of words, used in a clear and comprehensible style. My temerity in suggesting such a thing rests on my belief that there has been sufficient codification of words and grammar to make such

---

1. *Essentials of English Grammar*, by Otto Jespersen (George Allen and Unwin, 1933), p15.

an idea feasible. However, my mind is open on certain questions: notably that change may always be justified if it improves clarity, reduces ambiguity and does not violate logic. Some contemporary linguists talk about the "evidence" of how English is spoken and written as being the map by which the rest of us should proceed. They are entitled to their opinion, but should accept that their view is of limited use outside academic circles. It certainly would not help someone who wishes to, or has to, communicate for a living; or (more to the point) in order to secure a living.

As a professional writer, I happen to believe that the "evidence" of how I see English written by others, including some other professional writers, is not something by which I wish to be influenced. This is not because it is not to my taste: it is because in some degree it is, by the codified usage that seems sensible to me, wrong. The "evidence" is sometimes founded on the choice of the wrong word; the use of faulty grammatical constructions; and an absence of logic. So long as people are comprehensible to others they may write or speak as they choose. This book is designed for those who wish to ensure that they are speaking or writing the language in accordance with the widely understood, and accepted, rules of grammar; that they are choosing words according to their correct meaning; and that their usages are logical.

A presumption

There have been events in the last century-and-a-half that have helped those who wish to argue that, while English can never be fixed, the time is more propitious than ever for it to make a claim to being reasonably settled. This is a dangerous sentiment: others have tried in the past to argue that widespread change is unnecessary, and have failed. There was such a movement in the early 18th century, described by Jean Aitchison in her book *Language*

Change: Progress or Decay? "Around 1700, English spelling and usage were in a fairly fluid state. Against this background, two powerful social factors combined to convert a normal mild nostalgia for the language of the past into a quasi-religious doctrine. The first was a long-standing admiration for Latin, and the second was powerful class snobbery."[2] Aitchison describes the reverence for Latin, and the belief that its models should (or could) be uniformly applied to English. She also talks of the development, later in the century, of Samuel Johnson's dictionary. Anyone who knows Latin will appreciate its unsuitability as an exact model for English, and the foolishness of trying to make it one; and anyone who has read Dr Johnson will know that some of his definitions were not of the highest etymological purity. Aitchison's point about class is not the leftist kneejerk it may seem: at a time when so few people were educated, but when even completely uneducated people spoke the language, any attempt to regulate that language would inevitably fail.

As Aitchison also points out, not only did English have a questionable lexicographer, but it also had some questionable grammarians, such as Bishop Robert Lowth (1710–83). Lowth was Professor of Poetry at Oxford, and Bishop of St David's, Oxford and London: he turned down the archiepiscopate that had seemed otherwise to be inevitable. In 1762 he published his *Short Introduction to English Grammar*, a work reviled by linguistics scholars today with, it must be said, some reason. Some of the fetishes I shall dismiss in the course of this book – the ban on ending sentences with prepositions, or on using the possessive pronoun *whose* to refer to an inanimate object – originated with Lowth. His idea of English was that it should imitate Latin: but English cannot do that, despite its many points of correspondence. Also Lowth's grammar, like Johnson's dictionary, was aimed at

2. *Language Change: Progress or Decay?*, by Jean Aitchison (Fontana, 1981), p21.

that small and privileged class who could read: it would have no effect on the majority who could not, but who used the language nonetheless. Lowth's prescriptiveness was based on several false assumptions, and it went too far. Yet the desire to regulate and codify was not merely understandable, but also sensible. It merely required a more scientific and practicable basis. In time, more thoughtful grammarians than Lowth would provide it.

By the book

The need for a serious and reliable dictionary was glaringly obvious by the mid-19th century. A group of men connected with the Philological Society, led by Richard Chenevix Trench (1807–86), the Dean of Westminster, agreed in 1858 to pursue the project of a comprehensive dictionary. It was known as the *NED*, short for *A New English Dictionary on Historical Principles*. Trench's career in the church prevented his becoming editor (he would become Archbishop of Dublin in 1864), a post handed over to Herbert Coleridge (1830–61), grandson of the poet. He began the process of finding quotations to support the definitions of words but, after just a year's work, he died. The project stumbled and faltered for some years, its sheer scope intimidating those who engaged in it. It was not until 1878 that the Oxford University Press agreed to take on the project. The first volume was not published until 1888, 30 years after Trench, Coleridge and their friend Frederick Furnivall (1825–1910) had conceived the project. The final volume was not published until 1928, at which point work was already under way on a supplement of new words. The appearance of this authoritative and exhaustive dictionary gave great force to the arguments of those seeking to settle the use of English by codifying what words actually meant. Some of those who had assisted in its compilation, such as the brothers H W and F G Fowler (1858–1933 and 1871–

1918) and Charles Talbut Onions (1873–1965), the grammarian and lexicographer, went on to write English grammars and guides to usage that sought to consolidate the process of codification.

To some people such a process became daily the more necessary. After the 1870 Education Act literacy (or something approaching it) was no longer the preserve of a small educated class. The language ceased to be a dictatorship (albeit one that, as it was gradually codified, had been based on sound intellectual principles and rigid precedents) and became a democracy (albeit one rooted, like most democracies, in sentiment and convenience). The masses not only started to write, but they often wrote badly. Some of their solecisms and catachreses caught on. Educated men from our old universities began to notice the spread of this linguistic corruption. Determined to fight to preserve standards, they began to write their manuals prescribing what was right in English usage. Those who wished to aspire to the highest levels of English bought these books and learned from them. Those who did not continued in their acts of verbal butchery, usually unaware, and certainly unabashed.

Those who made such attempts in the early 20th century – notably the brothers Henry and Frank Fowler, whose manual *The King's English* appeared in 1906 – were prescriptive grammarians. This put them at odds with the main stream of linguistic scholarship, which was descriptive. Professional linguistics scholars of that age went out and documented languages as they were spoken; they were not interested in correcting errors, and certainly in nothing like the reactionary way that people such as the Fowlers did. It is a philosophical point to many linguistics scholars whether a language can, or should, be fixed. To people such as the Fowlers it was nothing of the sort. Books produced by them and their school are rigidly prescriptive: though, usually, the prescriptions are based on logic and precedent rather than on prejudice or what Aitchison and her school might call "snobbery". Even the Fowlers, though, saw that language was changing; and that technological change and other forms of progress would force English and other languages to embrace new words. In our own era, nouns such as *internet*, *iPod*, *blog* and (in an evolved usage) *tweet* and *text*, and verbs such as *google*, *text* and *tweet*, have been minted by force of technological need.

The Fowlers' struggle, and the struggle of others like them, was to seek to make what was often a perfectly good case for resisting new grammar, new spelling or (a hopeless case) new meanings for existing words. Other commentators have taken a different view of why language changes, and why some of these changes must in many instances be resisted. George Orwell, perhaps the finest stylist in English in the 20th century, argued in the late 1940s that our language was declining thanks to "political and economic causes". In his essay *Politics and the English Language* he said he could see English being manipulated by politicians in order to conceal their intentions from the public (a thought he greatly expanded in his novel *1984*). Politicians, as Orwell correctly noted, like to speak in code. Some truths are too harsh in their possible effect on the electorate, and too damaging to politicians, to be communicated directly. Code of this sort also has the advantage of being ambiguous: it can be sensible of different interpretations by different people. Since the task of a writer who is not a politician – such as Orwell, or the author of this book – is to communicate his message to his reader as clearly as possible, obscurity is the enemy. No wonder Orwell was so angered by it, and imputed the worst motives to those who practised it.

Politics and specific policy also, indirectly, distort language. A determination to dilute the teaching of English and of foreign languages in our schools has made recent generations of schoolchildren insensitive to language and particularly to its nuances. There is no serious attempt to teach grammar in most of our schools today, and there has not been for some time. There has been no serious attempt for decades to teach children why words mean what they do, and what certain words actually mean. This neglect has left most of them with nothing but a random (and often erroneous) understanding of the components of language. Literature is taught, even on English courses in our better universities, by means of asking the student to evaluate what an author was or the characters are feeling, and not by inviting students to examine first the words writers use, why they were chosen and what they mean.

Imprecise teaching of English, and a failure to enforce correct usage because of wrong-headed notions about a living language's being allowed to mutate as the majority of its users see fit, are not confined to state schools. Some of the products of our private schools show through their inarticulacy and semi-literacy that the problem is widespread. Good English, therefore, is now something popularly associated with a certain, usually over-privileged, class. In fact, it is not a middle-class trait at all. It is a trait of the far smaller educated class, and this class (by any strict definition of the term) is contracting all the time. There is a theory that the correct use of English is linked to social class, and that to correct mistakes made by children who do not share this imagined background of privilege denies them their right to their own form of self-expression: a form as valid, in the eyes of some, as what is still thought of as "correct" English. Others may feel that the fact a student can obtain a pass at GCSE in English without being able to write the language literately shows that the educational establishment is determined not to believe there can be such a thing as decline in a language, and not to care about the effect that illiteracy and inarticulacy have on those afflicted by them.

The consequences of this attitude are, in fact, far-reaching. Young people apply for jobs, or to take courses in tertiary education, and demonstrate in their letters of application that they cannot speak English properly. Some potential employers and university dons can and often do make negative assumptions about an applicant who shows an inadequate command of the language. When those who have been poorly educated in the language have dealings with those who have not, they may quickly be embarrassed. For anyone who has to communicate with anyone else – not just in the mass media, but even in writing to customers or clients, or writing a letter of application for a job or degree course – that can be highly damaging. This book, if read and absorbed properly, will help such people understand the essence of correct usage and good style. We should understand that some forms of English, in an old, class-ridden society such as ours, inevitably say things about us that we may not want said. The widespread use of slang, incorrect forms and the idioms of the uneducated classes is a badge for those who do so. If, as the old newspaper advertisement used to say, you are "shamed by your English", it can, with practice and application, be put right. It is also the case – and users of this book need to be warned of this too – that those who speak English precisely and well will also be labelled, and not always flatteringly: such is the value today put generally on upholding the highest standards of our language.

If something is worth doing it is, as the cliché has it, worth doing well. Why should language be an exception? Why should we be afraid of excellence and precision? If English is worth speaking or writing, then it is worth speaking or writing well. Good English is not the preserve of an elite: it is available to everyone who wishes to speak it. For that reason, this is not a book that will appeal to or interest the professional scholar of linguistics, whose work is undoubtedly valuable but irrelevant to those who wish to have a guide to how to use a certain tongue accurately and with the maximum clarity of expression. It is a book for people who wish to speak or write English to a high standard of precision and without illogicality or solecisms. While its author recognises the scholarly value of descriptive linguistics, this book is prescriptive;

for it is only by following certain prescriptions that those who wish to speak English correctly will succeed in doing so.

Stop all the clocks?

Yet language does change: read a page of Chaucer, Shakespeare or even Jane Austen or Dickens and compare the writing with what is regarded as the best prose or poetry of our times. Some changes are for the better, and language will continue to change as the necessity arises. New words enter the language all the time because of technological changes, or changes in the experience of those to whom the language belongs: centuries of imperial endeavour brought all sorts of words, from *kiosk* to *curry* and from *wigwam* to *boomerang*, into standard English.

Words also alter their meanings over the centuries. Whole books have been written on this subject: one of the best is C S Lewis's *Studies in Words*, published in 1960 and revised in 1967. Lewis took some of the most common words in the language, including *nature, sad, wit, free* and *sense* and described how their meaning had altered over the centuries. He had no objection to trying to settle the usage of the English language. He wrote that "I should be glad if I sent any reader away with a new sense of responsibility to the language". He rails against "verbicide, the murder of a word", which he describes as happening by inflation (writing *tremendous* where one could as easily have written *great*) and by verbiage, the use of a word that promises but does not deliver: "the use of significant as if it were an absolute, and with no intention of ever telling us what the thing is significant of, is an example". The themes of the inaccurate and illogical choice of words will recur often in the course of this book. So too will one of the other causes of poor usage, the refusal by writers or speakers to focus precisely on what they are attempting to convey through language. As Lewis put it, "most people are obviously far more anxious to express their approval and disapproval of things rather than to describe them. Hence the tendency of words to become less descriptive and more evaluative."[3]

The changes that Lewis referred to here, and in many other instances in his book, could be seen to constitute decay. It is a case of words losing their precise meaning, or of words that convey an exact idea being replaced, gradually, by words that do not. It is one thing to say that a man is handsome or a woman is beautiful; it is quite another to specify exactly why. Yet change is not inevitably synonymous with decay; that our language has, for example, lost many of its inflections, and ceased to function quite as Latin functioned, does not mean it has decayed: it means it has changed. It is as precise a weapon, in the right hands, as it ever was; it would have decayed only if the firing mechanism had ceased to allow that precision. However, its precision does depend upon its users being aware of its capabilities, and knowing how to use them.

Because ours is a living language it is inevitable that certain words will either change their meaning, or change their form from noun to verb, for example, over time: the dictionary (and when I use that term in this book I am referring to the *Oxford English Dictionary*) is full of such examples that are now accepted as good usage. With words that are evolving now there will always be a question of debate, or possibly even of prejudice. Pedants and conservatives will argue that words should stay as they are. They will support this argument by saying that enough words to supply all needs exist in the language as it is, and that corruptions of grammar or bastardisations of existing words are unnecessary and betray ignorance on the part of the writer or speaker. Progressives will argue the contrary: that a living language must change to

3. *Studies in Words*, by C S Lewis (Cambridge University Press, 2nd edition, 1967), pp6–7.

reflect the needs of those who use it, and that expansion and great choice of vocabulary is no bad thing. They can support that argument with reference to exactly what has happened to the English tongue (and to most other languages) during the last thousand years. This is not a question on which it is comfortable to sit firmly on one side or the other.

As I have argued already, the codification of spelling and meaning that comes with a standard dictionary such as the *OED*, and the detailed grammars that settled the framework of English of the sort written by Onions and Jespersen a century or more ago, mean that there are rules, and it is often unnecessary and confusing to break them. Much of what follows in this book is about where sensible rules have been and are still being broken, and how these infractions can be recognised and stopped. I shall attempt to argue these points not from a position of pedantry, but from one of logic. The ideal condition of a language is where it allows communication without ambiguity or confusion. Our language does allow that: it only stops doing so when those who use it break the rules that keep matters unambiguous and free from confusion.

Many of the solecisms identified in this book, whether of words used ungrammatically, or used to mean something they do not, or of faulty grammatical constructions, may be viewed as attempts by a body of users of the language to effect change; just as users of the language have effected change over the centuries. Pedants, conservatives and logicians would contend that such a move for change is motivated by ignorance, not by a desire to reduce ambiguity or confusion. It is certainly not a campaign, but rather an accident. Let me offer some examples. First, the noun *target* has in recent years become a verb; the dictionary finds various usages of this sort for the word since the 1970s. (There was a mediaeval verb *to target*, which the dictionary describes as obsolete, with which the new usage should not be confused.) One can see how and why people have been tempted to adopt this new usage. The first step was the metaphorical use of the noun. For centuries a target was something at which an archer, or a sniper, could aim. Then businesses had targets, abstract ideas of goals that had to be reached in each financial year. Then governments and bureaucracies had them too. Once one has metaphorical targets, one no longer aims at them; one *targets* them. Now all sorts of things are *targeted*. As I discuss in Chapter Eight, the very promiscuity of a popular metaphor warns intelligent writers or speakers to avoid it for risk of being considered boring. That aside, is *target* a legitimate verb? No doubt in 100 years' time it will be, and our descendants will wonder what all the fuss was about: just as we look in the pages of books such as *The King's English* and wonder why its authors became so exercised about the new usages of old words with which we no longer have any quarrel. For the moment, some of us cannot understand why spending cuts need be *targeted* on a specific department of state when they can just as well be aimed or directed there.

Second, consider the slightly different case of an adjective that has a distinct meaning but that is now being given a more widespread one, while remaining an adjective. The dictionary defines *viable* as "capable of living", and therefore a term that should correctly be applied to beings, organisms and plants capable of life. However, it also cites a number of uses of the word since the 1950s in which it is used figuratively "of immaterial things and concepts" (there are two from the 19th century too, but these seem to be consciously rather than unconsciously metaphorical, and it is clear that the writers understood very well the literal meaning of the word). So we hear today that, following an injection of cash, a business will be *viable*; or that a committee has looked at a plan, and it is *viable*. While the metaphorical meaning reflects the literal – the business will continue to "live", the plan will have "life" – one wonders whether those who apply the term in this way understand what its literal meaning is. Widespread metaphorical usages such as this also diminish the force of the literal usage, if that survives (as, no doubt, *viable* will). It is true that, without the development of metaphorical usages, our language would be far less rich than it is now. As with the verb *target*, however, there are plenty of other, more precise and more accurate words that could be used in the contexts above. There is nothing wrong with the adjectives *feasible*, *workable*, *reasonable* or even *possible*, all of which are easily understood by a reader, and none of which makes the sense any less precise. One of the features of pedants is that they seek to preserve the force that words have, something that metaphorical use may dilute.

Third, consider how attempts to alter grammar affect the language. We often read in newspapers that somebody has *warned* that something will happen. This is ungrammatical. The verb *warn* is transitive: it requires an object. Somebody has to be warned. If no such person or people is or are available (which is unlikely to be the case) then one has to write that somebody *gave warning* that such and such a thing would happen. Many writers and editors have run up the white flag of surrender on this matter. It is commonplace to hear the verb used intransitively in the broadcast media. Does it matter? Other verbs have acquired an intransitive as well as a transitive meaning, and that has done little harm to the language. All the pedant can do is appeal to logic, and to consistency. If this grammatical point is to be conceded, then why should not many others be? The logic of holding to the original use is impeccable. That does not mean that the infraction will not continue, and that the pass will not one day be sold entirely. What is happening to the verb *warn* is a sign of the constant evolution of our language. Those who continue to use the verb correctly have the consolation of knowing that they mark themselves out as understanding the correct – because it is logical – use of English. The value that may be set on that correctness is for others to judge.

That I set a high value on it, and on correct usage generally, is why I have written this book; that you are reading it suggests that you (unless you are a deliberate controversialist) set such a value on it too. What follows is a description of correct English grammar; and also a defence of it.

PART ONE

THE RULES

CHAPTER ONE

The building blocks of English

In Molière's comedy *Le Bourgeois Gentilhomme*, M Jourdain is told by his philosophy master that there is no way of expressing oneself other than in prose or verse. Jourdain replies: "By my faith! For more than 40 years I have been speaking prose without knowing anything about it, and I am much obliged to you for having taught me that." Like M Jourdain, we all speak and write prose too, unless we consciously divert into poetry. It is important to know, and define, exactly how we do this. Once we understand the structures, and the building blocks of which they are made, we can understand better the need to select the materials accurately in the sense of our choice of words, and to keep them in order through the conventions of grammar and punctuation. The basic building block is the word. It may be article (definite or indefinite), noun, verb, adjective, adverb, pronoun, conjunction or preposition. Depending on what it is, it will be used in a certain way in relation to other words to form the main vessel of meaning in language, the sentence.

The parts of speech this chapter describes and analyses will, despite the self-inflicted wounds of our education system, be obvious to many who speak only English, and should require no explanation to anyone who has been taught a foreign language. Because native English speakers learn English from the cradle rather than in a course of formal instruction they just get on and use it: they are not made to learn separately the declension

3

of nouns, the conjugation of verbs, the need to make adjectives agree with their nouns – not least because of the great simplicity of English in that it does not really have genders. However, this supposed ease with our own tongue should not prevent us from learning more about the precise use of certain categories of words within it.

The article

The most common words in English are articles. The **indefinite article** is *a* or (in front of a noun beginning with a vowel) *an*: *a dog, an armadillo*. The **definite article** is *the*: *the definite article*. Onions reminds us that it was originally considered "the demonstrative adjective".[1] Latin did without definite or indefinite articles; Greek had them and, like the unarticled nouns in Latin, they declined – that is, inflected or changed their endings according to the way in which they were used in relation to the verb – through several cases in both singular and plural. Although there are relics of declension in English (and I shall deal later with examples such as *whom* or *him*), the student of our language has an easy task compared with the classicist: or, indeed, with those learning (for example) French, who have to master the gender of nouns, or German, where articles behave rather as they do in Greek. The most strenuous intellectual exercise the user of the English article has to take is to add the *n* to *a* before the vowel, and to neglect to use the indefinite article at all before plurals: *a dog; dogs*. *The* is relaxingly consistent: *the dog, the dogs*. *The* also has an emphatic usage, in which it is deployed to convey authenticity or uniqueness – "his was one of the largest houses in the area – perhaps *the* largest" or "you say you are John Smith – not *the* John Smith?"

1. *Modern English Syntax*, by C T Onions (Routledge, 1971), p142.

This usage is more acceptable in speech than in formal writing.

Perhaps the only complication some find with the indefinite article is before some nouns beginning with *h*, and some with *u*, that defy the rules. However, once one grasps that they defy them in a logical way, all is straightforward. Some words beginning with *h* do not sound it, and so require *an*: "we shall meet in *an hour*", "it is *an honour* to be asked", "she was *an honourable* exception". Many users of English imagine that the words *historian*, *historic* and *historical* require *an* to precede them even though they are aspirated. It is hard to understand why, when we would say "*a history* of England", anyone would feel the need to call its writer "*an historian* of England" or to talk of "*an historic* feat by the English" or "*an historical* tour of England". (I shall discuss the important distinction between *historic* and *historical* later on.) Some speakers perhaps feel uncomfortable aspirating the unstressed syllable *hi*- so soon after the vowel *a*, and write it likewise; whereas they have no such problem with the stressed *hi*- at the beginning of *history*. In my view one should always write: "*a historian* of England", "*a historic* occasion", "*a historical* novel".

Some words beginning with the vowel *u* require *an* rather than *a*. It depends whether the vowel is pronounced *you* or not. So one would say or write: "he wanted to join *a union*"; "she went to *a university*"; "it was *a ubiquitous* feeling". However, one would say or write: "he was *an ugly* brute", "she gave *an upward* glance", "they had *an understanding*".

There are idiomatic usages where nouns seem to survive without articles. Some of these are in everyday use – we go to bed, we eat lunch, we drink beer, we visit grandmother and we do all these things without the need of an article. The article would only be used if we needed to create a sense of the specific – "*the bed* in the spare room is uncomfortable" or "*the beer* in that pub is disgusting". Certain other specialist idioms exist where the article is dispensed with. Anyone watching a meeting of trade unionists or Labour activists will have heard the noun *conference* thus stripped of its definite article. When reporting or describing such occasions, outsiders do best to maintain correct forms. Exotic communities put on an event called *carnival*, comprising brightly dressed women swaying to tropical music: "the carnival" is something genial provincial towns put on, in which a pretty girl sits on the back of a slow-moving lorry, and there may be a coconut shy somewhere on a field at the end of the procession. This is perhaps as good an example as any of how evolving social conditions do not so much change our language, as introduce new distinctions to it.

Nouns and pronouns

A **noun**, or substantive, is the name of something: *dog, cat, table, chair, aardvark* and so on. Sometimes they are **proper names**: *Jack, Jill, Mr Gladstone, Sir Jasper, Lady Muck*. Most nouns in correct sentences require definite or indefinite articles; proper names do not. Some nouns have been created from verbs: verbs can transmute into nouns, some more logically than others. For example, the verb *eat* gives us the verbal noun (or gerund) *eating*, as in "the proof of the pudding is in the eating". The verb *drive* supplies the noun *driving*, as in "his driving was dangerous". Verbs also supply adjectives that may be substituted for nouns, as in *the departed* or *the unwashed*, with *people, men* or *women* omitted and understood in the process of ellipsis. Adjectives themselves can serve as nouns, with a similar ellipsis, as in Housman's line "And many to count are the stalwart, and many the brave". Sometimes an adverb – the verb's equivalent of the adjective – may do the job ("I come *here* always"), sometimes it takes a whole clause ("please explain *what you have done*").

A noun may be the **subject** or the **object** of a sentence. In "John made the tea", the noun *John* is the subject (the agent of the verb) and the noun *tea* is the object (the target of the verb). There may be multiple subjects or objects in any sentence and, indeed, multiple verbs – as in "John, Mary and their parents locked the house, the garage and the garden gate before catching the train for their holiday". Sentences may also contain nouns that are direct and indirect objects of a verb. An example of this is "John gave the ice-cream to Mary", in which *John* is the subject, *the ice-cream* is the object of the verb *gave*, and *Mary*, as the person to whom the ice-cream was given, is the indirect object of the sentence.

Languages have a convenient system by which, in speaking or writing about a creature, object or person, a short word may be used as a substitute for the noun to avoid ugly repetition of it. These are called **pronouns**, and there are several types of them. The fundamental point about using a pronoun is that it has to be accompanied by the noun for which it is working, and nearby. For example: "Mr Smith sat by the fire. *He* felt warm" is a straight-forward use of the personal pronoun. *He* in the second sentence clearly refers to the proper name in the first. There are also possessive pronouns. Were the next sentence to be "his dog came and sat by him" it would be clear that the dog belongs to Mr Smith, and the *him* next to whom the dog is sitting is also Mr Smith. This leads us towards the dangers of ambiguity. Were Mr Smith with several other men, and they had been named, it might not be clear whose dog it was, and next to whom it sat. In those circumstances it is hard to avoid simply repeating the proper name.

Personal pronouns – *I, you* (singular and plural), *he, she, it, we, they* and the impersonal pronoun *one* – take that nominative form as the subject of a sentence, in other words when they are the agent of action. The pronoun with the verb *to be* therefore, as in Latin, is always in the nominative case. This correct usage has all but disappeared in speech – "it's me", "that's him", and so on – but it persists in looking right when followed by a clause in writing: – "it was *he* who killed the cat", for example, or "it might be *they* who called". When the action is happening to a person or persons, all except *you* and *it* require a distinct accusative form – *me, him, her, us, them*. So one would say "he hit *him* over the head" or "she gave *them* some cakes". These forms are also used after any preposition, such as in "we thought she would get on with *them*" or "I wanted to introduce you to *her*". Again, confusion is avoided when the pronoun is not too far removed from the noun or proper name to which it relates: we must assume that in those last two examples a preceding sentence has identified clearly who *them* and *her* are. Perhaps the greatest source of pronominal difficulty in our language is the accusative of the relative personal pronoun, *whom*. The correct use of this important word, whose disregard damages the English language but whose correct use marks out a precise and thoughtful writer or speaker, will be found in Chapter Four.

There are other varieties of pronouns. Possessive pronouns – *my, your, his, her, its, our, their* and the impersonal possessive *one's* – as the name suggests, describe ownership of a thing or of an action. They are essentially adjectival, describing the relation of one person or thing to another (*my* mother, *his* aunt, *her* dress). As with their cousins above, the use of these should be second nature to any native speaker of English – "Mrs Smith left *her* umbrella on the bus", "we took *our* holidays in France" or "it is impossible to make time for all *one's* hobbies". More complicated are the relative pronouns – *as, such as, that, what, which* and *who*. The first two most people would not recognise as pronouns at all, but the first is (though it sometimes pretends to be adverbial) and the second truly is.

A sentence such as "he resented the fact that he had no power to refuse the summons, *as* his colleagues had", is wrong. It is also ambiguous: do his colleagues have the power to refuse, or have they already refused? If the second clause began "*such as* his colleagues had" it would be correct: the *such* can refer only to *power*. *As* can be used as a pronoun when it refers to a verbal idea (or ideas) rather than to a noun: for example, when one writes "they go to the opera and dine afterwards, *as* one does", that is correct. This is but an hors d'oeuvre. The many grammatical pitfalls of the relative pronouns are explained in the next chapter.

This is a suitable moment to make an observation about *one* and *one's*. This useful pronoun has an elitist image. It is used in any caricature of what is deemed to be upper-class speech and is found in the most formal speech and writing. It has therefore attracted something of a stigma among anti-elitists. It is useful because it avoids ambiguity when one is stating a general principle. To say something such as "you don't want to go outside without a coat on" leaves the listener unsure whether it is indeed a general principle that is being enunciated, or a specific piece of advice to that person. Should one rephrase it as "*one* doesn't want to go outside without *one's* coat on" it is quite clear that one is expressing a general rule. Certain people will also use the *one* construction in order to avoid talking directly about themselves, for it was not long ago considered the height of bad manners to use the first person singular except when absolutely essential. So such people would say "*one* always used to go to the Riviera in July to meet *one's* friends", which sounds less swanky and proprietorial than "*I* always used to go to the Riviera in July to meet *my* friends". This usage does, these days, risk sounding pompous, and it is better to restrict usage of the pronoun *one* to circumstances where a generality is being expressed, for the avoidance of doubt or ambiguity. There should be no complaint about *one* when it is used to obviate self-advertisement, though. Understatement used to be a prominent feature of our speech and writing, but this has fallen into disuse in recent times. It remains a feature of the best writing style, even if the surrender has been signed when it comes to the spoken word.

Some other words we commonly use in speech and in writing are also pronouns: *the same* ("I had a beer and he had the same"); *some* ("he saw me eating a plate of beef and said he would like some); *each* ("each was spoken to"); *other* ("of the two girls, I preferred Jane but he preferred the other"); *certain* ("most people present supported him, but certain of them threatened to change their minds"); *any* ("I offered him some nuts, but he didn't want any"); *either* and *both* ("they both wanted money, but I chose not to give any to either"); *all* ("there is plenty for all"); *none* ("none has owned up to doing it"); and *neither* ("neither was ready").

Adjectives

An **adjective** is a word that describes a noun. They are common in our speech – *fat, thin, tall, short, bright, dull* and so on. As well as being simple descriptive words like these they may be manufactured out of verbs, as indicated in the section on nouns above, in instances such as "the *living* dead" or "a *standing* rebuke". Indicating possession is also adjectival, as in "the *prime minister's* car", which is the equivalent of the direct adjectival usage "the *prime ministerial* car". Use of a noun and a preposition may also be adjectival. "The road *to London*" is the London road; "a basket *of fruit*" is a fruit basket. Whole phrases may be used as adjectives, often satirically – "we'll have none of this *Jack's-as-good-as-his-master* nonsense here" is one such. Finally, two nouns may be taken together to give one the force of an adjective – "*fruit* basket" is one such, as are "*tractor* driver", "*running* shoes", "*casualty* list" and countless others. As I discuss in the next chapter, such compound nouns were once felt to need hyphenation, but this is not now the fashion; long phrases used adjectivally, however, manifestly do need hyphens.

Elsewhere I lament and advise against the overuse of adjectives: they are a habit many writers need to bring under control.

Verbs

Verbs, as teachers of small children are wont to put it, are "doing" words. They describe action, and the interaction of subject and object. In the sentence "the man read the book" the interaction of man and book – subject and object – is described by the verb *read*. The two main categories of verb are the transitive and the intransitive. A **transitive verb** is one where a subject does something to a direct object – "the dog ate the bone" or "the woman threw the ball". An **intransitive verb** has no direct object: "he slept soundly" or "he dreamt he was there". Some verbs can be both transitive and intransitive, such as *eat*. One can eat three times a day, or one can eat fish; the first use has no direct object and is therefore intransitive, the second has a direct object and is transitive. The distinction is the same with usages such as "I run every morning" and "I run a marathon". "The man walked to the shops" is intransitive, though like many intransitive verbs *walk* here takes an indirect object; "the man walked the dog" is transitive. Other examples of intransitive verbs taking an indirect object are essentially reflexive verbs. In the sentence "the boy sat on the chair", the subject is the boy himself, who sat the object – his person – down on the indirect object, the chair.

In rare cases there are similar but distinct verbs to describe the transitive and intransitive senses of an action. The verbs *lay* and *lie* are prominent examples. *Lay* is transitive: "he lays the book on the table" and "she has laid out her clothes for the morning" show how the verb is used with a direct object. *Lie* (in the sense to be recumbent, not to prevaricate) is intransitive: "he lies in a corner of a foreign field", for example, or "she has lain under the tree for several hours". I deal with these two verbs, and their pitfalls, in more detail in Chapter Four, and also with other confusions between transitive and intransitive verbs.

There are various other sorts of verbs. **Reflexive verbs**, mentioned above, are ones where one does the action to oneself – in French they are preceded in the infinitive by the reflexive pronoun *se*, as in *se pencher*, to lean, *se laver*, to wash oneself, *s'asseoir*, to sit down or *se tromper*, to be mistaken. There are also **auxiliary verbs**, which attach themselves to main verbs to provide variations of tense ("he *has* gone" or "we *shall* overcome"), to describe capability, compulsion or permission ("he *can* swim", "he *must* swim" or "he *may* swim"), possibility ("he *might* swim") or the passive voice ("he *was* beaten", "she *will be* found", "they *were being* overlooked"). These are the main types that should concern us, though the science of linguistics knows many more, such as catenative verbs – the technical term for those verbs that can only be used when followed by another verb ("he *hoped* to pass his exams" or "she *longed* to marry him") – and compound or phrasal verbs, such as *to go into* or *to take over*. Speakers and writers of English use these forms quite naturally and do not need to trouble themselves with their semantic properties.

Verbs also have voices and moods. The **active voice** is the more straightforward – "the boy waved his bat in the air". The **passive voice** turns the order around – "the bat was waved in the air by the boy". As I shall discuss later on, it is stylistically preferable to avoid the passive and prefer the active voice wherever possible. There are also political considerations of using the passive voice: the phrase "you will be taxed" differs from its counterpart "the government will tax you" only in failing to disclose who is doing the taxing. The passive voice is part of the language of evasion.

There are three moods, the indicative, the imperative and the subjunctive. (Some also decree that the infinitive is a mood, but, like the dictionary, I see it as just being the form of the verb that simply describes its notion – *to walk*, *to run*, *to stand*, *to sit* and so on.) The **indicative mood** is the most common of the three and is used for the most straightforward statements of positive description or intent: "I went to school", "I go to school" and "I shall go to school" are examples of the imperfect, present and future indicative tenses of the verb *to go*. In much modern writing and in demotic speech the indicative has also moved on to the ground once occupied by the subjunctive mood, which was used to describe nuances of intent or desire, and degrees of certainty and uncertainty. This is to be regretted, as the demise of the subjunctive removes some of the subtlety from the English language. The **imperative** is a truncated form of expression used when giving orders – *sit*, *stay* and various other commands used to dogs are all imperative, as are human instructions such as "*come* in", "*go* away" and "*give* me that". It is peculiar to speech and not found in formal writing except in accounts of dialogue and certain types of written text, such as cookbooks and instruction manuals.

The **subjunctive** is (or, since it is now largely the province of pedants, should be) used in dependent clauses for verbs that rely upon another in the main clause, and express will or desire, necessity or possibility. For example: "I command that he *be* executed" uses in the dependent clause the present tense of the subjunctive mood of the verb *to be*; "she wishes that he *were* here", "it is essential that he *be* brought here" and "he would be happy if he *were* here" are all examples of the subjunctive. Many people ignore its existence altogether; yet it is not entirely confined to pedants. It has a place in educated speech. Those who have studied the classics instinctively understand its nuances, for the subjunctive (and, in Greek, its cousin the optative) is an essential part of the Latin and Greek tongues. No educated person in France would neglect it. In English writing its use marks out a writer of a higher calibre and with greater powers of expression. In American English it is far more commonplace than in British, being a mark of that occasional conservatism that marks this otherwise capriciously progressive variant of our language. Its exact workings are outlined in Chapter Four.

Verbs also provide present and past **participles**: *going* and *gone* are the participles of the verb *go*. These participles have a more complicated use in gerunds. The **gerund** is another word for the present participle, and is a verbal noun: "He hates *working*" or "she wanted to go *skating*" are sentences that employ the gerund as a direct object. It can also appear as the subject of a sentence: "*smoking* is banned" or "*eating* chocolate will make you fat" are examples. The gerundive is deemed by grammarians not to exist in English, though it is prevalent in Latin, the language from which most grammarians took their template. In Latin it is a verbal adjective, identical to the gerund but used to qualify a noun rather than being a noun itself, and formed only from transitive verbs: "the detective found a *smoking* gun" and "the girl wanted a *crying* doll" use what seem to be gerundives. We had better just call them adjectives. The precise use of participles is also explained in Chapter Four.

Earlier, when considering nouns and pronouns, we noted how a verb can have an indirect as well as a direct object. Sometimes the second object of the verb is another verb, in the infinitive: as in "I asked him *to stop*"; "she taught her *to speak*"; "they allowed him *to walk* on the grass"; and so on.

Adverbs

An **adverb** does for a verb what an adjective does for a noun: it qualifies or describes more exactly what the verb indicates. One of the more disturbing trends in modern English usage, even among some educated people, is for the adverb to fall into disuse. "Kiss me quick" hats ought really to say "Kiss me *quickly*", though that is perhaps unduly pedantic in that context. However, there is no excuse for "he ran down the road so *quick* that he fell over", or "she thought he came on too *strong*" – if one must write such a thing, then one should remember that he came on too *strongly*. Perhaps some of the difficulty with adverbs is that some adjectives end in the usual (but not inevitable) adverbial suffix of *-ly* (*lovely*, *ugly*, *shapely*, *comely* and so on), which some may conclude makes such parts of speech interchangeable. It does not. If you want to qualify a verb, use an adverb. They cost the same as an adjective, but they sound much better. Of the peculiarly horrific popular use of the adverb *hopefully*, there will be more in the next chapter.

One of the first points to make about adverbs is that they do not all end in *-ly*; and that numerous words that do end in *-ly* are not adverbs, but quite often adjectives. One of those is *lovely*, and it has its own adverb: Eric Partridge (1894–1979), the distinguished grammarian and expert on slang whose *Usage and Abusage* is one of the more important books ever written on English, wrote in 1947 that "lovelily is good English and it means beautifully".[2] One can only assume that he was trying to give this strange word the kiss of life, but was too late. It is better now to stick to the alternative form that he gives, which is that one does something "in a lovely manner" – or possibly even just *beautifully*. *Lowlily*, which is also in the dictionary, should be avoided not just for reasons of euphony, but because it is almost certainly being used wrongly. *Lowly* means humble; if *lowlily* were being used to describe something that was low in any other sense (such as a voice, a ceiling or a mode of behaviour), then it would be an error. It is good style now to take the same course with other adjectives that end in *-ly* and write, therefore, that one did something in an ugly manner, or a costly fashion, or a courtly way rather than manufacture adverbs such as *uglily*, *costlily* or *courtlily* – even though the first two of those are in the *OED*, the second of them albeit not found since 1425.

In Chapter Four there is a list (not exhaustive) of words that

2. *Usage and Abusage*, by Eric Partridge (Penguin, 1973), p175.

are adverbs but do not look like them. Phrases, too, may serve as adverbs. "He walks *by night*" is one such, the prepositional phrase qualifying the verb. Similar usages are "she's cooking *with gas*", "it will go *a long way*" and "I have suffered *more than I can tell you*". When using adverbs it is important to position them properly within their sentence, in order to avoid ambiguity or confusion, and that too I deal with in Chapter Four.

Conjunctions

The dictionary says that a **conjunction** is "one of the parts of speech; an uninflected word used to connect clauses or sentences, or to co-ordinate words in the same clause". Conjunctions come in two categories: they are either co-ordinating or subordinating. A **co-ordinating conjunction** links two clauses that would stand just as well as independent sentences; a subordinating one introduces a subordinate clause. The co-ordinating conjunctions are *for, and, nor, but, or, only* and *yet*: examples of how they co-ordinate are "the door was open, *for* he was already inside", "I was awake, *but* I was not dressed", "they would have arrived sooner, *only* their car broke down" and the most usual of all such constructions "the dog was lying by the fire *and* he stretched out his legs". Onions also points out that some co-ordinating conjunctions are preceded at times by co-ordinating adverbs: *both* may precede *and*, *either* may precede *or*, *neither* may precede *nor* and *not only* may precede *but* [*also*].

If a writer seeks to make his prose easier to read by shortening his sentences he will often be able to achieve this by cutting them in two. This will be feasible only if the constituent parts are co-ordinating clauses, and the effect may be achieved by removing the conjunction, as in: "The dog was lying by the fire. He stretched out his legs." Orwell's prose, extracts from which I quote in the chapter on style, is remarkably lacking in conjunctions precisely because his sentences are so short.

The trick is less easily accomplished (and sometimes may not be accomplished at all) with sentences with subordinate clauses, for these include at least one that is not grammatically independent of the others. **Subordinating conjunctions** introduce either noun clauses or adverbial clauses. An example of the former is where a clause says that something *is, was, had, would* or *will b*e: such as in "she hopes *that he will come*", "I never dreamt *that she would do that*", "they wished *that it had stopped raining*", and so on. An adverbial clause is one that illuminates the main verb, as in "I used to go fishing *when I was a boy*"; "I was late *because the train was delayed*"; "she left her coat *where she could easily find it again*"; "we saved our money *in order that we might have a holiday*" and so on. Onions enumerates several different types of subordinate adverbial clauses. In addition to the types of which I have already given examples there are also conjunctions that introduce comparisons (*as, than, as if, as though*), conditional clauses (*if, unless, whether, so long as*, and *that* preceded by *supposing, provided* etc) and concessive clauses (*though, although, even if, even though, notwithstanding that*).[3] I say more about the correct uses of conjunctions of cause in Chapter Four.

In contemporary usage, some participles have been enlisted as conjunctions; they have become synonyms for words that already serve that purpose. "He didn't do too badly, *considering* his age" is one such example; an even more frequent usage is "the concert is postponed *owing* to illness". Partridge lists several of these but in the 70 or so years since he wrote their number has multiplied, to the point where all sorts of participles can serve as a conjunction: "it was a surprise that he ate anything, *seeing* he was so ill" or "they should be here by evening, *bearing* in mind the traffic".

3. *Modern English Syntax*, p63.

Sometimes the conjunction *that* is lost in an ellipsis, which is considered now to be acceptable if there is no ambiguity as a result: "they wished it had stopped raining" causes no confusion whereas "he believed she didn't" may well. This point is dealt with in Chapters Four and Eight, where the omission of conjunctions is considered in the context of style.

Prepositions

A **preposition** establishes a relationship between one word and another: often between a verb and a noun or pronoun. So one goes *to* church, one walks *from* the house, one sits *on* the lavatory, one loiters *by* a stream, one stands *for* parliament, one swims *with* the tide, one is tired *of* life, one lies *in* the sun, one is good *at* games. These are the most frequently used prepositions: there are many others: *between, around, about, through, over, below, until, into, beneath, inside, outside, notwithstanding* and so on. Some prepositions have become adjectives in modern usage – an *outside* table, an *inside* story.

In some languages, such as Latin, Greek or German, different prepositions take different cases. English having lost most of its inflections, one only notices the different cases taken by prepositions with certain pronouns. All prepositions take *me*, or *him*, or *her*, or *us*, or *them*. *You* does not inflect. They also take *whom*, an accusative that requires preservation. In Chapter Four I deal with the problems that occasionally arise after use of a preposition because of logical errors.

There is also such a thing as a postposition: "he threw it *away*", "he went there years *ago*", and so on.

CHAPTER TWO

From clauses to paragraphs

Without presuming to insult the intelligence of any of my readers, I have nonetheless made certain depressing assumptions. One is that many of you will not have been taught English grammar in any formal or systematic way. Few children have been so indulged in British schools since the Second World War; hardly anyone is now. Many children still learn a foreign language, and some are fortunate enough to learn some Latin or even some Greek. It is when encountering these tongues that a child often has his first encounter with grammatical terms, or with parsing a sentence – that is, breaking it down into its component parts. For that reason, this chapter deals with the structural framework of language, to avoid confusion later on when I deal with points of grammar, vocabulary and style.

All writing has a distinct structure, as does all coherent speech. Look at a page of prose – such as this – and you will notice that most obviously it consists of paragraphs. Within each paragraph are sentences. There are three sorts of sentence: the simple sentence, the complex sentence and the compound sentence. The dictionary defines a sentence as "a series of words in connected speech or writing, forming the grammatically complete expression of a single thought; in popular use often such a portion of a composition or utterance as extends from one full stop to another." Within the sentence, groups of words will be arranged – it is to be hoped with grammatical accuracy – within clauses. Let us start by looking at them.

Clauses

Charles Talbut Onions defined a sentence as an expression containing a subject and a predicate: the predicate being that part of the sentence that contains what is said about the subject. If that is all a sentence does, it is a simple sentence. If it has more than one subject and predicate, however, then each subdivision of the sentence with its own subject and predicate is a **clause**. The sentence then becomes what Onions calls "a compound sentence".[1] "I had no idea that grammar was so easy to grasp as this" is a complex sentence: it consists of a **main clause** followed by a **subordinate clause**, introduced in this example by the conjunction *that*. There are several different types of subordinate clause: those that take the role of a noun, an adjective or an adverb. One does not need to understand such technicalities to write English correctly, but these examples of each type may be useful:

"It is quite apparent *that the boy is a fool.*" (noun clause: provides a subject)

"The dog *that ran into the road* was run over." (adjective clause: describes the dog)

"He wrote the book *until it was time for dinner.*" (adverbial clause: complements the verb)

There are further varieties within these groups that only scholars of linguistics or grammarians need concern themselves with: full details are contained in Onions.[2] Many adverbial clauses are of time or place or reason, and so are introduced by *when, since,*

1. *Modern English Syntax*, p13.
2. *Modern English Syntax*, pp46–79.

until, before, after (time), *where, wherever* (place) or *because, why, how* or *whereas* (reason). The point about a subordinate clause is that it cannot stand alone and make sense: it is sometimes called a dependent clause because it depends on another clause to show its full meaning. The one I quoted near the beginning of this section – "grammar was so easy to grasp as this" – is meaningless on its own. The main clause, "I had no idea", however, can function on its own.

There are also **co-ordinate clauses**. These are clauses that do make sense on their own. They are commonly introduced by a conjunction such as *and, but, or* and *nor*. If you look at these examples you will see that what comes after the conjunction, or indeed before it, makes sense independently:

"I had been to Brighton, but John had never visited it."

"She put away the breakfast things and then she went to the village."

"He had nothing to contribute to the discussion, nor did he wish to do so."

"Either Mary would walk from the station, or John would collect her by car."

The main point that most speakers need to know about clauses is that they require careful examination to ensure that the logic of the sentence is maintained throughout all of them. There is more on this in Chapter Four, where the particular danger of clauses that include participles is demonstrated. To make matters more interesting, subordinate clauses may have further clauses subordinated to them, and subordinate clauses may co-ordinate with each other. When I express a prejudice for short sentences, there is method in my madness.

Sentences

In defining the **sentence** the dictionary goes on to make a more technical definition peculiar to grammar, which we must take note of: "the verbal expression of a proposition, question, command, or request, containing normally a subject and a predicate (though either of these may be omitted by ellipsis)." We had better define some of these terms. A **predicate** is what is said about the subject. "My wife cooked them dinner" has "my wife" as the subject and "cooked them dinner" as the predicate. A **simple sentence** is as just defined and exemplified – one that has a subject and a predicate. A **complex sentence** has a subordinate clause. "My wife cooked them dinner, which was delicious" would be an example of that. A **compound sentence** has more than one subject or predicate. "My wife cooked them dinner, which was delicious, and their driver came to pick them up at eleven o'clock" is a compound sentence.

Not all sentences contain the traditional subject, object and verb: some contain less, many more. A sentence may consist of only one word: "Yes!" "No!" "Hello?" are all sentences – Jespersen calls them "amorphous sentences".[3] Onions said there were four sorts of sentences – statements, commands (or expressions of wishes), questions and exclamations. A one-word sentence has an ellipsis, or series of missing words that are understood, that if undone would provide the missing matter – "Yes (you may)!" for example. A detailed knowledge of such things is not necessary to speak or write English correctly: many people manage to do so without a degree in linguistics. It is, however, valuable to understand a little about the structure of language, to ensure that any sentence one writes in formal English contains the components required to make it grammatical.

3. *Essentials of English Grammar*, p105.

In this book, I have followed the dictionary's "popular" definition of the sentence as being the matter between full stops. Not all grammarians choose to do this, and they are quite justified in doing differently. What I call a clause they call a sentence, provided it satisfies the rule above of having subject and predicate. Onions, for example, whose usage differs from my own, would call the first clause of each of the examples of a complex and compound sentence given above sentences in their own right, because "my wife cooked them dinner" satisfies the requirement for a sentence as codified in his grammar. The Fowlers took the same view. I do not dispute that they are right, but in the century since they wrote, even most educated people's definition of what constitutes a sentence has become what the dictionary now says it is: the matter between full stops.

Where Onions and the Fowlers remain unchallenged is on the notion that this matter must, in order to constitute a grammatical sentence, have a subject and predicate. One of the great and pervasive offences against good grammar, to be seen almost every day in a newspaper or magazine, is the "sentence" without a main verb and, more to the point, without a coherent ellipsis. "I saw the dog. Ugly brute" is such an example. The omission of the verb *to be* in the second sentence is not coherent because it is not idiomatic in the way that sentences such as "yes", "no" or "hello" undeniably are.

There are various different types of clauses. The main clause will introduce a subject and predicate, and there may then be various types of dependent clause – noun clauses, adjective clauses and adverbial clauses, named according to what function they perform in the sentence. A noun clause is found in "*the last thing I want to do* is to go". There is an adjective clause in "the house *that we saw* was sold" and an adverbial one in "I must eat something *because I am hungry*". A relative clause will be introduced by a relative pronoun, as in "she drank the cocktail, *which her friend had ordered for her*" or "he introduced his wife to the doctor, *whom he had met on holiday*". Clauses may also be fashioned to create a literary technique, such as paratactic clauses, that stand side by side with each other without any co-ordinating or subordinating conjunctions. Caesar's remark "I came, I saw, I conquered" is probably history's most famous parataxis. I deal with co-ordinating and subordinating conjunctions, and the types of clause they introduce, in the section on conjunctions in Chapter Four.

Paragraphs

Sentences may be constrained by the tenets of strict grammar, but paragraphs are a matter of taste. The dictionary defines a **paragraph** as "a distinct passage or section of a text, usually composed of several sentences, dealing with a particular point, a short episode in a narrative, a single piece of direct speech, etc." It will be indicated by a line break at the end of a preceding sentence. The definition in the writer's mind of the particular point, or thought, will vary from person to person. Therefore what constitutes a paragraph will vary too.

An especially complex thought may prompt one writer to break it down into constituent parts of the structure and present them as separate paragraphs, even though the point is only made using a number of them. Another writer will wish to contain one point in one paragraph, however long that paragraph may have to be. In Chapter Nine there are examples of writing by George Orwell, the master of the short sentence, and Enoch Powell: Orwell, though favouring the short sentence, likes a long paragraph; Powell, terse in his sentences, is equally so in his paragraphs. Orwell was writing an essay; Powell a piece of journalism. Journalism, even at the quality end of the spectrum, does not favour lengthy paragraphs. They look unappealing on the printed page and may deter readers. They can be better concealed in books.

The fashion today – and it is one that I endorse – is for short paragraphs. It is not merely that they do not put the reader off: it is that, once read, they make for easier comprehension. They help support and sustain the logic of an argument. They are harder to become lost in. Few points are really so complex that they cannot be broken down. The slightest change of tack – or the need to bring in new evidence, or to open up a subsidiary line of argument – provides the perfect excuse to end one paragraph and to start another.

Some teachers argue that there is an ideal paragraph structure: however, I feel this depends on the nature of the piece of prose that contains the paragraph. A glance at an article in the tabloid press will show that its paragraphs rarely contain more than two sentences. The ideal structure favoured by some teachers contains four sentences. First, there is the "topic sentence", which contains the theme of the paragraph. Second, there is a sentence in which the topic is explained or expanded upon. Third, there is a sentence that gives corroborative evidence for any contention the writer has advanced in the second sentence. Fourth, there is a closing sentence that refers back to the idea in the topic sentence. One can see that this prescription has its merits, not least in ordering the thoughts of those unused to such an exercise. Yet one can also see that it is artificial, restrictive and bereft of any sophistication. Those with more experience of using the language will instinctively see when the thought contained in a paragraph has reached the limits of its expression, and when the time has come to move boldly on to a new one – and, with it, a new paragraph. Variations in paragraphing are also an essential component of an attractive style.

Those seeking guidance on how to structure a sophisticated argument will find it in Chapter Nine.

Parsing

Those who have studied the grammar of any language at school may have done the exercise of **parsing** a sentence, or defining each term within it and identifying its role there. It is a remarkably useful exercise, for if we were in the habit of parsing every sentence we wrote we should make far fewer mistakes of grammar. Some grammarians and linguistics experts take parsing to an extreme level, but that need not be the case for those who simply wish to write or speak English correctly. Parsing may have a theoretical and intellectual value, but it can also be of practical use to those who make slips with their grammar. For example: working out that in the sentence "she gave the picture to John and me" the second personal pronoun is the indirect object of *gave* prevents the horrible, but all too frequent, error of saying or writing "she gave the picture to John and I". Similarly, in the more complex sentence "having taken my bath, I found myself on the terrace with her", by correctly identifying the personal pronoun *I* as the subject of both clauses, one avoids a mistake such as "having taken my bath, she found herself on the terrace with me", in which it would appear that the woman has taken the other person's bath.

Should you have persistent difficulty with grammar, get into the habit of looking at sentences – whether they be your own or someone else's – and parse them to identify subjects, objects and verbs. Learn to separate clauses into main, co-ordinate and subordinate ones; to categorise words as nouns, pronouns, verbs, adjectives, adverbs, conjunctions and prepositions; and to be sure that these words stand in the correct relation to each other, in the proper cases, and making the right sense of every clause in the sentence. With practice this becomes not so much second nature as utterly subliminal. Once one has a command of the roles of the different parts of speech such as comes with the ability to parse accurately, one has one of the fundamental skills needed to become a good writer and speaker of English.

Other necessary skills include the ability to spell accurately, and to punctuate sentences correctly: these I deal with in the next chapter.

CHAPTER THREE

Spelling and punctuation

Underpinning my approach to giving advice on good English is another assumption, less depressing than the one that I signalled at the beginning of the last chapter: that my readers can spell. I realise this is a bold assumption: it is possible to obtain a first-class degree in English from our best universities without being able to spell, as I have noticed when reading applications for jobs in journalism from those with such qualifications. Spelling has been standardised in this country effectively since the completion of the *Oxford English Dictionary* in 1928: as I noted in the Prologue, when I refer to "the dictionary" in this book it is to that magnificent, if occasionally flawed, work. I have a hardbound copy of the first edition, with supplements: but every definition I have had cause to use in this book has been checked in the online second edition. The latter is a valuable resource, and available to almost everyone with a library ticket and an internet connection. If one visits the website of one's local public library, there is usually a reference section. It will state whether the *OED* is available, and, by typing in the number on one's library ticket, one can access the work.

I dare to say the work is flawed because the *OED* and I have one serious difference of opinion. It can be best summarised as follows: I take the view that once the meaning of a word was settled with the publication of the dictionary, it had no great need to change. If a group of people insisted on using the word in an incorrect way, and were at odds with the dictionary's definition, then they and their usage were wrong. The *OED* has never dealt in arbitrary definitions. An etymology is always supplied, giving legitimacy to the defined meaning of any given word. However, on some words the *OED* has surrendered to usage: if people insist on using a word incorrectly, and that incorrect usage becomes popular, then the *OED* will record the fact and, to all intents and purposes, sanction it. I take a more conservative view. The incorrect use of a word happens because people confuse its meaning with that of another (such as people saying *flaunt* when they mean *flout*). Since this purports to be a book on correct English, I cannot see the logic or the value in proposing to the reader that he should use the language wrongly.

There is a small group of words in frequent use that many people have trouble spelling correctly. This does not pretend to be an exhaustive list, but it is one that contains the most troublesome of the words that cause difficulty in this respect:

Accommodation	Harassment	Publicly
All right	Humorous	Quandary
Bellwether	Independent	Questionnaire
Cemetery	Jewellery	Receive
Committee	Liaison	Recommendation
Consensus	Lightning	Restaurateur
Definite	Linchpin	Rhythm
(just) Deserts	Manoeuvre	Separate
Diarrhoea	Mantelpiece	Skilful
Drunkenness	Memento	Stratagem
Dumbbell	Millennium	Succeeded
Embarrassment	Minuscule	Supersede
Fulfil	Misspelt	Tyranny
Gauge	Possession	Weird
Harass	Privilege	Withhold

There are also words about which there is genuine dispute concerning the correct orthography. In most cases these disputes were raging before the dictionary was completed and no consensus had been reached on the spellings among the educated. The dictionary failed, in these instances, to settle them. As a matter of taste I would include the *e* after the *g* in words such as *judgement*, *acknowledgement* and *abridgement* as it seems necessary for correct pronunciation. As I note elsewhere, forms such as *connexion*, though still favoured by the dictionary, have long been regarded by most of us as archaic. Their alternatives were current and popular long before the dictionary was completed, which makes their rejection by it the more peculiar. The second edition of the dictionary continued to discount them. The third, now in preparation, will be interesting in this respect.

Pronunciation is outside the scope of this book. However, for the sake of clarity it is worth noting that before universal literacy there were traditional pronunciations of words that changed once people could read; for many words, notably proper names, were not pronounced as they were written. I mention this because sometimes it leads a person into the reverse error, that of spelling. *Forehead* was pronounced *forrid*; *waistcoat* was *weskit*. The days of the week were *Mundy*, *Tuesdy*, *Wensdy*, *Thursdy* and so on. Words with the vowel *o* were spoken as if they contained the vowel *u* instead: *cunstable*, *Cuvvent* Garden, *Cuvventry*, Denis *Cumpton*. In similar fashion, Montgomery was *Muntgummery*, Honiton was *Huniton* and Romford *Rumford*. The word *some* and its compounds (*something, someone, somewhere, somebody*) behave in this way still, and *Somerset*, *Somerton* and *Somers Town* with them, as well as *son, done, none, monger, honey, money, love, wonder* and numerous other such words. (This is nothing to do with the "great vowel shift", a phenomenon so named by Jespersen to describe the mutation in sound of long vowels and diphthongs.) Daventry was pronounced *Daintry*, Hunstanton *Hunston*, and Rievaulx Abbey *Rivaz*: the last of these has been transmuted not just by our ability to read English, but by the ability of some to read French. Perhaps in another century we shall pronounce *some* like *Somme*, *done* will rhyme with *gone* and *wonder* will sound like *wander*.

The rules of punctuation

Punctuation exists not merely for ease of reading, but also for ease of comprehension and the avoidance of ambiguity. If used correctly, it shows the reader how clauses in a sentence relate to each other; how sentences are delineated; and how an argument or exposition is broken up into paragraphs. The technical aspects of punctuation I shall deal with here; the stylistic ones will fit more logically into Chapter Eight.

A sentence begins with a **capital letter** and ends with a **full stop**. In between those two points may come one, or several, clauses. Clauses are often, but not always, separated from each other by commas. One important point about commas is both technical and stylistic: there are tendencies, according to the writer, to use these either excessively or insufficiently. It is the mark of the skilful writer that he uses them just when they are needed.

A **comma** helps define clauses that, if not so defined, could struggle to convey their accurate meaning. They also, as in this sentence and in the one preceding it, separate parenthetical matter from the main thrust of a sentence. It is vital when one introduces a parenthesis with a comma to remember to end it with one, otherwise the sentence fails to read logically. A comma may also be used, as in the preceding sentence, to introduce a contrast. The comma's purpose is as a signpost or aid to the reader in his understanding of what is being said: it has an important role in the maintenance of logic. I give more examples of this in the section on common mistakes, below, and discuss the use of the comma (and other punctuation) in relation to style and the attainment of elegance in Chapter Eight.

More profound breaks in meaning than enabled by commas may be introduced by the **semicolon**. One frequent use for the semicolon is in introducing a nuance, or a contrast between clauses. One such example is this description of Walter Hammond's batting: "he did not walk to the wicket; he strode". The semicolon creates a degree of emphasis for which a comma would be inadequate, and for which a colon would be incorrect – as we shall now see. The semicolon also separates what Onions and the Fowlers would have called "independent sentences" – or what I would call clauses, each of which has a subject and a predicate.

The Fowlers specified five correct uses for the **colon**, and they hold good today. The first was between two antithetical clauses that could stand as sentences on their own, such as "sentence was passed: the prisoner broke down". The second was for introducing a short quotation, as I have done frequently in this book. The third is when introducing a list, as in "those present were: Mr Smith, Mr Jones, Mr Brown, Mrs White". The fourth is when something that becomes expected as a result of a first clause is delivered in a second, as in "the jury considered its verdict: it found Smith guilty". The fifth is where the clause after the colon proves or explains the contents of the first, as in "always take care how you treat people on the way up: for you never know whom you might meet on the way down".

I think there is a sixth class, an amalgam of examples one and four. Were the fourth example to read, instead, "the jury considered its verdict: the judge went and watched tennis on television", it would be an example not quite entertained by the Fowlers. Example one has a direct relation between the two events described, of the prisoner's reaction to the sentence. The judge's going to watch tennis is a parallel event consequent on his having sent the jury out and not himself being required in court until they return, and not on the verdict they eventually reach. There is also another important distinction between a semicolon and a colon. A colon can be used to separate two clauses the second of which is not an independent sentence in Onions's and the Fowlers' definition of the term. Examples are "the murderer was revealed: Smith" and "there was only one thing for it: surrender".

A sentence will end with a **full stop**. Several sentences will constitute a paragraph.

Within a sentence, **parentheses** of a more emphatic sort than allowed by pairs of commas may be introduced to give some important explanatory information. These may take the form of **brackets** (such as surround this clause) or – in a somewhat more interrupting fashion – **dashes**. The Victorian habit of putting colons or commas before dashes should be considered barbarous. It is to be avoided. A parenthesis in brackets is almost incidental to the meaning of the sentence around it. One in dashes makes an important point relevant to the surrounding sentence, and which is included in it for rhetorical reasons. It is often deployed when compiling an argument, and so has an element of aggression to it. Ordinary brackets tend to be more helpful, and to supply information, almost by way of a commentary. Consider these two examples:

> It had become a rite, a sacrament (that was how John Beavis described it to himself): a sacrament of communion.

> But the smell of poverty when the twenty children were assembled in the dining-room was so insidiously disgusting – like Lollingdon church, only much worse – that he had to slip out two or three times....[1]

---

1. *Eyeless in Gaza*, by Aldous Huxley (Chatto and Windus, 1936), pp194 and 111.

Both examples come from Aldous Huxley's novel *Eyeless in Gaza*. In the first the matter in brackets simply provides further illumination to the reader about Beavis's state of mind; in the second a contention is made, and the matter within the dashes seeks to support it by way of comparison.

Huxley is also the master of the single **dash**, something that from the early 20th century did the work occasionally of the colon, but was also used for dramatic effect to provide a longer pause, or to aid conscious repetition. These, too, come from *Eyeless in Gaza*:

The old shyness, he noticed, as they shook hands in the lobby of the restaurant, was still there – the same embarrassed smile, the same swaying movement of recoil.

He spoke well – the right mixture of arguments, jokes, emotional appeal.[2]

Both of these examples could just as well have featured a colon: but that was not the fashion in 1935, when Huxley wrote the novel, whereas dashes were. The same interchangeability applies today. Whether to use a dash or a colon has in some cases become a question of stylistic prejudice. My prejudice is for the colon, though in some cases only the dash will do – like this. As with all forms of punctuation they can be overdone, and become distracting. It should also go without saying that logic and good grammar dictate that two dashes can be used in the same sentence only to form a parenthesis. If this is not the intention then confusion will result. I say more about this in Chapter Six.

If the prose includes dialogue, there will have to be **quotation marks**. These will also have to be used if the writer is using a direct

---

2. *Eyeless in Gaza*, pp370 and 415.

quotation from a specified source, to distinguish his own remarks from those of some other writer or speaker. If a quotation stretches over more than one sentence, do not insert the closing quotation marks until after the last sentence of the quotation has finished. If a quotation runs into a new paragraph, do not put the marks at the end of the paragraph break; but do open the first sentence of the new paragraph in the quotation with new marks, thus:

> "I told him that he was a fool. He seemed unable to grasp the point. I tried again, but to my frustration there was no recognition of the fact.
>
> "I hoped it would sink in eventually."

Other than in the instances cited above, quotation marks should not be used. If writing the name of a book, or a ship, italicise it: *The Canterbury Tales* or the RMS *Titanic*. It is a matter of taste whether to italicise the names of poems or give them within single quotation marks: my prejudice is to italicise poems known by a specific title and put ones generally known by their first lines in single marks: so *Paradise Lost* or *The Waste Land*, but 'I wandered lonely as a cloud' or 'My love is like a red, red rose'.

The positioning of punctuation marks relative to parentheses and quotation marks is often a source of confusion. It is entirely logical, however, and should not give any difficulty. When a complete sentence is given in quotation marks, the full stop must come inside them, thus:

> "I shall have none of that nonsense in here."

However, this is the correct punctuation for a sentence that includes both matter within quotation marks and matter without them:

Mr Smith said "I shall have none of that nonsense in here".

If you are quoting matter that itself includes a quotation, the positioning of the full stop is again logical:

"Mr Smith said 'I shall have none of that nonsense in here'."

Note the full stop comes after the internal quotation mark but before the quotation mark that comes after the end of the complete quoted sentence. Similarly, had the writer said

Jones remarked: "Mr Smith said 'I shall have none of that nonsense in here'."

that punctuation would be correct, as the full stop completes the sentence in direct speech and therefore must come between the single and the double quotation marks. In the following example, however, there is a problematic juxtaposition of single and double marks at the end of the sentence before the full stop:

Mr Smith said "my favourite poem is 'I wandered lonely as a cloud'".

Professional typesetters usually introduce a small space between the single and double marks in order to distinguish them. Note the punctuation required in a sentence that contains an insertion that is outside quotation marks, such as:

"I think we shall have breakfast now", said Mrs Smith, "and then go for a swim."

Mrs Smith's statement would not have required a comma between *now* and *and*, but the insertion requires a parenthesis to be distinguished, and the commas therefore come outside the quotation marks. The Fowlers were against such use of commas, claiming that quotation marks were stops enough. Subsequent practice and logic disagree with them.

In like manner, should a sentence include a statement in parentheses it should have any final punctuation outside the closing bracket, as in this example:

> He saw no reason to go to France for his holidays (and, in any case, he had plenty to do at work).

This could also be written as follows, with a subtle difference in punctuation:

> He saw no reason to go to France for his holidays. (In any case, he had plenty to do at work.)

Since the second sentence is contained completely within the brackets, the full stop comes before rather than after the second parenthesis. A good stylist would observe that, in the second example, the parentheses are not really needed at all.

Questions, literal or rhetorical, must be terminated with a **question mark**. Exclamations should be terminated with an **exclamation mark**, though in most intelligent writing such forms will be confined to dialogue. Exclamatory writing in most English prose betrays an excitable nature, something not always easy to reconcile with a desire on the part of the writer to be taken seriously. Sophisticates use the exclamation mark only in moments of jest or parody, and then rarely.

The codicil to our discussion of punctuation is the **hyphen**. In the 19th and early 20th centuries these proliferated in English writing, joining words that custom and practice have since completely fused: such as *road-sweeper* or *girl-friend*. They would also join words that have defiantly remained separate, but which we now see no point in hyphenating, such as *ballet-dancer* or *shooting-brake*. They also used to appear in street names, so one would read in Victorian fiction about people living in *Belgrave-square* or *Curzon-street* (note the lower cases of the ordinary nouns). Hyphens cause clutter. We do not use them in any of these instances today and our language is none the worse for it. We do still use them in certain restricted senses, notably to compound words as adjectives, and this is largely for the avoidance of ambiguity.

For example: it is quite correct to write that a girl with long hair is "a *long-haired* girl", or that a house with a flat roof is a "*flat-roofed* house". "A long haired girl" and a "flat roofed house" could well be interpreted as being very different in nature and in appearance from their hyphenated alternatives. The rule should be generally observed to avoid any misunderstandings. Certain (although now very few) nouns are hyphenated: one example is when we choose to describe a person according to age. We should write "the 19 *year-old* appeared in court". However, were we to make his age adjectival by giving him an extra noun, we should need an extra hyphen, thus: "the *19-year-old* youth appeared in court". All words in a compound adjective need to be hyphenated, as in "the *dark-greenish-blue* stamp", or "a *fin-de-siècle* moment". The exception is where a proper name becomes the adjective: one would not hyphenate "a Great Eastern Railway train", or a "Corpus Christi College tie". The most important point today is that hyphens are not nearly so frequent, or required, as they used to be.

The **apostrophe** at the end of a noun or proper name and before an *s* signifies possession: "*Mr Smith's* cat", "*the woman's* room", "*the child's* toy". It is also used in contractions such as *don't, won't, shouldn't* and *can't* to indicate a missing letter or letters. It is never to be used to signify plurals – the so-called grocer's or greengrocer's apostrophe (as in "*apple's*, 50p a pound"). I deal with this ubiquitous and tiresome atrocity below; in Chapter Eight I discuss the use of contractions. Care is also required in using the apostrophe with nouns that have unconventional plurals. One occasionally sees *childrens'* when the writer intended *children's*.

Common mistakes in punctuation

If writers stick to the rules of punctuation as set out above they will come to no harm. Sometimes, as with all sets of rules, the exercise of judgement may be needed to avoid ambiguity or confusion. One of the prejudices of this book is against hyphens, whose use was defined above. They have a place in compound adjectives, but rarely in compound nouns. No-one would hyphenate *test match*; but should one not, on the same principle, leave the hyphen out of *cross-examination*? I should say it is necessary. The word *cross* is susceptible of too many interpretations. A *cross examination* could be an exhibition of bad temper in examining somebody or something. At all times in such circumstances, apply common sense before proceeding.

The greengrocer's apostrophe is the term given to the illiteracy of inserting an apostrophe before the plural of a noun – such as in *apple's*, *carrot's* or *potatoe's*. A variant of this is to take a word ending in *s* and make it plural by adding another *s* after an apostrophe – for example, *a brass*, *some brass's*, or *Mr Harris*, *the Harris's*. It has become a near-ubiquitous fault of punctuation and perhaps the most common grammatical error in our language. It is a rare day, as one walks or drives around Britain, that one does not encounter it on a handwritten (or, occasionally, printed) notice somewhere. A variety of this irritating error is the insertion of the apostrophe in possessive pronouns such as *theirs*, *hers* and *yours*. The most frequent offender is *it's*, no doubt because of the existence of the identical, and legitimate, contraction: *it's* is the contraction of *it is* or *it has*, and must be used in no other context. One sees this solecism in newspapers, on signs and even on menus – "lamb in it's own *jus*".

Plurals require no apostrophe, though I would make one exception for the sake of clarity: which is when one is writing about individual letters of the alphabet. If one is writing about examination grades one has no difficulty with *Bs*, *Cs* or *Ds*; but when writing about *As* one may be interpreted as writing about the word *as*. So, for consistency's sake, I would counsel in favour of the usage *A's*, *B's*, *C's* and so on, to avoid ambiguities concerning *as*, *is* and *us*. This sensible convention is common in many newspapers, including my own.

Avoiding ambiguity is one of the great purposes of the comma. "Eats shoots and leaves" is a modern equivalent of Fowler's "he stopped, laughing" and "he stopped laughing". Fowler's two examples mean entirely different things, and the comma demonstrates a participle in the first sentence, while its absence shows a gerund in the second. Along similar lines is the venerable children's joke "she cooked, grandma!" "Eats shoots and leaves" is an extreme example because each of the verbs could be a noun: the installation of a comma or commas removes any such ambiguity. The same game may be played with "books plays and travels", and there are numerous other examples.

A comma in the right place may stop serious misunderstandings as well as those that are merely amusing. I would not favour using a comma before a conjunction in a sentence that, without it, holds no danger of ambiguity. Therefore I would regard "she closed the door, and removed the key" as exhibiting an unnecessary use of the comma by the writer. However, in a sentence such as "she closed the door, and the window, which was open, blew shut", the comma before *and* is essential if the verb *close* is not to be seen to apply to *window* as well. Dividing the sentence would provide a more elegant and less cluttered solution:

"She closed the door. The window, which was open, blew shut."

One should not put a comma before a conjunction at the end of a list: so "punctuation marks include commas, semicolons, colons, and full stops" has a final superfluous comma. A comma's use after an introductory subordinate clause is a matter of taste. One may write "before I left for the airport, I checked I had my passport" just as correctly as one may write "before I left for the airport I checked I had my passport". If one is concerned about style, and there is no risk of ambiguity, simply turn the sentence around: "I checked I had my passport before I left for the airport."

In Chapter Four I detail the circumstances in which one should use the conjunction *which* as opposed to the conjunction *that*. When *which* is used as a conjunction it should always be preceded by a comma, to emphasise that it is amplifying something about the contents of the clause that precedes it. So "I wore my green hat, which I bought in the sale" has the correct punctuation. Were the comma removed the *which* should be replaced by a *that*. "I wore the green hat that I bought in the sale" has a different emphasis, suggesting that the person bought several hats in the sale, and on this occasion is choosing to wear the green one.

As I have mentioned above, do not forget that when a comma is used to open a parenthesis, another is required to end it. Also, once one has used a colon one cannot use another in the same sentence: a semicolon, or a comma, must be used if any other break is to be signalled before the final full stop. After the use of a semicolon there can only be a comma.

It is important to use apostrophes correctly when signifying possession. Usually their use is straightforward: "*Mrs Brown's* car", "*John's* house", or "*Mary's* doll". Some writers feel that when they are not using this form, but the more formal *of*, the possessive is also needed: as in "a friend of *Tony's*". This is wrong, for it invites the question: a friend of Tony's what? All one needs to write is "a friend of Tony". The possessive apostrophe and *s* are ungrammatical. Onions charitably points out that the origins of this are in an ellipsis, signifying that what is imagined is a full phrase like "a friend from among Tony's friends". This seems unwarranted now when the possessive form with *of* is correct enough.

There is often debate about what to do with the possessive when the singular word requiring it ends with an *s*. Does one write *Paris's* or *Paris'*? It is my unequivocal view that one writes the former. One pronounces the *s* twice, so one writes it twice. One uses the device of a lone apostrophe after an *s* only when the word is plural, for one pronounces the *s* only once: therefore, one writes "the *dogs'* home", or "the *porters'* lodge".

As mentioned in the preceding section, think logically about the placement of quotation marks and brackets in relation to full stops. "If a complete sentence is within quotation marks, put the full stop before the final marks." (If a full sentence is quoted in brackets, put the stop inside the final bracket.) If only part of the section is included within the punctuation marks, then the stop comes beyond the final mark.

Having now learned the basic rules of punctuation and grammar, we must examine the ways in which – and the abandon with which – they are broken.

PART TWO

BAD ENGLISH

CHAPTER FOUR

Bad grammar

Correct grammar – the use of words in their orthodox relation to other words – is not difficult to master. It is a question of logic, and if regarded as such it will, by all but the most resolutely illogical minds, become second nature in anyone's usage of English. Grammar is designed to keep our language comprehensible and free from ambiguity. Although some writers and speakers of English (notably politicians) actively seek ambiguity, most users of English attain it only by accident. It is unfortunate when they do, because those with whom they seek to communicate are left in doubt about what they are trying to say. This defeats the purpose of communication.

Good grammar alone will not be enough to guarantee a good writing style: that depends too on the choice of words and the concision and originality with which they are used. The precise selection of words, with which I deal in Chapter Five, is also essential to conveying accurate meaning. However, grammar is the foundation of good style. Its violation or disregard has the same effect on language as filleting and removing the skeleton from a healthy being has on the body. The orthodoxy of its use has been established not only by logic, but by custom, practice and precedent. In educated and formal usage there is agreement about what that orthodoxy is. Users of English depart from it only if they wish to display a lack of conformity, which in formal contexts may cause those with whom they communicate to make assumptions about their intelligence and grasp of the language.

Those who have studied a foreign language tend to have a reasonable knowledge of grammar, though they are unlikely to have learned very much about it when acquiring their mother tongue. In preceding chapters we have examined the structure of a sentence, the building blocks of language and how to punctuate; grammar is the science of using those components correctly. It is about ensuring that nouns and verbs agree; that verbs take the correct prepositions and govern the right pronouns; that adjectives and adverbs are used appropriately; that tenses and participles are accurate; that clauses have the right subject and do not go off on an unplanned course of their own; and how in some instances the choice of the wrong word can lead to grammatical error. Above all, grammar is the means by which language remains logical, comprehensible and clear. If we learn to spot that offences against grammar are in fact offences against logic and clarity, we will come close to winning this particular battle in the war against bad English.

What follows is a discussion, broken down into sections according to the main parts of speech and other considerations, about what the main grammatical errors found in English are; and how to avoid them. In my experience of editing the writing of others, or simply reading it in newspapers, magazines and books, a surprisingly large proportion of mistakes seem to have had their origins in the writer's failure to understand, or remember, whether the items or people being discussed in a particular sentence are singular or plural. Therefore, let us begin with matters of number.

Number

One of the most common mistakes in writing or in speech is a variant of "none of us are free tonight". The pronoun *none* is singular. It derives from the old English negation of *one* and means "not one". Therefore one writes "none of us *is* free tonight", "none of us *was* there", "none of us *has* done that", and so on. The dictionary now says that the use in the plural is common. That does not mean it is correct. Partridge, writing in the 1940s, also sanctioned this usage in certain instances, but in quoting a usage by Dryden reflects the dictionary's view that the usage in the plural was common from the 17th to the 19th centuries, but has since been rectified. Partridge quotes a correspondent who dismisses the singular *none* as a "superstition", claims *no* is a contraction of it, and argues therefore that the plural usage is acceptable. The dictionary declares the etymology of *no* to be a variant of *none*. That does not settle the point about its usage, however. There was enough precedent before the 17th century, never mind the time of the creation of the alleged "superstition", of *none*'s being singular. So it should stay.

None is also an adverb whose usage is not subject to this error – as in "he is none the worse for his ordeal" or "they were none the wiser having read his book".

Other confusions of number include resistance to the correct "one in five is" and the like, where one now routinely reads "one in five are". It is easy to see how this mistake comes about: the writer or speaker knows that there are a number of groups of five, resulting in a multiplicity of ones that form a plural. That is not the point. It remains "one in five is"; the noun *one* is always and forever singular. If that is unbearable to some minds, then their owners should feel free to say instead that "20 per cent are".

Where one is describing one of a group that has a common characteristic, any verb must refer to the group and not to the individual item. So one would write 'he was one of those men who *refuse* to be beaten" rather than "he was one of those men who *refuses* to be beaten", as the relative clause describes the group and not the individual. The same would apply to "it was another of those things that *make* you mad" rather than "*makes* you mad".

Neither is singular when it refers to a pair of individual people or things, but has to be plural when it refers to a pair of groups. It must also be followed by *nor*, never by *or* or *and*. So one would write "neither John nor Mary was at the funeral" but "neither the Smiths nor the Browns were at the wedding": the latter for the obvious reason that each of the nouns is plural. Whether referring to individuals or groups, it can only refer to one in two. If there were three or more people, or groups, then use *none*, remembering to use a singular verb: "none of John, Mary or Jane was at the funeral," or "none of the Smiths, Browns or Whites was there": the singular is correct with the groups as, in logic, not only are the entire families not present, neither is any single member of them.

That last clause raises a point worth emphasising: that where individual alternatives (or more than two individual things or persons) are conjoined by an *or*, the verb remains singular. It would be plural only when groups are listed, as in "men or women are invited to apply".

Neither can cause difficulties when used with a mixture of pronouns. It is tempting for some to write that "neither she nor I are used to that", but it is wrong. The pronoun used second in such constructions is the one that must govern the verb. Therefore one should write "neither she nor I am used to that", "neither he nor you are allowed to go there" or "neither we nor she has been invited to the party". A construction such as "neither John, nor you, nor I is available" is simply wrong, as *neither* cannot be used with a greater number than two. As above, write "none of John, you or I is available", or "not John, nor you nor I". Fowler says this adverbial use of *neither* with more than two nouns is acceptable, an assertion of which I fail to see the logic.

Either, the positive of *neither*, is one of two, and is often misused. "Would either of you three get me a drink?" is so obviously wrong as, I hope, to require no further elucidation. "Would one of you three" or "would any of you three" would both be correct. However, fewer writers or speakers understand that "she had rouge on either cheek" is wrong (Fowler calls this construction "archaic")[1]; it is on *both* cheeks: *either* in such a context means one or the other, not both. "She had rouge on each cheek" would not be wrong but, since as a rule there are two cheeks on the face, "both cheeks" is to be preferred. Being one of two, *either* is also singular: "either of them is well-placed to win the match" is correct. As with *neither*, prefer "both John and I are happy to help" to "either John or I am happy to help". The second is not incorrect, but it requires the use of the verb to be in the number of the pronoun immediately preceding it. *Or* is the inevitable complement to *either*, never *nor* or *and*: "Either John or Mary would fetch the children from school."

Either also has an adverbial use, in negative sentences. "I don't want to do that either" is the natural response to an invitation to take an alternative course to one already offered. A positive response would be "I want to do that too".

Each is singular too. So one would say "Mr Smith, Mr Brown and Mr White each has his own house" rather than "have their own house". With groups, use *all*: "the Smiths, the Browns and the Whites all have their own family tree"; but "each family has its own family tree". Sometimes there appear to be pronoun problems with the use of *each*, as in "John and Mary each ate their apples". That is wrong. The clumsy "John and Mary each ate his or her apple" would be correct. The problem is avoided by using *both* or, where there are more than two subjects, *all*, as in "John and Mary both ate their apples" or "Mary, John and Jane all owned their own houses". The phrase *each other* can only apply to two people or things – "John and Mary wrote to each other" is correct

1. *A Dictionary of Modern English Usage*, by H W Fowler (Oxford, 1926), p129.

but "John, Mary and Jane wrote to each other" is not. "John, Mary and Jane wrote to *one another*" is.

It is incorrect to write "they each went to London". If you must use *each* (and it would be better to write *both* or, if more than two, *all*), write "each of them went to London". The same is true with other persons; *you each* should be *each of you*, *we each* should be *each of us*, and so on. I think there is also a subtle distinction between the usages of *each* and *both* or *all*. To say "we each went to see mother" may imply we went separately; "we both went" or "we all went" implies we went together.

Every is singular, as are its derivatives *everything, everyone, everybody* and *everywhere*. Correct usages are "every boy is good", "everyone has arrived", "everybody knows she is ill" and "everywhere is covered with snow". Instead of writing the correct but wordy "every man and woman must make up his or her own mind", write "all men and women must make up their own minds", or even simply "all must make up their own minds".

Any may be singular or plural, depending on the noun to which it refers. "Any people who go there are mad" is perfectly good grammar, as is "any woman who goes out with him wants her head examined". However, all derivatives of *any* are singular: "anybody who sees this will value it", "anyone knows she is foolish", "anything is better than nothing" and "anywhere is better than here". The usage "she is a more beautiful girl than any I have known" is a solecism. It should be "than any other I have known". The other abuse of *any* is in the Americanism "I don't think that helps any", where the correct English is "I don't think that helps at all".

Some words apply to specific numbers and are misused. There cannot be "the lesser of three evils"; it is the *lesser* of two, or the *least* of three or more. A similar misunderstanding applies to many comparatives and superlatives. One often hears reference to "the eldest son" when there are only two sons available; or "the youngest child" when there are only two children. For a **superlative** (normally

50

an adjective with the suffix *-est*) to be used there have to be more than two things or people being compared. If there are just two then the **comparative** (normally ending in *-er*) must be used. Therefore, in the two examples just given it would be "elder son" and "younger child". Another common mistake is found in the use of *former* and *latter*. These words can be used only when there are two things or people described in sequence. One cannot say *the former* of three or more, it is *the first*; or *the latter* of three or more, it is *the last*. All this is logical; it only requires an observance of how many people or things are being discussed for any solecisms to be avoided.

The construction **both...and** can obviously be used only with two subjects; and it is important to take care where the *both* is placed. "He killed both his mother and his wife" makes perfect sense in a way that "he both killed his mother and his wife" does not. It is also important to ensure that there is a parallelism in the items joined in this construction. If one writes "both the meat and vegetables were undercooked" it implies something is missing: the absence of the definite article before *vegetables* suggests that they and the meat are being taken as a single item and something else is about to be added. "Both the meat and vegetables and the sauce were undercooked" would make logical sense in one respect, though not necessarily in another. "Both the meat and the vegetables were undercooked" is grammatically correct.

A rearguard action against the neglect of the valuable word *fewer* was launched a few years ago when a supermarket put up signs over some of its tills that invited customers with "10 items or less" in their baskets to use them. It should have read "10 items or fewer". One has *less* of a single commodity; *fewer* of a multiple of them. So one has less sugar, less heat, less cheese, less grief, less work, less money; but one has fewer days off, fewer friends, fewer worries, fewer soldiers, fewer cream crackers and fewer pets. A related illogicality comes with the nouns **majority** and **minority**.

As nouns of multitude they may legitimately be used with a plural verb, as in "a majority of people vote no". However, the nouns may only be used correctly when applied to something that is a multitude: so to write or utter a phrase such as "I do that the majority of the time" is simply wrong. Time is one commodity; *majority* may often be a synonym for *most*, but it cannot be so in this context, or others like it. One may write "I ate the majority of the sweets" but not "I ate the majority of the soup".

Two final points on the question of number: first, remember that (as I mention elsewhere) there can only ever be one choice, which may be between no more than two alternatives, or any number of options; second, "the wages of sin are death" is correct, as is "the nastiest vegetable of all is Brussels sprouts". The verb takes the number of the subject governing it. Were these two examples inverted they would have to be written "death is the wages of sin" and "Brussels sprouts are the nastiest vegetable".

Plurals

Related to the question of number is that of which words are, or are not, plural; and therefore how the constructions in which they appear should remain grammatical by ensuring that all the words within them stay in the correct relation to each other.

Are institutions, teams, public bodies and so on plural? Does one write "the cabinet was divided last night on the question of the economy" or "the cabinet were divided"? In many cases there are established idiomatic usages for what Fowler calls "nouns of multitude". However, in many other cases there are not. Nor, as may be expected, is usage common throughout the English-speaking world. As cricket lovers will know, England *are* either batting or bowling when the commentator is English, but when they [sic] tour Australia England *is* batting or bowling.

We need only concern ourselves with what should pertain in British English. Fowler's point about the importance of remaining consistent is perhaps the most important. If one is writing about a body and starts by saying "the committee were agreed that Mr Smith be elected chairman", the committee must remain plural. If, later in the piece, it becomes singular, and possibly even reverts to the plural later on, the reader can only be confused and annoyed by the mess and inconsistency of the writing. One needs to make one's own rules, to some extent. Mine is that institutions are singular except where the overwhelming force of idiom says the opposite – such as with the England cricket team. So I would write "the government is...", "the Labour party is...", "the Brigade of Guards has...", "the royal family was..." and so on. This is a matter of taste, my own taste being shaped by what I regard to be the logic of the matter: but one must, having made up one's mind, stick to it.

Certain words, usually of foreign origin, are not always recognised by people as being plural. *Data* and *media* are the plurals of anglicised Latin neuter nouns and should take verbs as such – "the data were wrong" or "the media are scum". A popular fast food in recent years has been the *panino*, as it is not called: the singular as used by cafés and stallholders is always the plural, *panini*: "a cheese *panini* is £2". A *panino* is a bread roll in Italian. They are *panini* only when in a multitude. One often reads of how a celebrity was "chased by a *paparazzi*", which is the *panino* problem again. This useful word, which describes a particularly ruthless and unprincipled brand of press photographer, is in the singular *paparazzo*.

The plurals of most foreign words are now anglicised, since the singular words themselves are, though *media* and *data* prove that this is a question of idiom. It is quite correct to write *referendums*, *forums* and *dictums*; although *referenda* is still in common use and is not incorrect, *fora* and *dicta* passed out of idiomatic usage long ago. Nor would *formulae, tabulae rasae* or *copulae* be considered current. Some Greek words observe strict etymology in the plurals: for example, *criterion* becomes *criteria* and *phenomenon* becomes *phenomena*; no-one has yet tried arguing that *clitorises* should be *clitorides*, however, so there are limits. *Omnibuses* have always been *omnibuses*, despite occasional Victorian jokes about *omnibi*.

With words from modern languages the idiom may be less certain: one is as likely to hear someone from the musical world talk of *concerti* as of *concertos*, but one never hears anything except *sopranos, altos* and *impresarios*. If one heard *inamorata* in the plural it would doubtless be *inamoratas* rather than *inamorate*; a beloved man, should one wish to make his status Italianate too, would be an *inamorato*, and more than one would be either *inamorati* or *inamoratos*, the last sounding somewhat fruity, and comical.

Certain compound nouns have unusual plurals. A *court martial* becomes *courts martial* because in English we do not decline adjectives. Similarly we have *queens mother, lords lieutenant, lords privy seal, attorneys general, solicitors general* and *directors general*. Where the adjective precedes the noun there is less scope for confusion, which is why we know the plurals are *field marshals, major-generals, lieutenant-colonels, rear admirals* and *air marshals*.

It used to be the case that almost all English nouns ending in -*f* changed to -*ves* in the plural. Some still do: *loaves, halves, hooves, knives, dwarves, calves, leaves* and even *sheaves* are normal. However, *rooves, handkerchieves* and *beeves* are all now of varying degrees of antiquity, and *wharves* is probably on its way with them. There probably never were *chieves* or *oaves*. This is a question of idiom now, and of judgement: as with any English usage, using something that is obsolete or self-consciously archaic will detract from the message in the writing by drawing attention to itself.

Some common English nouns have irregular plurals with which

we are all familiar: *mouse* and *mice*, for example, or *louse* and *lice*. It never fails to surprise some literate people how many of their peers think that *dice* is a singular. It is a plural. The singular is *die*. *Spice*, it may be worth adding, is not the plural of *spouse*.

Jespersen points out that some singular nouns either inevitably do change their meaning, or may change their meaning, when they become plural.[2] It is our *custom* to shake hands, and shaking hands is one of our *customs*; but *customs* are also the formalities by which one enters or leaves a country. The plural of *colour* can also mean the flags and banners carried by soldiers on parades or hung in regimental chapels. Other examples are *spirit* and *spirits*, *honour* and *honours*, *order* and *orders*, *writing* and *writings*, *quarter* and *quarters*.

Although it irritated Partridge, who becomes quite cross about it (he headlines his article on the subject "plurals, snob"), it is also the case that idiom in Britain has for centuries spoken of plural quantities of game in the singular.[3] This remains current among those who engage in these activities or who have businesses connected with them, such as game dealers and sporting agencies. So one shoots a brace of pheasant, grouse or woodcock; one sees a covey of partridge (but a flock of geese), a flight of duck and a leash of hare; and one sees a herd of deer when out stalking. It applies to big game too: those who went pigsticking in India would talk of "plenty of pig in these parts", and might on their sporting travels around the world have seen a herd of elephant, buffalo, giraffe or rhinoceros. Perhaps Partridge had pacific scruples that caused him to be angry with people who pursued such quarry; but the fact is that if one wishes to describe such beasts in the plural, that is how to do it. It is not about being a snob, it is about being idiomatically correct. Using singulars as plurals also

2. *Essentials of English Grammar*, p205.
3. *Usage and Abusage*, p232.

applies to fish, something almost everyone does idiomatically and without a second thought. One would not dream of talking about *salmons, trouts, cods* or *skates*, and people who have nothing to be snobbish about quite happily talk of *haddock*.

As well as odd plurals, let me conclude this section with a note about odd singulars. *Physics, ethics, econometrics* and other studies or sciences ending in *-ics* are singular. Also, the singular of the plural noun *troops* does not mean a single soldier. A *troop* is a small group of soldiers. *Troops* are large numbers of them. It is nonsense to use the singular as a synonym for *soldier*.

Negation

To negate any word is, depending upon its sense, to create a sense of its direct opposite. Almost anything can be negated: nouns ("not John"), pronouns ("not him"), adjectives ("unappealing"), adverbs ("inelegantly"), verbs ("not to say"), conjunctions ("not until") and even prepositions ("not among"). This variety of usage means that the creation of ambiguity or downright incomprehensibility is sometimes possible if the negator – such as the word **not** – is placed thoughtlessly in the sentence. The negator must accompany the word it is negating. Where it acts as an adverb (as *not* does) it should come between the subject and the predicate; though there are certain idiomatic exceptions. For example, there is the emphatic negative response to the statements of others ("I should say not!" "I should think not!" "I hope not!" and so on), and the use of the negative to introduce a participle ("never having been here in my life…" and "no-one having told me that was the rule…").

In most statements one must place the negative carefully in order to convey precisely the meaning one wishes. Think of the difference, for example, between "she did not want a glass of wine" and "she wanted not a glass of wine". In earlier times the meanings would have been regarded as synonymous, though they could also have meant that the woman did not lack a glass of wine. In current idiomatic usage, in which word order is more regular, they have acquired further subtleties. The first is that she wanted no wine; the second is that she wanted more than a glass of it, or that she wanted a glass of something else. Understanding the context of a negated statement will also help to overcome ambiguity. "He could not eat breakfast" means something entirely different depending upon whether one has already been told that the subject has a terminal illness, or that he has a terrible hangover, or that there is no food in the house.

Sometimes, negating a word will not give the direct opposite of its original sense because of its inherent meaning. We know what *always* means. Yet *not always* does not mean *never*: it means *occasionally* or *sometimes*. The same applies to various words with an absolute meaning; the opposite is not absolute, which means it is partial. *Not everywhere* means *somewhere* rather than *nowhere*; *not everyone* means *someone* rather than *no-one*; and so on. It should be immediately apparent that there is a distinction between "not all could see" and "all could not see". The positioning of the adverb *not* in such sentences requires precision. If the negation of absolutes logically creates something that is partial, one has to find another means of illustrating the opposite of the absolute: which is the simple word *no*, or its cousins *none*, *never* and the like. The opposite of one's *always* doing something is one's *never* doing it; *not* is sometimes inadequate.

Avoid ***double negatives***. They are offences against logic and, if they are an attempt at being funny, they fail. Sometimes they occur by accident: not obvious stinkers like "he said he would not never go there", which can only be the product of illiteracy and stupidity, but a phrase (which I discuss later) such as "of all the casualties, she was the least unscathed". *Unscathed* is entirely the wrong word; it needs to be one of its antonyms, *injured* or *hurt*. Statements such as "it was impossible that she could not succeed" are mind-twisters; it is much better to say "it was certain she would succeed". Further down the literary scale still, phrases such as "not inconsiderable" and "not inexpensive" are unfunny if they attempt to be humorous, arch if they attempt to be anything else. They have no place in civilised writing, except in the most obvious forms of parody. Any clause that contains more than one of *no, nothing, never, nowhere, none, nobody* or *no-one* is almost certain to have a logical problem within it and should be examined with great care before being allowed out of captivity. If one is about to use a negative to imply a positive, it is always preferable to pause, reflect and use the positive. Why write "no-one is missing" when one means "everyone is here"? Or "nothing is wrong" when one means "all is right"? Such phrases should only be used in response to a direct question – "is anyone missing?" or "is anything wrong?"

Jespersen, quoted extensively by Partridge, pointed out the peculiar idiomatic senses of the negative with auxiliary verbs. He noted that the opposite of telling someone he *must not* do something was that he *may* do something else. This is logical, given that *must* is an absolute term. There is a difference between saying "you mustn't swim when the flags are flying, but you may swim when they are not" and "you must swim when they are not". Jespersen also notes the idiomatic usage of a negated *may* to imply, ironically enough, possibility: "I may not be the brightest light on the seafront, but I do know that..." and so on. Fowler highlights the danger of beginning a sentence with a negative, then forgetting that the subject of the second clause should not be negative: sentences along the lines of "no candidate may take a calculator in to the examination, and must complete both papers", the second clause of which should correctly begin "and all must complete...". A similar difficulty may arise in sentences beginning with *nor*: "Nor does he accept the force of his opponents' case, and argues that…" must become "and he argues that". As with so much written English, difficulties and ambiguities will be more easily avoided if the writer keeps sentences short and stops clauses proliferating. Otherwise, the logic of what is being communicated may fail, in this case most often because of the unwitting insertion of the double negative.

The use of *neither* I have dealt with in the section on number above. I merely reiterate here that it requires *nor* in the sentence, and should not be used with more than two items. *Nor* may also be correctly used after other negatives, as in "I had never seen him, nor her" or "He was nowhere to be seen, nor heard".

On the question of how to make a word (usually an adjective, sometimes an adverb) negative, Fowler sets an etymological rule: "It may be safely laid down that when adjectives ending in the obviously English *-ed* or *-ing* are to be negatived, the English *un-* is better than the Latin *in-*; *indigestible*, but *undigested*; *indiscriminate*, but *undiscriminating*."[4] There are inevitable exceptions: one would never say or write *irregenerate*, but rather *unregenerate*; though the dictionary finds four attempts at the former since 1657, by writers adhering to Fowlerite principles, the last of them in 1892. Nor would we countenance *inforgettable* or *unconvenienced*. However, generally the rule holds good. Sometimes the prefix can make a profound difference in meaning: see the example, in the next chapter, of *irresponsible* and *unresponsible*.

Always ensure that any negation is consistent. There can be a problem when a main verb covers two acts, both of which are supposed to be negative. In the sentence "he concentrated more on not crashing his car on the ice than on driving it in to a tree" a second negative has been omitted, rendering the sense absurd.

4. *The King's English*, by H W and F G Fowler (Oxford, 1906; 3rd edition, 1931), p51.

In such instances a recasting of the sentence is often the best route out of a construction that may end up sounding clumsy. "He concentrated more on not crashing his car on the ice than on avoiding the tree" does the job satisfactorily.

Negation, even when done properly, can confuse readers. If a sentiment can be expressed using a positive rather than a negative, always do so. "No-one was likely to fail the examination" is not so direct as "everyone was likely to pass". The more complicated the potential negative, the more desirable such a solution becomes.

Verbs: some general observations

Given the tenses, voices, moods and other properties of verbs (are they transitive, intransitive, or both?) there is plenty of scope to mangle their usage. When one adds auxiliaries into the mix the prospect can become even more daunting. However, if one keeps a clear head and cool demeanour, all will be well. One should not pretend, though, that mastering the use of verbs will not require mastering a lot of detail, because it will: and this reflects the significance of verbs in our language. As "doing" words, they communicate what is happening, has happened, will happen, might happen or should happen; and they have to do so precisely.

First, let us clarify the distinction between transitive and intransitive verbs. Some verbs that are only intransitive are sometimes wrongly used as transitive, and vice versa. A house of cards can collapse, but one cannot *collapse* a house of cards. One can make it collapse, or knock it down. Similarly, one can halve the price of something, or halve a grapefruit; but a price cannot *halve*. It has to be halved. It is also becoming common in American English to read that somebody who is the spokesman for a particular pressure group *advocates* on its behalf. *Advocate* is a transitive verb and it requires an object, so the spokesman must advocate ideas, policies or suggestions on the group's behalf. The verb *grow*, which is both transitive and intransitive, has in recent years acquired a separate form of transitive use that is peculiar and wrong. People can grow potatoes, or trees, or plants, but can they *grow* a business? They cannot. They can, and may, make it grow.

One complex misuse of an intransitive verb is found with the verb *exit*. It has long offended the logic of pedants, being the third person singular of the Latin verb *exeo*, to go out. So when people said, as they have done for 400 years, "they exit" or "I exited", Latinists would wince. However, this became an accepted English usage as an intransitive verb. Then, thanks to America, it became a transitive (or perhaps, in the light of subsequent developments, semi-transitive) verb, the first use of which the dictionary puts at 1976. Since then we have had people exiting buildings, exiting cars, exiting motorways, and so on: an unnecessary abomination, given the reliability of the verbs *leave* or *quit*. Now we have the verb in a fully transitive sense, where the exiting is something somebody does to something else: in January 2010 a newspaper had a businessman say "we are going to exit our business from the City of London", with *exit* now meaning *remove* or *take away*. Perhaps those who use the term would argue that it puts new precision into the language. The businessman was talking not simply about taking his custom elsewhere, but about closing his enterprise in London and re-opening it somewhere else. However, why could he not simply have said that he planned to relocate from the City of London?

The verb *to be* is the fundamental verb. It is intransitive and has no object. It describes a subject of a sentence: "I am tired"; "you are angry"; "he, she or it is lost"; and so on. Having no object, it must take a nominative pronoun, which in speech (and not just demotic speech) it hardly ever does. It is second nature for us to say "that's her", "it's him" or "it's me", and in speaking or writing dialogue it would now sound pompous or unreal to say anything else. However, the correct forms are "that is she", "it is he" and "it is I". In formal writing, in contexts longer than those simple statements, one should always stick to the correct form. "It was them who were there at the time" must be "it was they who were there at the time"; similarly, write "it was I who sent for you", "it will be she who will see you" or "it is they who must be held to account for this", rather than be seduced into any barbarism.

The other popular obsession about verbs is the **split infinitive**. This began with Latinists, notably Lowth, arguing that since the infinitive was intact in that language, it had better be as intact as possible in our own too. There is no reason in that sense why this should apply in English. However, the division of *to* from its verb was seized on by the Fowlers, correctly in my view, as inelegant. This rational observation carries more weight than a dubious precept such as Lowth's. It is hard to see why the phrase "to boldly go" is any less direct or forceful than "to go boldly" or "boldly to go". The meaning is as clear in any of the three forms as in another; but for the sake of logic and clarity *to* and the verb whose infinitive it forms are always best placed next to each other rather than interrupted by an adverb. In nearly 30 years as a professional writer I have yet to find a context in which the splitting of an infinitive is necessary in order to avoid ambiguity or some other obstruction to proper sense. Some writers may feel that complications arise where auxiliary verbs are brought into the phrase: "she used frequently to visit her mother at weekends", or even "she frequently used to visit her mother at weekends", will always seem to some writers more problematical and unnatural than "she used to frequently visit...". However, the principle is the same as with the present tense, and a correct usage with an auxiliary is just as easy to grasp as one without one. When dealing with the passive infinitive, such as in the sentence "she knew what it was like to be overlooked", the infinitive would be split by the entirely unidiomatic "she knew what it was like to repeatedly be overlooked". There is nothing wrong with "to be repeatedly overlooked" (or, for that matter, "to be overlooked repeatedly"). What is stylistically important is that the elements *to be* are not separated. I deal with the question of the positioning of adverbs in a sentence in greater detail below.

The **perfect infinitive** of verbs – the infinitive of the past, such as "to have loved" or "to have eaten" – is often misused. One sometimes reads "he would have wanted to have been there", which is wrong. The correct usage is "he would have wanted to be there": the sense of the past is conveyed by the finite verb and it is illogical to repeat it in the infinitive. Similarly, one would say "to be there would have been delightful", not "to have been there would have been delightful". Note also the logical difference between "I should have liked to see her" and "I should like to have seen her". The first implies that the opportunity of his seeing her may still be current; the second that the opportunity is in the past. The perfect infinitive should be used only when attached to a finite verb in a past tense, as in "to have seen her meant more to him than anything" or "to have lived in those times would have been glorious". Usually, though, where one may have the instinct to use a perfect infinitive, one ought correctly to use the present. One of the rare legitimate usages is to refer to a completed action after a verb of perception: "he appears to have broken his leg" or "she seems to have been lucky".

Writers sometimes use the infinitive where it would be more idiomatic to use the gerund. This is dealt with in the section on **participles**.

One fundamental problem with verbs in all moods, voices and tenses is the failure to observe the correct rules when using *shall* and *will* as auxiliary verbs, and therefore the imperfects *should* and *would*, the perfect tenses *should have* and *would have*, the future perfects *shall have* and *will have* and the continuous futures *I shall be going* and *I will be going*. The Fowlers dedicate enormous amounts of space to this question and, I fear, complicate it unnecessarily. Onions is more amusing on the subject: "The traditional idiomatic use of *shall* and *will* is one of the points that are regarded as infallible tests of the true English speaker; it offers peculiar difficulties to Scots, Irishmen, and Americans, the main difference being that these use *will* in many places where the Englishman uses *shall*."[5]

It may be helpful if we seek to distinguish between two sorts of unconditional futures: let us call them the simple future, in which the writer makes simple statements of fact about future events, and the future of resolve (I should have written "the future of will", but it is probably best to avoid that ambiguity in this context), in which he expresses determination or compulsion. In the simple future, the auxiliary verbs are as follows: in the singular, *I shall, you will, he, she or it will*; in the plural, *we shall, you will, they will*. So we write that "I shall go to town tomorrow" or "they will have jam for tea tonight". However, when the action in the future is a question of will – whether a person being determined to do something himself, or to ensure that another does it, the use of auxiliaries is reversed: in the singular, *I will, you shall, he, she or it shall*; in the plural, *we will, you shall, they shall*. Therefore we write "I will never smoke again", "he shall be punished" or "you shall go to the ball". The Victorian schoolmaster had a way of impressing this distinction upon his charges, with the story of the boy who drowned: for he had cried out "I *will* drown, and no-one *shall* save me". This applies also in the past and other tenses; and *should* and *would* also have subjunctive and conditional usages that I deal with below.

As Onions also illustrates, *shall* and *will* retain an existence as independent verbs that dates back to Old English. He defines it,

---

5. *Modern English Syntax*, p126.

in a passage leading up to the one I have quoted above, as follows: "The fundamental meaning of shall is 'to be under a necessity', 'to be obliged'… the fundamental meaning of will is 'resolve, intend'." Fowler writes of the sense of "intention, volition or choice" that must be conveyed by the statement "I will" or "we will", and how therefore it is nonsense to say it in a context such as "I will get up in the morning" (my example, not Fowler's).[6] So when the commandment says "thou shalt not commit adultery" it is seeking to place you under an obligation not to do so, just as the drowning boy, his grammar askew, was putting any potential rescuers under an obligation not to save him. "Thou wilt not commit adultery", by contrast, has the status of a straightforward prediction. There is logic, once one understands this, in the use of *shall* and *will* to provide the future tense. I can predict that you *will*, or they *will*, do something. Since I know my own obligations, I know I *shall* do it. If I have an extreme determination or resolve to do it, then I *will* do it. If I am seeking to compel others, then they *shall* do it. These rules today are widely flouted, and not just by Scotsmen, Irishmen and Americans, and this dereliction has caused our language to lose precision.

"Shall I go to London tomorrow?" is a straightforward question. "Shall they go to London tomorrow?" has the force of "must they?" or "is it inevitable that they will?" "Will they go?" is the simple question for the third person plural. Partridge contends that it is idiomatic to answer a question with the same auxiliary used in asking it, so writers of dialogue should be alert to this if they agree with him: I am not sure that I do. By his rule, if one asks "*Will* you go away?" the answer should be "I *will*". I cannot see what is wrong with answering "I *shall*", particularly if (as Fowler would observe) whether I went or not was not a matter of "intention, volition or choice", but merely a straightforward

6. *A Dictionary of Modern English Usage*, p527.

confirmation of what was going to happen anyway. *Should*, as the past tense of *shall*, denotes all the feelings that *shall* does; as does *would* for *will*. Some of these usages now seem archaic, such as the simple expression "I would not" for "I didn't want to", or Rupert Brooke's "would I were" for "I wish I were there".[7]

When these auxiliaries appear in dependent clauses that relate to a main verb in the past tense, they must be in the past too. "She realised that if she sat in the bar a moment longer, she would be late" is one example; "We understood that if we failed to pay the bill on time, we should be taken to court", is another. In the latter the impulse today is to use the solecistic "we would be taken to court". On the subject of solecisms, Partridge attacks the usage "I shall go; he doesn't want to", as being unacceptable in formal writing. So do the Fowlers. They prefer the repetition of the verb. Today it seems not so much a question of this pass having been sold as usage accepting that it is more elegant to avoid the repetition, and that to do so does nothing to impair meaning or accentuate ambiguity.[8] One can avoid repetition by writing "he doesn't want to do so", but that does not seem necessary either, and also risks the overuse and debasement of *do*. I fear that what was once branded as "colloquial" is now standard, but it is hard to see how the language has suffered because of it.

The conditional

The conditional usages of **should** and **would** in main clauses follow the same rules that I have just outlined. "I should like to do that" is correct for simple conditional futures. "I would like to

7. *The Old Vicarage, Grantchester*, line 33, in *The Poetical Works of Rupert Brooke*, edited by Geoffrey Keynes (Faber, 1970), p68.
8. *Usage and Abusage*, p335; *The King's English*, p341.

do it" carries with it an additional expression of will, and would be justifiable only in response to an assertion such as "you don't want to do that". Fowler was unhappy with what he regarded as the tautological use of the phrase *would like*, since the notion of *like* was contained in *would* in this sense, conveying a meaning of desire or intention. He attributed this to confusion between the idiomatically correct "I should like" and the archaic "I would", and I am sure he was right. It remains correct to say "I should like to thank all those present for their understanding"; in reported speech, this would become "he said he would like", to reflect the exact meaning of what he actually said.

There are a number of ways to express a conditional sense in using verbs. "I should go", "I would go", "I could go", "I ought to go", "I may go", "I might go", "I should like to go" and "I would like to go" are the main examples. Partridge observed that "conditional clauses have always caused trouble to the semi-educated and the demi-reflective; to the illiterate they give no trouble at all."[9] To avoid being herded into one of those categories, let us take each example above in turn. "I should get married if I had any money" expresses a simple fact. "I would get married if I had any money" expresses a determination that, should money arrive, I would be resolved to marry. "I could get married if I had any money" notes that my ability to marry is dependent on my being able to afford it. "I ought to get married if I had any money" means that I would feel an obligation upon me to marry if I had the means to do so. "I may get married if I have any money" denotes that I have the option to marry should I come into funds. "I might get married if I had any money" denotes a possibility of my marrying if only the money to do so were available. "I should like to get married if I had any money" and "I would like to get married if I had any money" are variants of the first two meanings above.

9. *Usage and Abusage*, p82.

Onions divided conditional clauses into three main sorts. The first, the open condition, covers those sentences "in which the main clause does not speak of what *would be* or *would have been*, and the if-clause implies nothing as to the fact or fulfilment".[10] These use the indicative mood: Onions's example is "if you are right, I am wrong". Other examples are "if they win the toss, they will bat" or "if she wears that dress, she will catch cold"; nowhere is it implied that the other person is right, that they will win the toss, or she will wear that dress.

The second, the rejected condition, are "those in which the main clause speaks of what would be or would have been" and the if-clause implies a negative. His example is "if wishes were horses, beggars would ride", it being obvious that wishes are not horses. Writers and speakers using this construction may not realise it, but they are using the past subjunctive; and it is the use of the subjunctive in the if-clause that signals the rejection of the condition. Other examples are "if you had any sense you wouldn't do that", the clear implication being that you have no sense; or "were you to let me help you, I should show you another way of doing it", the implication being that you are so stubborn that you probably will not. In these clauses, *would* and *should* are imperfect subjunctives, and they follow the rules for *shall* and *will*.

The third type of conditional sentence has a main clause identical to that of the first type but has an if-clause that "marks the action as merely *contemplated* or *in prospect* or implies a certain *reserve* on the part of the speaker".[11] Onions's first example is "if this be so, we are all at fault". Acute readers will note the indicative is used in the main clause and the subjunctive in the if-clause; the subjunctive is there to indicate the "reserve" on the part of the speaker. Another example is "were she to drive over to see me, I

10. *Modern English Syntax*, p67.
11. *Modern English Syntax*, p71.

shall show her my garden". Onions pointed out a century ago that this sort of sentence was largely in rhetorical or formal use, and it has become distinctly less idiomatic since then. The first two types cover most of today's eventualities.

Clauses of the first type operate in the future and past as well as the present. They always remain in the indicative and not the subjunctive mood. Examples are "if she drove that fast, she was stupid" or "if he goes to France, he will spend all his money". (As Onions points out, it has long been idiomatic for the future tense in an if-clause to be replaced by the present tense, as an equivalent to "if he shall go to France".) The second sort of clause can also be in the past or future tense, and requires the appropriate subjunctive. For the present tense, we have noted that it requires the past subjunctive: "were she to leave her husband, she would make a terrible mistake". The past tense requires the pluperfect subjunctive: "had she left her husband, she would have made a terrible mistake". The past subjunctive is also used for the future, making it indistinguishable from the present and therefore conveying an ambiguity that can only be eliminated by a specific reference to time: "were she to leave her husband in the months to come, she would make a terrible mistake", for example.

There can be a shift of time between clauses of the second type, and most sophisticated users of English have no difficulty mastering this. "Had I not drunk so much I should not have so bad a hangover now" is an example: the rule with clauses of this type is to stick to the subjunctive mood. In formal writing always keep to the rules.

Conditional clauses do not need to contain *if* to make them conditional: there are many other words or forms that convey an idea of possibility or eventuality. Among them are Fowler's despised *provided* ("provided he passes the examination, he will get a job"). Here are some others: "supposing you won the lottery, what would you spend your winnings on?"; "in the event that he comes, what shall we feed him?"; "in case of fire, break glass"; and "on the condition that you drive carefully, you may borrow my car". It will be noted that, like *provided*, most of these forms are merely a verbose alternative to *if*. In sentences containing the subjunctive, *if* may also be dispensed with by an inverted word order. Instead of "if I were to go, it would cause a disturbance", one can say "were I to go"; instead of "if I had seen her, I would have told her the truth," one can say "had I seen her"; and so on.

There are two degrees of conditional sentence. One sometimes reads a sentence such as "if Smith plays for United next Saturday he will be making his hundredth appearance for the team". This is fine, for it assumes there is a possibility that Smith could play for United. Sometimes, however, one will wish to make a conjecture about something that simply is not going to happen. If there were absolutely no prospect of Smith's playing for United – because he has broken his leg, or has dropped dead – then one would write "if Smith *played* for United next Saturday he *would* be making his hundredth appearance for the team. Most idiomatic writers would realise that, having used the first verb correctly in the conditional tense, a *would* would need to follow. As we shall see in the next section, the writer could also have started with a subjunctive – "were Smith to play for United…" which would naturally precede a *would* in the following clause.

Before leaving the matter of conditionals, it is important to note that the vogue for using *may* and *might* as though they were interchangeable is wrong. The distinction can be summed up in the difference between "the boy may still be alive" (but we cannot verify the fact) and "the boy might still be alive" (had he not caught the plane that crashed). In the first sense we simply do not know; either outcome is possible. In the second we know very well he isn't alive, but we are reflecting that had he acted differently he might not have died; *might* is a post-conditional usage. Perhaps a further confusion is that *might* is also the past tense of *may*: so where we would correctly write, in the present tense, "I hope I may be able to see you in London", in the past it would be "I hoped I might be able to see you".

The usages of *may* and *can* are also often confused these days, with a consequent loss of precision. *May* is about having permission to do something, or entertaining the possibility of doing it; *can* is about having the ability. If a man asks a woman whether he *can* kiss her the answer will, unless he has some shocking disability that restricts his movements, probably have to be "yes"; his ability to complete the manoeuvre is not in doubt. Were he to ask, as he more correctly should, whether he *may* kiss her, she can at least express an opinion on the matter. So when one hears someone ask "can I sit down" and we establish that his ability to do so is not in question, it more accurately becomes a matter rather of whether he *may*. *Can* is usually used wrongly for *may*; it is difficult to imagine abuses in the other direction – "can you swim?" and "may you swim?" clearly ask two completely different questions, and "might you swim?" asks a third. The first is a query about whether the person interrogated has the ability to swim. The second is whether he has permission to do so. The third is about whether there is a possibility that he could go for a swim – his ability to do so and his freedom to do so being taken for granted.

The subjunctive

Consideration of the conditional leads us naturally on to the question of the subjunctive, whose acquaintance we have already made in conditional sentences of the second and third type. It has a far wider use than we have so far encountered. As well as being the mood used for certain sorts of conditional expressions, it is (or was) most frequently used in dependent clauses of sentences expressing will, desire or hope. In certain forms it is markedly different from the most common mood, the indicative; in others it is indistinguishable. Over the last century-and-a-half or so it has come to be regarded by most British English speakers as an unnecessary facet of language. Few will have heard of it unless they have been taught Latin or French to a reasonable level. Since some archaic usages of it survive in everyday speech, everybody will have used it without realising he was doing so. This will have been not merely in the conditionals already described, but in phrases such as "God save the Queen", "lest we forget", "so be it", "far be it from me to say that", "may he rest in peace" and "be that as it may".

However, much of the subjunctive is now regarded as the preserve of pedants and reactionaries. This is to be deplored. Its correct use adds precision to meaning. It distinguishes a certain family of verbs, and the meanings and sentiments they convey, from certain others. Onions argues that one reason the subjunctive fell out of favour in English was because we lost so many of our inflections as the language evolved. However, the subjunctive has decayed visibly in the era since most of the inflections went. This, I fear, is for another reason offered by Onions: "the loss or decay of precision in expressing thought-distinctions; hence the substitution of indicatives for subjunctives". We no longer, unlike the French (or the Germans, for that matter: credit where it is due), summon up the clarity of thought that tells us there is a distinction of mood between those verbs that express will, hope or desire, and those that do everything else. The French especially remain particular about the subjunctive. Anyone who cannot deploy it when required (which is in circumstances similar to those in English, and others besides) is regarded as an inadequate speaker of that language. In English usage, it is one area where the Americans (with, as I have already noted, their peculiar combination of conservatism and gratuitous innovation) put us to shame.

It should be understood that in outlining the scope and correct usage of the subjunctive here I am making a case not merely for its retention, but for its renewed usage.

Let us jump in at the deep end, and imbibe a pure subjunctive of the sort that our American cousins drink every day, but which we would find not to our taste, or unpleasantly intoxicating: something such as "I order that he be brought here". The third person present subjunctive of the verb *to be* is "he be". It naturally, in this mood, follows the verb of will. It is easy to memorise the present subjunctive of the verb *to be*, for in all persons it is *be*. Let us drink deep of these, for example:

"If I be wrong, I shall be defeated."

"Though you be old, you are handsome."

"Unless she be reasonable, I shall not continue."

"He commanded that we be silent."

"He desires that you be comfortable."

"It is necessary that they be strong."

No educated American would blink at any of these. For our part, the current idiomatic usage has us reaching either for an auxiliary verb, which is tolerable, or for an indicative, which is demotic, almost idiomatic, and downright wrong. A careful person may write "if I should be wrong", which is a subjunctive (albeit a diluted one); most would use the indicative and write "if I am wrong". The same applies to the other examples. Even in instances where the subjunctive is used by more than just pedants, it is in increasing disuse. "I wish it were that simple" is increasingly rendered as "I wish it was".

If we make up our minds that we wish to use the subjunctive, where, and how, do we do so? We have already seen its use in certain conditional clauses, which are its main survival. The more specialist use of it is in dependent clauses. "It is the committee's decision that he be admitted to the fellowship" is an example of a dependent clause expressing desire or will. "It is desirable that a gentleman hold open the door for a lady" is another, and one that demonstrates how the subjunctive of ordinary verbs in the present tense does not add the *s* in the third person. Another example is "her father demanded that she tell him where she had been". This also demonstrates how the present tense of the subjunctive is used in reported speech after verbs of will and desire. Today, except in America, these usages would usually include the auxiliary *should* before the verb. The point is that they do not need to do so. In addition to its use in subordinate clauses after verbs of will and desire, the subjunctive also has a role after what we may term verbs of exhortation and suggestion: "she urged that he be included", or "I propose that she come". What will be seen to link all these verbal usages is that the outcome of the exercise – whether it be *hoping, suggesting, willing, urging*, or even *ordering* or *commanding* – is not certain: it relies on the actions of others. The subjunctive is a mood that is used to convey an underlying ambivalence or uncertainty, hence my use of it after "whether" in the preceding sentence.

Clauses beginning with *if* often need a subjunctive, as do some sentences where the if-clause is an ellipsis, and so imagined. We say "I should like to have some champagne" because there is an imaginary clause that says "if it is (or *be*) permitted" or "if there is (or *be*) enough left". Similarly, "what would you call your dog?" imagines "if you had one" and "she might have telephoned" imagines "if she had been considerate", or something of that sort. All those verbs are subjunctives. More obvious is the usage after *if* itself, as in "if he were to join us, would you mind?" Clauses with *as if* or *as though* also take a subjunctive: "it was as if she were up in the clouds" or "I felt as though I were drowning". *Though* itself takes one too: "though I be prejudiced, I feel my wife is beautiful", as do clauses with *whether* that raise a doubt about outcome, such as "whether or not he be qualified, he intends to drive the car" or "we tried to discover whether he were the culprit".

Both *until* and *unless* can take a subjunctive. The sentence of the law once was "that you be hanged by the neck until you be dead". Less finally, it would be correct to write that "he has decided to bide his time until his father come"; or "she said she would not enter the house unless the rat were dead". It was once asked of students reading English at Cambridge University to say where the verb was in Donne's line "Till Age snow white hairs on thee".[12] Once one realises that *till* takes a subjunctive, and that that subjunctive is the verb *snow*, all is clear. *Lest*, too, takes this mood, and it remains a very useful but underused word: "he refused to drink any whisky lest he have to drive" or "I took an umbrella with me lest it rain" are examples. *Lest* never takes a subjunctive auxiliary such as *should, would* or *might*.

Words like *however, whatever* and *whoever* may take a subjunctive in relative clauses expressing doubt or uncertainty: "however it be depicted, what he did was still wrong"; "whatever be your excuse, you had no right to do it"; and "whoever it be who told you, he was lying" are all examples, though they sound archaic today. There is also a past tense of the subjunctive that may be used in reported speech: "She said that whoever it were who told him, he was lying." Again, such a usage may be hard to defend against archaism. It is a question of idiom, but it seems to be that a subjunctive usage after verbs of will or desire sounds the least anachronistic when used today. Whether even that can survive another generation or two ignorant of classical and other modern languages is a matter for conjecture.

12. *Song* ("Go and catch a falling star") in *The Complete English Poems*, by John Donne (Penguin, 1971), p77.

Passives

The **passive voice** of a transitive verb is used to create the form that no longer has someone doing something, but has that something being done by a person. It is the difference between "I drank the beer" and "the beer was drunk by me". In good style, writers should avoid passives wherever possible. As is clear from this example, they are verbose. They are also indirect. As I have discussed elsewhere, they have political implications: they can be used to create distance and to de-personalise an action. There is a difference between "I have decided to sack you" and "it has been decided that you should be sacked" that should be too obvious to require further comment. There are more sinister applications, of the sort that turned writers and thinkers such as Orwell against them. A government finds it easier to say "restrictions will be placed upon the movement of people and upon their liberties" than "the government will place restrictions" because the apportionment of responsibility for so unpleasant an act is so much more blatant, and therefore damaging, in the second example.

In grammatical terms, the formation of the passive is straightforward. Another reason to avoid it is the complex mess of tenses that it tends to attract, rather like flies: from the mildly tiresome "the girl was being pursued" to the exceptionally irritating "the girl had been being pursued". This voice also becomes extremely unattractive when compounded. Many verbs require another verb to complete their meaning. This is straightforward in the active voice ("he hoped to see her again"), but it may lead to an abomination ("it was hoped that she would be seen again") in the passive. If an active sentence must be turned into the passive, only the main verb need change ("it was hoped to see her again"). Similarly, "they attempted to climb the hill" just needs to be "it was attempted by them to climb the hill", and "we intended to cut the grass" would be "it was intended by us to cut the grass". However, why anyone should want to turn an active into a passive is beyond me.

For all the political considerations of the passive, there remain fundamental problems of style. In her memoir of her late husband Harold Pinter, Lady Antonia Fraser writes that "technically, since my father was an earl and my mother a countess, I could be argued to be an aristocrat".[13] Such an abomination is strange from so good and experienced a writer, and the tortuousness of the phrase indicates some moral difficulty that lies behind her admission. Her use of the passive leads us to question how it is that a *person* – even one so elevated and aristocratic as Lady Antonia – can ever *be argued*. A point of view can be argued; so too can a contention or a policy. But can a person? Lady Antonia could have avoided this jumble had she used the active voice ("some will argue that I am an aristocrat") or, had she felt the need to retain the passive for purposes of distance, had she written "it could be argued that I am an aristocrat".

On a pedantic note, the passive voice of the verb *to work* is, correctly, *wrought* when the object that has been worked is some sort of material or substance. *Wrought iron* is iron that has been worked – *wrought* – by a farrier.

Sequence of tenses

This is another of those rules that come so easily to those who have learned Latin or Greek but can seem a struggle for those who speak English. It is the matter of ensuring that, in reported speech, everything remains logical by observing the need to put everything into the past. Onions defines it as "the principle in accordance with which the tense in a subordinate clause 'follows'

13. Quoted in the *Times Literary Supplement*, 12 February 2010, p34.

or is adjusted to that of the main clause".[14] This means that when the main clause has a present, perfect or future verb any subordinate clause is in the present; and if the main clause has a past or pluperfect, then a subordinate clause is in the past. "I have laid the table so that we can eat dinner" and "she will buy the tickets so that we may take the train" are examples of the first; "they went to the shop and bought some ham" and "we had some champagne and it made us drunk" exemplify the second. Onions specifies an exception to this rule, which is where something is "universally" true or at the time of speaking. I do not entirely agree with him. His first example is an arguable point ("he had no idea what economy means") and one can see how it may apply to other such concepts – "he did not believe that the earth is round". Yet in reported speech one would now, I think, be within the idiom to write "he had no idea what economy meant" or "he did not believe that the earth was round" without conveying any sense that economy now meant something different, or that the earth had changed shape.

So we should stick to the rule that once the verb in the main clause goes into the past tense, so must every other verb. Logic demands this, however strange the outcome may seem to untutored eyes and ears. Suppose a man says at this moment: "When I look into the bathroom mirror I see that I am bald." If he chooses to record this statement in writing tomorrow, or in a year's time, he must say: "I said that when I looked into the bathroom mirror I saw that I was bald." Were he to put what he said in quotation marks, quoting directly what he had said, then he would not have needed to alter the tense. However, since he has decided to use an indirect quotation, he must put everything into the past tense. In some minds confusion will arise because the man, who presumably is still bald, is saying that he *was* bald, as if that condition

14. *Modern English Syntax*, pIII.

has passed. However, to say "when I looked into the bathroom mirror I saw that I am bald" is simply wrong and illogical. It is not only with practice that one learns how to master the sequence of tenses; it is also with practice that one comes to understand that it is logical and makes sense.

The sentence "the leader of the party said he had ordered a review, and Mr Smith will repay the money immediately" is wrong. It should be "Mr Smith would repay the money". If the main clause is in the past tense, so must everything else be, even if one of the subsequent clauses refers to action in the future. "I said that I shall go there" is also wrong: it should be "I said I should go there". Perhaps in instances such as this there is a problem with the ambiguity of *should*, which as well as being the past tense of *shall* may also be interpreted as *ought*. The problem needs to be resisted. Precise writers will use the correct past tense of *shall* in reported speech. Should they wish to convey a sense of duty or obligation in the action they would write "I said I ought to go there", which removes any ambiguity.

The basic rule of not switching tenses in order to preserve the logical sequence is straightforward. In reported speech, every-thing, even the future, is in the past ("he said he would be going there the following day"). However, there are other considera-tions of the sequence of tenses that the usage of verbs throws up. Sometimes one reads sentences such as "the government has not and will not pretend to have all the answers", which is gram-matical nonsense; it must be "has not pretended to have all the answers, and will not". If one chooses to mix up tenses in a clause and use different auxiliaries, it is important that the verb works for both or all of them; and, if not, to adjust it accordingly. A report of actions that have taken place and are completed requires the past tense. In some journalism writers use the present tense even when reporting past events in order to convey a sense of immediacy. This may have its place in writing, for example, an account of an interview, but it has no place in news reporting, where it simply conveys a tone of cheapness and sensationalism. In more formal writing, in which a writer may be giving an account of events, it is simply wrong.

One final point about reported speech: in its purest form it contains no question marks, because no direct question is asked; and no exclamation marks either, for there are no exclamations. Both question and exclamation are neutralised by the report. Were one reporting "Will you come to dinner with me?" one would write "he asked whether she would go to dinner with him". Note also the change of verb, to make it impersonal in the report. "I don't believe it!" is reported as "he said he did not believe it".

Irregular verbs and verbal irregularities

We learn when very small that if we wish to put a verb into the past tense we simply add *-ed* to it. We also learn very quickly thereafter that in many cases, especially with the most simple English verbs, we would be wrong. That is because the English verbs that are the most essential to our life, because they describe some of the most essential actions of our lives, are of Germanic roots. As with many equivalent verbs in German even today, they change their whole form in the imperfect tense and have, quite often, another form altogether in the perfect and pluperfect. We call them **strong verbs**. So when a child says "I *drinked* my lemonade" we have to tell him that he *drank* his lemonade. Should he become more sophisticated yet and say that he *has drinked* his lemonade, or even *has drank* it, we have to tell him he *has drunk* it. There may be similar problems in learning how to use verbs such as *eat, see, sleep, run, ride, steal* and *tread*: but these are everyday verbs that we soon master and give no trouble to anybody.

There are difficulties with verbs that we use infrequently, however.

A resurgence in popularity towards the end of the last century for P G Wodehouse, in which an aunt or two always "hove into view", persuaded some people who chose to adopt this cliché as their own that there was a verb *to hove*; so one reads horrors such as "she hoves into view". *Hove* is the past tense of the verb *to heave*, just as *wove* is for *weave*. Should one wish to write the past tense of the phrase *stave in*, it is *stove in*. We know the past participle of *strike* is *struck*; but there is also the metaphorical usage, used these days almost exclusively to describe an emotional blow, which is *stricken*. It is not the case that *struck* is used only in a literal sense: one who is *struck dumb* has probably suffered no physical blow at all. A verb that seems similar, *strive*, has *strove* in the imperfect and *striven* as its past participle in all senses, though that does not prevent the occasional sighting of the illiteracy *strived* in either the imperfect tense or the perfect and pluperfect tenses.

There seems to be uncertainty in the minds of some writers about whether some verbs have a distinct past tense at all. *Fit* certainly does, though that does not prevent some people from writing "it *fit* me perfectly" when they mean "it *fitted* me perfectly". Does one write "I *quit* my job" or "I *quitted*"? In British English, the latter, though a battle has been raging on that question for about 300 years and is not won yet: the former usage is an Americanism. What about *cast* and *broadcast*? They are both irregular and do not add *-ed* in the past: so we have "he *cast* his bread upon the water" and "the concert was *broadcast* last Friday". Nor is *cast iron* known as *casted iron*, for this very good reason. Partridge disputes the point about *broadcast* and cites the dictionary in support. He was doubtless right in the 1940s; but the latest revision of the dictionary says the form *broadcasted* is now "rare", and our knowledge of idiom tells us that is correct. *Broadcast* works like *cast* and only failed to do so briefly in the early days of the use of the term to mean a wireless transmission. One sees occasionally usages such as "he had *hid* in the forest" or "it was *hid* in the bookcase". In both cases – the past participle and the passive – the correct usage is *hidden*. *Hid* is the imperfect of *hide* – "she *hid* in the cupboard".

Other irregular past participles from strong verbs include *mown, sawn, dreamt, spilt, leapt, slept, swept, kept, wept, rent, sent, bent, spent, sewn, sown, shown, spelt, smelt,* and *spoilt*. *Spoilt* is a special case: a dish kept in the oven too long may be *spoilt*, but somewhere that is pillaged has been *spoiled* (a contraction of *despoiled*). American English has the odd strong past participle that we do not share, as I note in Chapter Six, such as *dove* from *dive* and *gotten* from *get*: these must be avoided in British English. Some grammarians have decreed a distinction between certain of these irregular words when they are used as adjectives and when they are used as past participles or preterites (the technical term for the imperfect tense of verbs). It has been argued that there is a *well-mown* lawn, but that the lawn is *well-mowed*; and that one *spilled* the milk but cries over *spilt* milk. If this was ever the case it certainly is not now. All the words in the list above, and many others like them, serve perfectly well as the imperfect tense of their verbs.

Some verbs behave in special ways, or have to be used in specific ways if they are to convey the desired meanings, and these have to be learned. In British English (though not in American) the nouns *practice* and *licence* become *practise* and *license* as verbs. Pictures and pheasants are *hung*, but a man is *hanged*. As discussed in the section on transitive and intransitive verbs, *lie* and *lay* need to be deployed accordingly. A man *lies*, he *lay*, he has *lain* in bed; but he *lays* a hedge or a table, he *laid* it and he has *laid* it. The two participles are *lying* and *laying*. Confusion often comes with the similarity between the imperfect of the intransitive verb (*I lay* and so on through all the persons) and all but the third person singular of the present tense of the transitive one (*I lay, you lay, we lay, they lay*). If one is clear what action is being described – the choice being between a person *lying* down and *laying* something else down – there should be no confusion.

Because of the difference between transitive and intransitive forms there may be confusion with *wait, await* and *wait for. Wait* is intransitive ("I *waited* three days for the letter to come"). *Await* and its synonym *wait for* are transitive ("I *await* your reply with interest" or "let us *wait for* the dawn"). One never writes "I *awaited* in the rain", or "a terrible fate *waited* him", or any similar barbarisms. As I have already noted, *warn* has not developed into an intransitive verb, despite an enormous effort by semi-literates over the centuries to make it do so. One can *warn* somebody, and one can *warn against* something; but one cannot simply *warn*. If for some reason one cannot use an object, use the phrase *give warning*: "he *gave warning* that the weather would be terrible".

Adverbs

As discussed in Chapter One, an adverb qualifies a verb just as an adjective qualifies a noun. Perhaps it is this similarity of function that causes so many people, particularly in speech, to substitute an adjective for an adverb; or perhaps those people simply wish to spare themselves the effort of uttering an extra syllable, usually *-ly*. The main point one needs to remember about adverbs is that adjectives are not a suitable replacement for them. When one reads the sentence (as I did, in a newspaper, in November 2009) that "the economy shrank steeper than expected", one realises that even some professional writers have failed to grasp this point. An economy shrinks *steeply*. If a comparison is required, it shrinks *more steeply*. If it has outdone every other economy in the world in the steepness of its shrinkage, it has shrunk *most steeply*. This leaves aside the question of whether *steeply* is the right adverbial metaphor to apply to something shrinking, which it almost certainly is not. Logic, as always, matters.

Most other verbs and adverbs behave in a similar way. Dogs bark *loudly*; children cry *plaintively*; a footballer tackles *more daringly* than any other on his team. Some adjectives are abused as adverbs more easily than others. One often hears "it barked loud" whereas one has probably never heard "he cried plaintive". The more common the adjective, the more likely it is to be enlisted as an adverb. "Buy cheap and sell dear," "get out quick", "talk slow", "sleep sound" and "speak soft" have all suffered that fate. So has "run fast", though the dictionary gives a longish history of that particular abuse. However, "stand fast" is all right: the adverb *fast* means to hold firm or stick to one place, and has a long history.

Occasionally there are adverbs that look like adjectives. *Hard* has been an adverb for a thousand years (and *hardly* means something quite different). *Big* has been one since the 16th century, though its most popular application in this part of speech ("think big") has been current for a mere century; and few sophisticated writers would use it as an adverb. Kingsley Amis, in his book on English, berates those who do not see that the adjective *single-handed* is also an adverb. However, he is wrong, and the dictionary confirms this. It is a solecism to do something *single-handed*: it is *single-handedly*.

One adverb in particular, **hopefully**, has been extracted from its correct usage and is used (following American influence) as a self-functioning statement of faith before a clause to whose verb it is unconnected: as in "hopefully, Mary will be given a better report next term". Needless to say, it is not the giving that will be done hopefully, even though it is the only verb around with which this lonely adverb might associate itself. What the writer meant was "it is to be hoped", "I hope" or "one hopes" that Mary will be given a better report. This tiresome usage is now so ubiquitous that those who object to it are sometimes dismissed as pedants. It remains wrong, and only a barbarous writer with a low estimation of his readers would try to pass it off as respectable prose.

While in this strict temper, I should remark that other adverbs are used to introduce sentences in this way, and are not inevitably more acceptable when they do. Fowler sneered at *incidentally* in 1926. In the last 50 years it has become a standard filler, often used, as Fowler observed, to apologise in advance for an irrelevance: "naturally, those who find it most useful are not the best writers".[15] Whether explaining an irrelevance or not, fastidious writers may, if they have to use such a formula, use instead "by the way", or something similar. What is one to make of "interestingly, I saw Smith today"? The act of seeing may perhaps have been interesting, but that is not what we should imagine the speaker meant. It is an ellipsis of sorts, and we are to understand that he is also saying "it may be a matter of interest to you, or to both of us, that I saw Smith today". Much worse things happen in speech; but whether a civilised writer wants to commit such a thing to paper is a matter of taste. "As a matter of interest", or simply good old "by the way" again are equally serviceable. Other such adverbial sentence-starters (*arguably*, *actually*, *theoretically*, *obviously* and so on) are candidates for consideration for rephrasing, perhaps not least because they now come under the heading of "cliché" and as such show a paucity of thought on the part of the writer.

When it comes to forming conventional adverbs, there has been some debate about which should end in *-ly* and which should end in *-ally*. Several grammars present the rule that adjectives ending in *-al* naturally become adverbs ending in *-ally*, and all the rest take the ending *-ly*. This is not always so, however. Only the first part of that rule is right, and the process for other adjectives remains a question of idiom. Adjectives ending in *-ic*, for example, take *-ally* (with the exception of *publicly*); no-one

15. *A Dictionary of Modern English Usage*, p264.

would write *tragicly, dramaticly, idioticly* or *roboticly*. If in doubt, remember it costs nothing to consult a dictionary.

It is easier to make a rule about the adverbial (and indeed adjectival) use of words ending in *-ward* or *-wards*. It seems that in most idiomatic usages the adverbial type ends in *-wards*: "they went forwards", "she fell backwards", "the boy came towards me", "carry on downwards", "the road goes upwards", "proceed inwards" and so on. By contrast, the adjectival usages drop the last *s*. Stevenson wrote "I have trod the upward and the downward slope", a soldier takes a *forward* position, there are *backward* children (or there were before political correctness), *outward-bound* courses and *inward-looking* people.

There are other adverbs that do not, at first glance, appear to be adverbs, because they do not end in *-ly*. There are many of them: any word that qualifies a verb in a grammatically correct way is an adverb. Here is a just a selection of them: "they *also* serve", "I'm coming *now*", "she *just* left", "we're *almost* there", "he *always* eats there", "you will go *far*", "she *even* wept", "time *never* drags", "it went *well*", "do you come here *often?*" and most ubiquitously "they have *not* seen me".

Because of the influence of slang or vulgar usage, some adverbs (as with some prepositions: see below) attach themselves pleonastically to certain verbs, whose meaning is complete without them. Examples of such are: park *up*, revert *back*, watch *out*, test *out*, lose *out*, dry *out*, go *up until*, freeze *up*, tie *up*, free *up*, duck *down*, close *down* and shake *down*.

One of the fetishes that used to affect a certain adverbial usage was that one wrote, in listing things, *first, secondly, thirdly*. There was no logic to this. If one is writing a simple list the form is "First, he went to the bar. Second, he asked for a drink. Third, he drank it." It should be clear that the words *first, second* and *third* do not adhere to and therefore qualify the verbs; they are really adjectives with elliptical nouns ("his first action…his second action…"

and so on). However, if one were telling a story about a separate sequence of events, and using a verb common to separate actions, then one would use the numbers adverbially: "he went firstly to the bar, secondly to the table and thirdly to the car park".

Finally, adverbs may not just qualify verbs. They may qualify adjectives too: "*graphically* stupid", "*repulsively* ugly", "*stunningly* beautiful" and "*mildly* abusive" are all examples of that usage. Certain adverbs, like *somewhat* and *rather*, do little other than modify adjectives; in the contemporary idiom applying them to verbs ("he *somewhat* doubted it" or "he *rather* hoped she would come") is becoming quite restricted.

For where best to put an adverb, see the section immediately below.

Word order

The loss of inflections in English is one reason why word order has such significance. Once nouns lost an inflection in the accusative it was important that they were placed after the verb that had them as its direct object: as in "the cat sat on the mat". There is no problem of comprehension with "sat on the mat was the cat", though in most types of prose today it would be considered rather arch and breaking out of the idiom. "On the mat sat the cat" has the same problem. "On the mat the cat sat" and "the cat on the mat sat" convey the correct meaning but completely defy idiom. "The mat the cat sat on" is a different matter altogether, being comprehensible only in answer to a question about a number of mats. All other combinations are nonsense or change the meaning completely.

In Latin prose, word order, while not irrelevant because of its use in providing emphasis in a language without punctuation as we understand it, has less significance because one can always tell by looking at the nouns which is the subject, and which the object.

Take, for example, Sir Christopher Wren's celebrated epitaph in St Paul's Cathedral, *Lector, si monumentum requiris, circumspice*. It translates as "Reader, if you seek his monument, look about you". Put those words into any other order and they mean the same thing. *Lector* will always be vocative and will be the person to whom the imperative *circumspice* is addressed; *monumentum* will always be accusative and must be the object of the second person singular verb *requiris*; *si* will always, as a conditional conjunction, govern that main verb. It doesn't work in English: "Monument, if you look about his reader, seek you" is gibberish. In English, poetry is a rule unto itself, though the best poetry adjusts conventional word order only when there is no danger of ambiguity from the absence of inflection. At the opening of Book II of *Paradise Lost*, Milton, though he puts the main verb near the very end of a long sentence, creates no doubt about the meaning of his verse:

> High on a throne of royal state, which far
> Outshone the wealth of Ormus and of Ind,
> Or where the gorgeous East with richest hand
> Showers on her kings barbaric pearl and gold,
> Satan exalted sat, by merit raised
> To that bad eminence.[16]

Milton was an exemplary Latinist, and his word order could have been borrowed from Virgil. We may linger for a moment in doubt over whether the kings were barbaric, or whether the pearl and gold were, though we are helped by the meter to a correct understanding of the sense; but the delay in meeting the main subject and the main verb, even after clauses in which the word order is itself inverted, does not harm our comprehension of the passage.

16. *Paradise Lost*, by John Milton, Book II, lines 1–6, in *Poetical Works* (Oxford Standard Authors, 1966), p232.

Contemporary prose demands a more logical order, not least because it contains no metrical devices to steer us towards an understanding of the sense of a passage. Subject, verb, object is a good rule for the foundation of the clearest writing. In some prose, notably fiction or descriptive writing, there is plenty of scope to alter that order. That is not to say that inversions may not be used by writers even in the most formal prose, or in reporting; but these days a departure from the normal word order draws attention to form at the expense of content. In reporting dialogue "said Mr Smith" is no more exceptional than "Mr Smith said". However, such usage has the status of being formulaic now. An attempt to pass off a more esoteric verb in this way – such as "asserted Mr Smith" rather than "Mr Smith asserted" may find less favour with the reader. Sometimes a distinctive effect is desired; and an unorthodox word order, by drawing attention to itself, may create that effect. The Authorised Version has countless examples: "In that night was Belshazzar the King of the Chaldeans slain"[17] ;"and when they came that were hired about the eleventh hour, they received every man a penny"[18]; and "then drew near unto him all the publicans and sinners for to hear him"[19]. The Bible was written 400 years ago in this translation and its prose is consciously poetic; which makes a point about the effect of departing from the normal word order.

Two other points, already made, should be repeated here: that split infinitives are to be avoided, but the fetish of not putting a preposition at the end of a sentence need not be respected unless the idiom demands it. Sentences that begin with *and* or *but* are not wrong but unhappy, for they suggest incompleteness, and refer to sentences preceding that have, presumably, been inadequately

17. Daniel 5:30.
18. Matthew 20:9.
19. Luke 15:1.

completed. *Yet*, *however* and *furthermore* are less troublesome in this respect.

These are straightforward matters: other questions of word order are more complex. Chief among these is the **positioning of adverbs**. With transitive verbs, the rule is clear: something like "she loved with all the force of her being her husband" is abominable. With any transitive construction, the direct object follows the verb immediately. The adverb usually follows the direct object: "She drove the car *fast*", "he hit the ball *hard*", "they painted the room *well*". Those adverbs, not ending in *-ly*, do not function idiomatically anywhere else in the sentence; *-ly* adverbs just about do. One could write "she *carefully* drove the car" as well as "she drove the car *carefully*"; or "he *gracefully* hit the ball" or "they *cheerfully* painted the room". What one cannot do with any sort of adverb in such sentences is put it between verb and object, as in "they painted *cheerfully* the room", as it defies idiom and sounds like nonsense. The rule continues to apply where there are indirect objects: "she drove the car *fast* to the town" is more idiomatic than "she drove the car to the town *fast*". So too is "he hit the ball *hard* to the offside" rather than "he hit the ball to the offside *hard*". Some usages with indirect objects require *-ly* adverbs to come early in the sentence: "they *willingly* gave money to the boy" (or "they *willingly* gave the boy money") is preferable to putting the adverb anywhere else, unless there was some doubt about how willingly they gave it and the adverb needs to be emphasised: in which case "they gave the boy money *willingly*" is correct.

If it is so vexing to split an infinitive, how can one split a pronoun and verb with an adverb? It is a legitimate question. I should sooner write "he went boldly" than "he boldly went" for the same reasons that I should write "to go boldly": the sense of the verb phrase seems to my ear and to my senses to be reinforced by its being directly attached to the pronoun. While the matter is clear in sentences with simple transitive constructions there are, as we have seen, variations when indirect objects come into play, and there are (as we shall shortly see) more when auxiliary verbs are introduced. With intransitive verbs, lacking as they do a direct object, there is more flexibility about where to put an adverb; it is a matter of taste and idiom and a question perhaps best considered under the heading of style. Another option with intransitives that take adverbs is to write "boldly, he went", but that seems to me to become self-consciously poetic. If one puts an adverb too far from the verb it is modifying, confusion may result. "She went to the office with her new dress on happily" appears to mean that the garment was being worn with great contentment, which is unfortunate if the meaning to be conveyed is that her going to the office was happy, irrespective of what she was wearing.

The problem is magnified when there is a compound verbal phrase. "He had tried quickly to run down the road" suggests that the attempt was launched with haste; whereas if it was his running that was supposed to be quick, the order has to be "he had tried to run quickly down the road". With most usages of auxiliaries the adverb must be placed between auxiliary and main verb for the avoidance of ambiguity. "We shall definitely take John to France with us this summer" has a clarity not achieved by "we shall take John to France with us this summer definitely" and is stylistically superior to "we definitely shall take John…". The last of those forms would be used only in response to an assertion that they would not be taking John. An adverb such as *almost* has such a wide application that it must be anchored to the word it modifies: "she almost fainted when she saw him" means something quite different from "she fainted almost when she saw him". The first example describes her closeness to swooning; the second is a statement about chronology.

As above, the presence of an auxiliary can be complicating. "He had almost finished when the bell rang" is quite different from "he had finished almost when the bell rang". "They must nearly have been killed" is subtly different from "they must have been nearly killed": the first suggests that an intervention of fate prevented death, such as a lorry's having swerved and missed completely a car in which they were travelling; the second suggests that an accident took place, and injuries were sustained, but they did not quite prove fatal. When it comes to positioning adverbs one must take care to put them where the desired meaning is achieved. In sentences with auxiliaries, that will normally be before the main verb.

This is especially true of compound tenses. To insert the adverb *gladly* into the phrase "I should have had him shot" requires a little thought. It most naturally and logically goes after the auxiliary *should*, but an argument may be made for it to go after *have*. Sometimes, the idiom dictates a different positioning, especially if the adverb is the main point of the statement. In a sentence such as "this is not to be entered into *lightly or frivolously*" the desired emphasis puts the adverbs at the end. It is the same with other statements that are by way of a warning or an injunction, such as "I will not tell you *again*" or "please treat your children *kindly*". The shorter the sentence, and the less scope for ambiguity, the easier it is to displace the adverb to the end, as in "we went to work *happily*". With a construction such as "we used to visit my grandmother *weekly*" the idiom again puts the adverb at the end, since one senses that the point of the statement is to describe how regularly grandmother was visited. If a statement about one's feelings about visiting grandmother were to be the main point, the idiom dictates "we used *happily* to visit my grandmother weekly".

The adverb *always* usually precedes the verbal construction, as idiom also dictates: "we always used to visit my grandmother" or, to take other examples, "it always rains on Sunday", "you always say that to me" or "I bet you always do that". Putting *always* at the end of a sentence makes something of a point of it – "he said he would love me always" – and its effect should be noted. *Never* conventionally takes the same position, though there is not, outside poetry, an emphatic use of it at the end of a statement. *Sometimes* is more like *always* in that respect, in that a statement such as "we come here sometimes" creates no difficulties, though it has a force hardly different from "we sometimes come here".

Putting adverbs almost as a balance between clauses is also liable to create ambiguities. For example: "The dresses made by Dior *lately* have been worn by some of the world's most famous women." Were the dresses *made* lately, or *worn* lately? Probably both, but it was equally probably not the intention of the writer to say so. It should have been either "the dresses made lately by Dior…" or "have lately been worn by…". The danger of adverbs is that if they are not clearly attached to a specific word they will float off and look to be attached to whatever else is near. That last example could have had two interpretations. The next can have only one, but the comic effect of the positioning of the adverb means it must be moved to avoid becoming a distraction: "the man she saw regularly died" has to become "the man she regularly saw died" or even "the man died whom she had seen regularly" (sense dictates that, the verb of finality coming early in the sentence, the tense must change). If there are two verbs close together in a sentence the adverb must be allocated specifically to one of them. "The minister was said months ago to have signed the letter" does not make it clear whether he signed the letter months ago and this rumour is only now being broadcast, or whether it was being said months ago that he had done so. *Months ago* must go either after *was* or after *letter* according to the meaning desired.

One of the most important questions of word order arises when the word *only* comes into play. *Only* should be positioned as close as possible to the word it qualifies, otherwise it will qualify a word the writer does not intend it to. "She only went to the house to see her friend" means that seeing her friend was the sole purpose of her visit. "She went only to the house to see her friend" means that she went nowhere other than the house to see the friend. "She went to the house only to see her friend" means that when at the house she engaged in no activity other than seeing her friend. "She went to the house to see only her friend" means that she went there to see her friend and nobody else. "She went to the house to see her only friend" means that the unfortunate woman has but one friend. This is a relatively straightforward example; in sentences with longer clauses or a multiplicity of clauses the positioning of *only* is fraught with even more dangers. One should be similarly careful with words such as *even* or *at least*. The difference between "even she could not believe it" and "she could not even believe it" should be obvious; as should "he hoped he would at least be invited in" and "he at least hoped he would be invited in".

Here are two contemporary journalistic examples of infelicity that stem from a thoughtless word order. The first is "the Queen sent a letter of condolence to a pensioner whose dog died after he wrote to Buckingham Palace about the death". Were the order of that sentence changed to "the Queen sent a pensioner whose dog died a letter of condolence after he wrote to Buckingham Palace about the death" we should be in no doubt about the sequence of events, or about the literary and supernatural powers of the dog.

The second is "the body of a 45-year-old darts fan was recovered from beneath ice in a frozen lake in Frimley Green, Surrey, where he had been watching the darts world championships". This problem is caused by ellipsis – the elimination of structural matter that removes the nonsensical consequence of the statement – as much as by word order. The best we can do is recast the sentence as "the body of a 45-year-old darts fan who had been watching the darts world championships at Frimley Green, Surrey, was recovered from beneath ice in a frozen lake nearby"; or it can be divided into two sentences, with a full stop after "Surrey" and the elimination of "where". The longer the sentence, the more scope there is for an infelicitous word order that distorts the writer's intended meaning. It is another reason to keep sentences short.

The importance of careful word order when using negatives is dealt with in the section on negation above: but it must be emphasised what difficulties a misplaced *neither* can cause with word order. It is illogical to write: "I neither saw the accident nor how the driver ended up in the ditch"; it should be "I saw neither the accident nor how the driver ended up in the ditch". *Neither* would only precede the verb if there were a different verb in the next clause, such as "I neither saw the accident nor heard how the driver ended up in the ditch".

Variations of word order are used to emphasise certain ideas in response to specific questions or assertions. The difference between "they drive on the right in France" and "in France they drive on the right" is the difference between two possible preceding statements. The one preceding the first is "everyone drives on the left", and the main point that someone wishing to contradict this assertion must make is that some people drive on the right; and France is an example of where this is so. The one preceding the second is somebody saying that in France specifically they drive on the left; the main point about the response is that in France they do nothing of the sort. Word order will depend, as in these examples, on what has to be emphasised. "Yet again he has made this mistake" suggests the most important thing about the statement is that the mistake has been made for the umpteenth time; "he has made the mistake yet again" is more about recognising culpability.

I have dealt with split infinitives in the section about verbs, and have mentioned the mythology about not ending sentences with prepositions earlier in this section. I have already noted the problem with beginning a sentence using *and* or *but*; but beginning sentences with other conjunctions is a matter of individual taste. In journalism I have never worried about it – not just *however*, but not even *but* nor *and* has ever distressed me. However, I am not sure I would introduce a sentence with these conjunctions in writing more formal than journalism, though *however* (as the alert reader will have noticed) provides me with no difficulties at all. Fiction writers, for rhetorical effect, have licence in these matters, notably when reaching a climax: whether in Hardy's antepenultimate sentence of *Tess of the d'Urbervilles* ("And the d'Urberville knights and dames slept on in their tombs unknowing"[20]) or in John Cowper Powys's sublimely bathetic conclusion to *Wolf Solent* ("And then he thought. 'Well, I shall have a cup of tea.'"[21]).

One final matter of word order: when using the construction *rather a* do not be tempted to invert it when an adjective comes along. There is nothing wrong with "she was rather a harridan" and a good writer would add an adjective as follows: "she was rather an ugly harridan". The construction "she was a rather ugly harridan" is to be avoided; if the adjective is removed the construction "a rather harridan" makes no sense, whereas "rather a harridan" would. The same stricture applies to *quite*.

Participles

Every verb has participles. They can be used adjectivally in both the active and the passive voice. The most frequently encountered is the present active – *eating, seeing, reading, watching*. There is also the past participle, which requires an auxiliary verb – *having eaten, having seen* and so on. The future participle also requires one – *being about to eat, being about to see*. There are comparable tenses in the passive voice, though with more subtle shading.

20. *Tess of the d'Urbervilles*, by Thomas Hardy (Macmillan, New Wessex Edition, 1974), p449.
21. *Wolf Solent*, by John Cowper Powys (Jonathan Cape, 1929), p644.

There is both a present tense (*seen*) and a continuous present (*being seen*); and a past participle (*having been seen*) and a future (*about to be seen*). Certain participles can also serve as nouns, and these are known as **gerunds**. For example: "they saw her *drinking*" uses the participle adjectivally, to describe *her*; but "her *drinking* is becoming a problem" uses it as a noun, and therefore it is a gerund. The past participle can also serve as a gerund: "His *having watched* it showed him how boring it was" for example. So too can the passive past participle: such as in "her *having been forgotten* presented a problem". It should be noted that correct use of the gerund requires the possessive pronoun, and the possessive of any noun. One would say "I deplored *his* having been left out" or "she remembered *their* coming last Christmas".

If there are risks of ambiguity, or clumsiness of construction, do not forget that there are other ways of conveying the same sense: "they saw her drink" avoids the participle (though it creates an ambiguity, since "her drink" could be the possessive pronoun and a noun), just as "the amount she drinks is becoming a problem" avoids the gerund. With the past participle, turning the sentence around obviates a gerund: "it presented a problem that she had been forgotten" or, given the preference for the active voice, "it presented a problem that they had forgotten her". The Fowlers, in a lengthy article on this subject, say there is a "hybrid" usage between gerund and participle, and the example they give is "I do not mind you writing it".[22] This seems to complicate matters unnecessarily. The phrase is a straightforward use of the present participle, it seems to me, a substitute for "I do not mind that you write it". The gerund would be "I do not mind your writing it", which would be as correct and, it may be argued, more elegant stylistically. Other typical usages are found in constructions like "he admitted the idiocy of his driving while drunk", "she saw the

22. *The King's English*, p117.

point of his going" or "they acknowledged the wisdom of her dressing warmly".

Accomplished use of the gerund suggests sophistication because it also suggests a grasp of grammar usually associated with those who have been taught English grammar, or (sometimes and) the grammar of foreign languages. It is not a usage that comes easily to the uneducated.

In many cases, use of a participle will be as correct as use of a gerund. "I am most unhappy with my son wasting all his money in that way" is no less correct than "I am most unhappy with my son's wasting all his money". Stylists, however, will prefer the second usage. The Fowlers talked of the "fused participle" to indicate the use of a participle that was not a gerund but remained correct. An example they gave was as follows.[23] They used the sentence "I dislike my best friend violating my privacy" which they pointed out could also be rendered "I dislike my best friend's violating my privacy". In the second instance the gerund was used correctly. In the first, what they termed the fused participle effectively became the compound noun "the-violation-by-a-friend". Like some other explanations they advance, this seems a needless complication. All one needs to note is that the usage without the possessive is a clumsy one, though much validated by repetition in the last 100 years or so. The usage with the possessive is the correct use of the gerund, and to be commended. Justifications for other usages are, by this stage, purely academic.

Where the gerund follows a verb there may sometimes be doubt in the writer's mind about whether to use the possessive. This needs to be removed. It may seem instinctive to write "I regret him leaving his wife", since transitive verbs seem to cry out for a direct object. However, the correct form is "I regret his leaving his wife". In the same way, one would say "we have no

23. *The King's English*, pp124–125.

hope of its being sunny tomorrow", not "it being sunny". There is also a tendency to feel that the possessive may be dispensed with where a proper name is used, such as in sentences like "no-one took account of Mr Smith having the right to vote": yet there is nothing wrong with its [sic] being "Mr Smith's having the right to vote"; indeed, many would argue that such a usage was entirely correct and desirable.

With abstract nouns the correct use of the gerund seems even more important, as in "the committee believed the decision's being taken would bring an end to the matter". To lose the possessive would leave a sense of incompleteness, not to say ambiguity or lack of clarity. Like many sentences in which participles or words that appear to be participles occur, confusion can be avoided by making them short and structuring them properly.

There can be a potential problem when the noun that must take the possessive is long and complicated, and possibly multiple, as in the sentence "he deplored the foreign ministers of the allied countries' having spoken so bluntly". When a problem such as this arises it is not the fault of the gerund, but the fault of the writer's having cast his sentence so badly. There is nothing wrong with "he deplored the blunt speaking by the foreign ministers of the allied countries".

The Fowlers expended much ink and energy on when, in certain constructions, to use a gerund, and when to use an infinitive. Is it – to use their examples – "a duty to make" or "the duty of making"? Or is it "aiming to be" or "aiming at being"? A century later, the idiomatic usages in each case appear to be better established. The Fowlers tried to point the way, arguing that after a noun the usage is usually of the gerund, after a verb it is usually an infinitive. This is sometimes true, but not inevitably. It may sound, and indeed be, as correct to say "he relished the chance to play against Smith" as it would be to say "he relished the chance of playing against Smith", but good style prefers the latter. By contrast, "she was aiming at buying the dress before the weekend" is clumsy and unnatural compared with "she aimed to buy the dress". Yet most of us today would say "I had a duty to look after him" rather than the more pompous-sounding "I had the duty of looking after him". Perhaps a subtle difference has grown up between the two usages. The former gives the impression of a moral obligation, the latter, with its definite article, of one ordained by some rule or statute. The Fowlers concede that if a noun takes an indefinite article it probably requires a gerund, but with a definite article it needs the infinitive. This is still true today, and one can discern a natural distinction between "he wanted a chance of playing against Smith" and "he wanted the chance to play against Smith". Both are correct.

Many verbs of intention or desire naturally take an infinitive – *hope to, long to, wish to* – and no-one would seek to make a construction using the gerund instead, not least because no precedent exists. It does with *aim*, which is unusual. Over the last century the gerund does appear to have retreated in the face of the infinitive. If one used a construction today such as "she had the ability…" It would be the ability *to do* something, not *of doing* something. It is much more likely, though, that a writer would simply say "she could…". Indeed, deciding to be less verbose may eliminate many difficulties with this construction. Does one write "he had the intention of seeing her" or "he had the intention to see her?" Again, good style demands the former, but "he intended to see her" is shorter, says the same thing, and avoids any doubt. Where once we would have said "I did not think to do that", the idiomatic usage has become "I did not think of doing that".

There are verbs where a following infinitive is mandatory, though this is often concealed by sloppy usage of the conjunction *and*. "I will try and do better", "she was going to go and see him" and "will you come and see me" can all have the conjunction replaced by *to* in formal English.

Fowler defines a usage called the "converted participle" where a participle, by idiom, stands alone: his first example is "talking of test matches, who won the last?" and the subject of the second clause deliberately has no relation to the participle in the first.[24] This he relates to the gerund, saying it is a shortened version of the archaic *a-talking*. In the last century the idiom has taken root and no longer seems worthy of comment. The participle does not need a noun because it is, as a gerund, a noun in itself; that is why it is not solecistic to adopt this usage.

There is alarming scope for participles to go wrong. Onions gave a simple example in his grammar: "After fighting the flames for several hours the ship was abandoned."[25] The ship did not fight the flames; but that is the logical sense of this construction. One should note how the problem comes about: it is through the use of the passive voice in the second clause. Using the passive removes the people who were fighting the flames. Had the sentence been left in the active voice and read "after fighting the flames for several hours the men abandoned ship" the sense would have been clear and logical. If one way of avoiding problems with participles is to shorten sentences, another is to avoid eliminating the natural subjects of a participle by keeping the sentence in the active voice. As we shall see below, however, there are some rare circumstances where the passive improves sense rather than destroys it.

In the century since Onions drew attention to this trap many thousands of writers have chosen, nonetheless, to fall into it. The following examples were culled from the press over a few days in the winter of 2009–10. First, "stricken with grief by the tragedy, her father attempted to console her". That does not even have the excuse of confusion with the passive; it is simply the wrong subject,

24. *A Dictionary of Modern English Usage*, p675.
25. *Modern English Syntax*, p123.

the writer's mind confused by the presence of the "attempted to" construction in the second clause. In a case like this, the sentence has to be recast. "Stricken with grief by the tragedy, she was attempted to be consoled by her father" is hideous. It would be better to turn the whole idea around and to write: "her father attempted to console her, stricken with grief by the tragedy as she was". Better still would be: "she was stricken with grief by the tragedy, but her father attempted to console her".

Second, "the day before he died, David Cameron and his wife played with their son". It was not Mr Cameron who died, but his unfortunate son. Simple inversion of the clauses solves the problem. The writer, who clearly had not thought of this, had thought neither of what the subject of his sentence was. Third, this reporter was too busy reminiscing about his career to see that he had attributed it to somebody else: "as a young reporter, Mrs Smith told me that...". Alteration of the word order to "Mrs Smith told me, as a young reporter, that...", or, better still, "when I was a young reporter, Mrs Smith told me that..." is required. Insertion of the correct subject – in this case *I* – must always rectify the problem.

Fourth, "several Japanese tourists filmed the couple for 20 minutes before being arrested". The tourists were not arrested; the couple were. In a sentence such as this perhaps the passive is the answer: "for 20 minutes before the couple were arrested they were filmed by Japanese tourists" leaves no-one in any doubt who ended up in the cells.

Politicians do appear to be especially vulnerable to participle abuse. Edward McMillan-Scott, an MEP, published a press release on 14 January 2010 in which he wrote: "As a Conservative Party member for 42 years, an MEP for 25, leader of the MEPs for four and a Conservative Board member for three years, this is no longer the party I knew." It is hard to know where to start with this jumble, other than to note that the party was not a member of itself, an MEP, the MEPs' leader or a board member. Mr McMillan-Scott could say only what he intended to say by having two sentences. "I have been a Conservative Party member for 42 years (and so on). This is no longer the party I knew."

This sort of abuse is variously known as the **hanging participle**, the suspended participle or the misrelated participle. Sometimes participles are left dangling because of the thoughtless shift in a sentence from the active to the passive voice, in which confusion the logic of the sentence is lost. "Though refusing to concede that he had a point, it must be said that I started to see the force of his argument". The use of the passive and the arrival of *it* as the subject of the second clause destroys the sense of the sentence: it was not *it* that refused to concede the point, but *I*.

The rule for avoiding them is deceptively simple. If you are going to use a participle construction, make sure the subject of it is the subject you intend. This must always be the actor of the verb and not somebody or something else. When one writes "Going into the garden…", one needs to have a clear idea of who is doing the going. If it is *I* there is no sense in following that clause with the statement "she greeted me while she was pruning the roses". It has to be "I saw her pruning the roses, and she greeted me". As Onions says, "the participle must always have a proper subject of reference".[26] If it does not have one the result will be an illogicality; so give it one.

The shorter a sentence is, the less likelihood there will be of misusing participles. The problem arises when over two or three clauses the main subject ceases to govern the ensuing participles. Here is an extreme example: "The children went into the barn and, being dark, they could see nothing." The participle *being* can only correctly refer back to the children, not the barn: but we sense it is intended to refer to the barn. The subject of the third

26. *Modern English Syntax*, p124.

clause – *they* – seems to refer to the children's being dark again, but even if they were that would be no reason for them to see nothing. "The children went into the barn. Because it was dark inside, they could see nothing" would obviate the problem. The iron rule about participles is that each must be closely connected with a subject; including when, as gerunds, they may be subjects themselves.

Punctuation is important in all contexts, but especially with participles. The sentence "the man having refused to open the door, the woman did it herself" is correctly punctuated. Inserting a comma after "man" would make an absurdity of the sense. Sentences with participle constructions tend to be long; there should, therefore, always be proper regard to the use of punctuation.

Pronouns

Jespersen stops the traffic in his *Essentials of English Grammar* when writing about pronouns with his example "if the baby does not thrive on raw milk, boil it".[27] The great Dane contends that "there is really little danger of misunderstanding *it*", and he is right. There is, though, a danger of misunderstanding the British sense of humour. Knowing very well to what *it* refers, the average Briton will still chortle at the ambiguity, which means that the writer – who was seeking to make a serious point – will instead have created a distraction. There is a place for jokes in writing, but they are best when they are intentional.

The most common difficulties with pronouns occur when they lack the correct antecedent, or when (as in Jespersen's example) it becomes unclear what the antecedent is. Take this example: "the woman bought a lottery ticket and proceeded to win it". We all

27. *Essentials of English Grammar*, p153.

know what the writer is trying to say, but through lack of thought he has ended up saying something quite different. *It* can refer only to the lottery ticket, not to the lottery itself. Sometimes, confusion of thought causes writers to use a verb and then refer to it using a pronoun as though it were a noun, as in "John decided to propose to Mary, but she turned it down". She could have turned *him* down, but since a proposal is not mentioned there is nothing for *it* to refer back to, other than something understood by the verb. Simply paying attention to what one has written, and thinking of the logic with which one uses a pronoun, will normally prevent such confusions as these. Idiomatically, there is one regular usage in English of a pronoun that requires no antecedent. This is when *they* is used to describe a generality of opinion or people as in "they would, in those days, open a door for a lady" or "they say she is going to marry him". This usage would not normally be found in formal writing.

There is also a danger of ambiguity when more than one subject has been introduced early in a sentence, or in a previous sentence, and it becomes unclear exactly to what the pronoun is referring. "Smith and Brown both pleased their teacher with their answers, and he rewarded them with excellent marks" gives no-one any difficulties. Although there are three masculine subjects it is quite clear that the *he* can only be the teacher. However, a sentence such as "Smith met Brown and he gave him a drink" is properly ambiguous, unless it has been made clear to the reader already who has control of a drinks cabinet. Logic may seem to dictate that the *he* automatically refers back to the subject of the sentence (Smith) but there is no reason why that should be so. There would be nothing ungrammatical or illogical about "Smith met Mrs Brown and she gave him a drink", after all. In a sentence such as this another formula has to be used: either the use of "the former...the latter", which is rather stiff, or simply the repetition of one of the proper names in the second clause in order to remove doubt. I would favour "and he gave Brown a drink". Jespersen presents the example "John told Robert's son that he must help him", which he points out "is capable of six different meanings".[28] Only one extra meaning should be sufficient evidence for a writer to know he has to find the means of eliminating the ambiguity.

Beware, in long sentences, of estranging the pronoun too far from its antecedent, as this too may give rise to doubts. As with much that can go wrong in writing, this fault may be rectified by the short sentence. This is true too of statements such as "Jane had eaten up everything on her plate, but her dislike of the salad dressing caused her mother to leave the lettuce on hers". Until we get to the words "her mother" we think the possessive pronoun in "her dislike" refers to Jane. It is always better if the pronoun does not precede its antecedent.

There can be trouble, too, with accusatives. As I have noted elsewhere, the obvious need for an accusative pronoun when it is the object of a verb ("I hit him", "he kissed her", "we saw them" and so on) tends to get lost after an *and*. "He gave Mary and I his card" is clearly illiterate. **Whom**, the accusative of the pronoun *who*, is now so in disuse that many who hear or read it regard it as an affectation. This is ridiculous. However, as bad as not using *whom* at all is the art of using it wrongly. In the winter of 2009–10 this appeared in a newspaper: "the task of cutting is likely to fall to George Osborne, whom we hope will embrace the bold ideas…". Take out the "we hope" and it clear that the *whom* has no place there. Mr Osborne, or rather his pronoun, is the subject of the clause and not its object. It is more often that one encounters the problem in reverse, as in "Mr Osborne, who we used to see in the House of Commons", which cries out for a *whom*. It is sometimes possible, and always if possible desirable, to obviate such difficulties by splitting sentences into shorter ones. In collo-

28. *Essentials of English Grammar*, p154.

quial speech *whom* has almost entirely disappeared; it should not do so in formal writing. As noted in the section on verbs above, the pronoun with the verb *to be* always takes the nominative case in formal writing; "it's me" is colloquial and acceptable in informal speech.

When using the pronoun *one*, be consistent. Within a passage of prose, should one use *one*, one should use it all the time. Do not shift to *you* in the following sentence, and then, quite possibly, back again. Some consider the use of this pronoun pompous. I would agree that in certain circumstances and contexts it very much can appear to be. I have used it throughout this book to describe the activities of an indeterminate third person, much as the French do not hesitate to do with the impersonal pronoun *on*. This little pronoun has a use that is both the same as our *one* but also rather wider in its idiomatic usages; yet the ground it covers is theoretically the same as that covered by *one*, which is why it is worth considering how exactly it is deployed. When a Frenchman says "*on dit qu'elle est folle*" he is saying "they say she's mad", without having to specify that "they" are any specific people other than the general run of his acquaintances. If he says "*ici, on boit du vin avec nos repas*", he is saying "here, we drink wine with our meals". If he says "*on ne veut pas le faire*" he is saying "you don't want to do that". This breadth of usage, still common in France (and enormously useful to the Francophone) is steadily being lost in English.

The pompous usage of *one* is most perceptible when it is used as a substitute for *I*. It is hard these days to excuse statements such as "one spent the weekend in the country with one's friends" unless one is being satirical, or sending oneself up. Its use for other persons, as in the examples given in French above and as I have mentioned in Chapter One, is however much to be commended. If enunciating a general principle to someone else, either in speech or in writing, it is far better to say or write "one shouldn't run off with other men's wives" than "you shouldn't", in case the listener or reader thinks he specifically is being addressed and aspersions are being cast about his moral character when, in fact, that is not so. Using *one* for the first person plural risks pomposity, as it does for the first person singular, even though *on* as a substitute for *nous* is perhaps its most frequent usage in French. It is perhaps idiomatically most acceptable when outlining general principles rather than describing what the speaker and others have done: no-one ought to find fault with "one votes at general elections in order to ensure one has a say in the running of the country" as a preferable way of saying "we vote…". As with the *you* usage, to say *we* implies that that is why the speaker or writer and others associated with him take a specific course of action; rather than the intended meaning, which is to say why the generality of people do such a thing. *One* also has a role as a pronoun that creates distance between the speaker and the people whose activities he is describing. If, for example, referring to a shocking crime, a speaker were to say "I don't know why one does that sort of thing" it is quite clear that *one* is a third person usage, meaning a person or persons unknown; it does, however, risk the rejoinder "but one doesn't do that sort of thing". I repeat, though: however one uses *one*, one must be sure to use it consistently.

Reflexive pronouns such as *myself, yourself, himself, ourselves, yourselves* and *themselves* are horribly misused today. Perhaps it has something to do with the increasing self-obsession of modern life. It should have purely an emphatic use, as in "I did it myself" or "he attended to the matter himself", which suggests a point of contrast – he did it himself as opposed to someone else doing it for him; or it should serve as the object of a reflexive verb, as in "you should be ashamed of yourselves" or "she promised to take care of herself". What it emphatically is not is a synonym for the personal pronoun in any of its cases. Phrases such as "he gave it to myself" or "I saw yourself there" are sheer abominations.

With what Fowler so charmingly calls "nouns of multitude", think carefully before choosing a pronoun. As I have noted elsewhere, the idiom about whether certain nouns of multitude are singular or plural is not always settled; I also prefer the singular unless (as with the England cricket team) there is a prevailing idiom of plurality. So when one reads in a newspaper a story about a crime and about "the Victim Support Unit, who have been in touch", it jars. First, should the personal pronoun *who* be applied to an impersonal body like the Victim Support Unit? I think not. The moment one changes the pronoun to the impersonal *which* in the example above, one sees that the idiom demands a change of number too; so one has "the Victim Support Unit, which has been in touch", which is idiomatically far happier. The same is true of all such impersonal bodies: it should be "the Government, which has advised", or "the county council, which has offered", or "the governing bodies of the three schools, which have agreed to work together on the question", and so on.

Some accidents with pronouns are the result of carelessness or illiteracy. The most notorious is a version of the greengrocer's apostrophe, where *it's* is used for *its* as in "the business has had *it's* worst year for decades". Variations of this horror include "mind *you're* language" or its equally objectionable converse "let me know when *your* here". The third person pronoun *their*, because of an abundance of homonyms, is a minefield. In correct usage one writes "they could not believe *their* luck"; yet one from time to time sees "they could not believe *there* luck" or even "they could not believe *they're* luck". As with "your", there may be abuses in the opposite direction: "she could not see why *their* should be a problem," and so on. Few people are sufficiently stupid to make such mistakes; many more, however, are sufficiently careless.

The final pronominal difficulty is one that I noted at the start of this book, one created by linguistic history and evolution: there are no relative pronouns meaning *he-or-she*, *his-or-her* and *him-*

or–her. Almost daily, one reads or hears utterances such as "the teacher told each member of his class that they were to stand up" or "neither John nor Mary had remembered their books" or "every boy and girl had a present given to them". The problem is at once apparent: the prolixity, in the first example, of "told each member of his class that he or she was to stand up"; in the second of "neither John nor Mary had remembered his or her book"; and in the third of "every boy and girl had a present given to him or her". Being a pedant, I regard these usages of *they*, *their* and *them* as unacceptable. However, the alternative forms verge on the absurd. Often, in cases like this, it is easy to recast the sentence to obviate the problem. In the first example one would avoid the need for a singular by writing that the teacher "told all his class that they were to stand up". In the second, one would write "both John and Mary had forgotten their books", which also removes the need for a singular. In the third, one would recast it as " a present was given to every boy and girl". Perhaps the next development in our grammar will be to rectify this deficiency; though progressives would argue that it has already happened, and we pedants should overcome our resistance to *they*, *their* and *them*. No doubt in another century we shall have done. It is interesting to note that when a plural pronoun is required in French to cover both genders, *ils* has always been deemed to suffice; but then the French have always had a distinction between the masculine *they* (*ils*) and the feminine *they* (*elles*), which we have lacked. We seem a little way behind.

Relative pronouns

Perhaps the most common mistake of all with pronominal usages is the misuse of **which** and **that** as relative pronouns. It is probably not an exaggeration to say that almost everyone believes they are in most contexts interchangeable. They are not. The two sentences "the dog that was run over belonged to Mrs Smith" and "the dog, which was run over, belonged to Mrs Smith" say different things in two quite different ways. The first suggests there were a number of dogs, and the one that happened to be run over belonged to Mrs Smith. The second supposes there was only one dog. It happened also to be run over, which (unfortunate though that may be) is not the point of the story. The point is that it belonged to Mrs Smith. *That* defines; *which* is parenthetic, or non-defining. If one is having a conversation with another about the merits of various cars, and one wishes to make the point that a car one used to own broke down, one would say "the car that I used to own broke down", implying that cars one did not own did not break down. If one says "the car, which I used to own, broke down" one suggests that the main point one is making is that the car broke down and, incidentally, one used to own it. The reverse also applies. If one says "the coin that I found in the garden is valuable" one implies that one has found coins all over the place, but it is only the one found in the garden that is worth anything. If that is the only coin one has found, and one wishes to stress its value but provide the incidental information that one found it in the garden, then one must say "the coin, which I found in the garden, is valuable".

A book review in a magazine early in 2010 exemplified in two successive sentences the incorrect, and then the correct, usages of *which*. "It was not surprising that they rejected the UN partition resolution which gave them only half of their country," read the first. Perhaps it was a stylistic consciousness that prevented the writer from using a second *that* after the conjunction earlier in the sentence; yet it led him to use a parenthetic *which* when he should have used a defining *that*. To avoid repetition he could have omitted the conjunction without any danger of creating an ambiguity; or he could have inserted a comma before *which*, making it into a parenthesis without disturbing the sense of what he was writing. The next sentence – "There followed a war between

the Palestinians and the Jews, which saw 200,000–300,000 Palestinians driven, one way or another, from their homes" – uses the
pronoun correctly.

In talking about people rather than things or abstracts there
appears to be no such distinction; there is only the relative pronoun *who* or *whom*. (*Who* should be used only with reference to
persons; I write more about this below.) So one would have to
distinguish the two meanings by use of punctuation. "The girl
whom I saw was wearing a pink dress" is a statement that suggests that a number of people have seen girls, but the one that this
person saw was (unlike the others) wearing a pink dress. "The girl,
whom I saw, was wearing a pink dress" conveys the information
that we know there was one girl, that the important point is that
the speaker saw her, and he can disclose she was wearing a pink
dress. However, there is another way to make the distinction. It
was quite common, and accepted, usage until the early part of the
last century to use *that* for *who* or *whom* just as in clauses featuring objects or abstracts: so one would have said "the woman that
had a hat on broke her arm" to indicate that she was one of a
number of women being considered but the only one who had a
hat on; but "the woman, who had a hat on, broke her arm" would
be used to indicate that the woman has already been specified,
that she broke her arm, and that (by the way) she was wearing a
hat. Of the two types of usage, I prefer the first. The second is not
incorrect, but it now seems archaic; and if one punctuates correctly there is no risk of ambiguity.

Lest these sorts of distinctions seem pedantic in the extreme,
Onions gives an example that shows their value. It is "all the
members of the council, who were also members of the Education Board, were to assemble in the board room".[29] The meaning
to be conveyed is that only those members of the council who

29. *Modern English Syntax*, p59.

were members of the Education Board as well were to meet in the board room; and Onions argues this would be clear only if the punctuation were to be removed and the relative pronoun *who* were replaced by *that*. That may have been true at the time he wrote a century ago, according to the prevailing idiom; and, as I have said, his point shows the importance of the distinction. However today the idiom requires simply that the two commas in the sentence be removed, dispensing with the parenthesis, and then the meaning is clear.

What is always wrong, it must be stressed, is to use the pronoun *which* to refer to people, and the pronoun *who* to refer to objects. Less heinous is the use of the possessive pronoun *whose* when not applied to people. Its usage in a phrase such as "John asked Mary whose book she had borrowed" is straightforward and understood; but during the last century usages such as "he despised a government whose policies could have brought about such a thing" or "she collected her car, whose damaged windscreen had been repaired" have become accepted, to avoid the apparent clumsiness or pomposity of the strictly correct alternative. That would be "a government of which the policies…" and "her car, of which the damaged windscreen…". Pedants may legitimately stick to such usages, which are not yet universally regarded as outmoded, and which I would argue are still more acceptable than the alternative in the most formal writing. We are lucky we have a word such as *whose* at all; there is no equivalent in French, for example, where a construction using the pronoun *dont* – meaning "of which" – has to be used instead.

That, when used as a relative pronoun, may in certain idiomatic usages be omitted, even now in quite formal writing. "The car that I bought had an interior that I thought was very tasteful" over-does the *that*s, and one of them may without difficulty be omitted – preferably the first. Some grammarians have sought to lay down rules for when the relative pronoun, and indeed *that* when used as a conjunction, may successfully be omitted: but to my mind each case has to be judged on its merits. If there is a danger of ambiguity or confusion, leave it in. If there is not, take it out, on the principle that any superfluous word should always be removed from a piece of writing. So one ought to leave the conjunction in a phrase such as "he saw that the dog, being run over, would have to be put down", as removing it would give the hasty reader the impression that the man had seen the dog being run over, which he had not necessarily done. The verb is susceptible of two meanings, which makes the conjunction especially valuable in removing a possible ambiguity. However, in a sentence such as "she wore the dress that she had ironed", where *that* is a pronoun, no ambiguity is created by removing it; "she wore the dress she had ironed" can mean only one thing. However, were the sentence to read "she wore the dress she had bought in London" one might be led to think that London was the place where she wore the dress, not where she bought it. Were it to read instead "she wore the dress that she had bought in London" the meaning would become a little clearer: she has many dresses, and may have bought them in various places, but she wore the one that she had bought in London. We are not sure what to make of the dress if the pronoun is removed. It should be obvious that the pronoun *which*, if used correctly in its non-defining and parenthetical sense, may never be removed. A correctly-framed sentence, such as "she wore the dress, which she had bought in London, to the party that evening" must change its meaning if the *which* is removed. The punctuation has to be removed too, and the sentence then ceases describing a specific dress and describes instead one of many dresses she has – one she happens to have bought in London. The entire emphasis is altered.

Something that is always ugly is the construction *that which*: "I chose to wear a dress different from *that which* I had worn the previous day", or "he would not order a claret other than *that which* he chose every time he ate in the restaurant". If one must write such a sentence, the correct usage in both cases is the only slightly less inelegant, and much more confusing, *that that*. No doubt it is its propensity to confuse that causes it to be replaced by *that which*. The elegant writer would recast both sentences: "I chose to wear a dress different from the one I had worn the previous day" and "he would not order any claret other than the one he chose every time he ate in the restaurant".

Case

Case – the modification of nouns and pronouns to reflect their relation to other words in a sentence, also referred to as **declension** – is dealt with in passing in other sections of this chapter, notably under pronouns and verbs. English nouns do inflect in a limited way, but not as Greek, Latin or German ones do. With the exception of the case used to signify possession, there are no fancy endings for the writer or speaker of English to master so far as nouns are concerned. As illustrated in the section about pronouns, certain of them do inflect when they are the direct or indirect object of a verb or after a preposition, and their inflections must be observed in the correct contexts.

The two case distinctions in pronouns are the accusative, or the case that one uses in writing or speaking when the pronoun is a direct or indirect object (the words that have inflected are *me, him, her, us, them*); and the genitive, which signifies possession (*my, your, his, hers, its, one's, our, their*). English has the equivalents of the Latin cases, but, in the absence of inflections, uses prepositions to activate most of them. The nominative case is the straightforward noun – *a table*, say. The vocative is the case of addressing it – *O table!* (This made generations of schoolboys hoot when learning Latin, a testament to the puerility of much English humour.) The

accusative case is for English nouns identical to the nominative
– *a table*. The genitive signifies possession: *of a table*. Its shortening
(*a table's*) is perhaps not so much an inflection as an appendage.
The dative is *to* or *for a table* and is also the indirect object – "I
sent the food to a table" or "she asked the restaurant for a table".
The ablative signifies *by, with* or *from a table*. Latinists will recall
the ablative absolute, in which a noun and a participle were put in
the ablative case to signify a completed action by certain people,
and which was translated by the ugly formula "which boys having been kicked" or "which flies having been swatted". There is
no equivalent in English, and modern style hardly permits such a
stilted construction in contemporary usage.

We cannot entirely do without a sensibility of case in English,
even if English has tried to do without it by losing most of its
inflections. Anyone trying to say "me went to the pub" or "I told
he to stop" will be laughed out of town; but there will also be a
frisson when a more sophisticated user of the language makes
a common slip such as "this did not come as a shock to John
and I". It is important to make sure that a preposition always
takes an accusative: a usage such as "I was afraid of she who must
be obeyed" will simply not do. The direct object of a verb must
always be in the accusative too: we can have no truck with "I was
appalled to find only one woman, and she a foreigner, who understood English grammar". It should be "and her a foreigner" as the
phrase remains the direct object of the verb *find*. Were the verb
to be supplied (though that would be pleonastic) and the phrase
were to become "and she was a foreigner", that would be all right.
The verb *to be*, as I have mentioned, always takes the nominative
case – hence the wrongness of the occasionally-heard pomposity
"be you whom (or whomever) you may be".

It is when we use the possessive that we are perhaps most alert
to distinctions of case. There is scope for difficulty with compound possessives – phrases such as "my wife's sister's boyfriend"

or, to note a different form, "the driver of the car's behaviour". In instances such as the former, remember to ensure that all the necessary possessives are included. In instances such as the latter, make a stylistic judgement: it may be better to say "the behaviour of the car's driver". A phrase like "we saw the woman who lives in the house on the corner's dog" is so obviously clumsy that one needs little urging to recast it as "the dog of the woman…".

Prepositional problems

We established in Chapter One that a preposition usually governs a noun or a pronoun, and relates it to a verb. The main difficulty with prepositions is that some writers choose the wrong preposition for this relation. However, it is the perception of many writers that there is a bigger prepositional problem still: whether a preposition may legitimately end a sentence. Most grammarians dismiss this as a fetish, and the Fowlers dismissed it as "a modern superstition".[30] I am, as I have already said, with them. The very notion gave rise to one of Churchill's most renowned *bons mots* "this is the sort of English up with which I will not put". Churchill, with his instinctive feel for the rhythms of language, identified the main obstacle to this rule, fetish or superstition, which is the problem it causes with compound verbs such as *put up with*.

There is no rule, but there is a matter of taste. When I write I usually avoid putting a preposition at the end of a sentence, for reasons that are a mixture of logic and of style. However, when the preposition concerned is part of a compound verb I usually find myself, for Churchillian reasons, putting the preposition last, as to do otherwise sounds contrived and clumsy. Therefore, I would write "the man to whom I was writing" rather than "the man I was

30. *The King's English*, p71.

writing to". I think it sounds and reads better than the alternative (and the musical effect of our words on the page is something to which I fear we pay too little attention), and I like the logic of "the man to whom" running together. Yet I would sooner write "it is an event we are greatly looking forward to" than "an event to which we are greatly looking forward" because I feel the former is less of a distraction to the reader in its lack of awkwardness, and will communicate my meaning more effectively.

Prepositions require accusatives. In our largely uninflected language the writer will need to make no effort when using single nouns or proper names. The difficulties set in with pronouns, and are compounded with plurals. Few would be so barbaric that they would write or say "I gave it to *she*" or "the bird flew over *they*", but many are barbaric enough to write "the man to *who* I gave it" when *whom* is required. Indeed, it is in usages such as this that those (and they exist) who argue for the redundancy of *whom* are at their weakest. When using a construction with nouns and pronouns it appears to be second nature to forget that the pronoun must be in the accusative, especially if it comes second after the noun. So we are always reading, or hearing, "between you and I", "she invited John and I", "it was a present to my husband and I" (a solecism for which perhaps we must blame the influence of the Queen, despite Her Majesty's own immaculate grammar), "I sent it to John and she" and so on. If a pronoun is on the receiving end of something after a preposition it has to be in the accusative, however distressingly far it may be from the verb.

Here are some of the most common mistakes with the choice of prepositions: they are often made when a demotic usage seeps into the consciousness of supposedly educated people. A person is absorbed *in* a task, not by it; but liquid may be absorbed *by* a sponge. One acquiesces *in* something, not with it, and one connives *at* something, not in it. One aims *at* something, not for it. One becomes angry *with* someone, not at him. One is ashamed *of* bad behaviour, not by it. A decision is *between* one thing *and* another, not one thing or another. One is bored *by* or *with* something, never of it. Something is different *from* something else, not to it or, even more abominable, than it. One is disgusted *with* something, not by it. One becomes fed up *with* things, not of them. Something is identical *to* something else, not with it. One inculcates something *on* somebody, one does not inculcate somebody with something; and one instils something *into* somebody. There is an interaction *of* two people or things, not between them. Two things merge *with* each other, not into each other. One is oblivious *of* something, not to it. One prefers something *to* something else, not than something else. One is prohibited *from* doing something, not prohibited to do it (a confusion, one supposes, with *forbidden*). One thing is replaced *by* another, not with it. One has a reputation *for* something, not of it. One is sensible *of* something, but sensitive *to* it. One is sparing *of* something, not with it. One substitutes one thing *for* another, not another thing with the first. One suffers *from* something, not with it.

Care should be taken with the verb *informed*. If one is told some news, one is *informed about* or *informed of* a fact or facts. However, if one decides to go on holiday to the South of France because one learns that the weather is hot there, or the food is good, one takes a decision *informed by* such knowledge.

Into is a valuable preposition, indicating the passage to a state of being *in* somewhere. There is a distinction, and not always a subtle one, between it and *in to*. One says "I went into the room", "I got into trouble" and "I walked into the wood" but "I walked in to a lamp-post". The choice to be made in selecting what sort of preposition to use is based on a simple criterion: does the action described result in the subject's ending up within the object? If it does, then use *into*. If it does not, use *in to*. There is no such problem in distinguishing when a writer or speaker should use *onto* and *on to*, because *onto* does not exist.

Another problem with the contagion of slang and vulgar usage is that some verbs acquire pointless prepositions. Here are some examples: *be inside of, be outside of, infringe upon, comprise of, meet with* and *get off of*. Also, some vulgar usages have prepositions put to uses for which they were not intended. *Unless* does not mean *except*, so do not write "I shall not go there unless on Wednesdays" when you mean "I shall not go there except on Wednesdays".

Although the English verb *compare* is partly formed by the Latin preposition meaning "with", the dictionary has from its earliest days drawn a distinction between contexts in which one writes *compared with* and those in which one writes *compared to*. If one is using *compare* in the sense of to liken something to something else, then one uses *to*: the most famous example in our literature is "Shall I compare thee to a summer's day?"[31] If one is simply establishing a comparison ("I wouldn't compare prosecco with Pol Roger"), one uses *with*.

A common mistake no-one will admit to is the use of the wrong pronoun after *than* in a comparative clause. There is a sense of certainty that "she was so much taller than I" is correct. It is not. As Onions points out: "than, when introducing a contracted comparative clause has (at least from early Modern English times) been treated as a preposition and has been followed by the accusative".[32] So it would be correct to write "she was so much taller *than I am*", which is not a contracted clause, but if the verb is absent it must be "she is so much taller *than me*". To reinforce the point, *than* in these circumstances must take an accusative pronoun – "a woman *than whom* I was much shorter", or "she is taller *than him*".

In a sentence such as "he likes cherries more than me" the only legitimate meaning can be "he likes cherries more than

31. William Shakespeare, Sonnet 18.
32. *Modern English Syntax*, p98.

he likes me". If the meaning that is sought is "he likes cherries more than I like cherries", then one should say or write "he likes cherries more than I do", or the elliptical "than I", which is permissible here. There is a distinction between the first person pronoun being the object of the sentence (as in "she is taller than me" and its being a subject, with an ellipsis (he likes cherries more than I (do)). Partridge seems to have misunderstood Onions on this point, and argues the accusative is needed only with relative pronouns such as *whom*: but this is expressly not what Onions says.

Partridge's assertion that the use of other accusatives is "colloquial, not Standard English" is contradicted by Onions's point that *than* has been "prepositional" for half a millennium, and his conclusion that any other use is "pedantic". The same applies to *as*: either "she is not as (or *so*) tall *as I am*" or "she is not as (or *so*) tall *us me*". Lest this be thought a radical departure into demotic English, I should stress that Onions, one of the foremost academic grammarians of his day, took no issue with this usage as far back as 100 years ago.

Be sure that where verbs routinely need a preposition to complete their sense, those prepositions are supplied: they can go missing in long sentences, especially when the writer is overcome with the desire to avoid ending a sentence with a preposition. The quite obviously deficient "he was not drawn to what all her friends were attracted" is the type of sentence that omits an essential *to* at the end of it. This error happens when there is a common object, often pronominal (in this case *what*), of two verbs, each of which is prepositional. Using *to* once is not enough. In some rare instances, a prepositional usage dies out. It is common to read in British novels of the 1920s or 1930s – Evelyn Waugh, Graham Greene or Aldous Huxley – that one character has *telephoned to* another. By the end of the Second World War they are simply telephoning them. Since the verb itself was relatively new – the

OED cites its first use as 1877 – there were not centuries of custom and practice to cite as authority; and the use of *to* seems to have been a precious and somewhat exclusive affectation in any case.

Odd little words

As and *so* are a morass of potential difficulties. In the examples given at the end of the previous section, *so* would be regarded by pedants as the correct word – "I am not *so* stupid as that" or "it isn't *so* bad as all that" – because of the emphasis that *so* correctly places on the adjective. During the 20th century the colloquial usage of *as* became more frequent. It cannot now be considered incorrect, but pedants will stick to *so*. *As* is correctly used for straightforward similes, as in "she thought it was *as* cold as the Arctic". The distinction between the phrases *as far as* and *so far as* is simple: the former is used in positive expressions and the latter after a negative. Therefore one would write "the police jurisdiction ran *as far as* the border", but "his illness had not advanced *so far as* I had feared". Some combinations of *as* and other words are simply pointless ("I simply have no idea *as to* why he came" or "she has not *as yet* signalled her intentions") or preposterous ("could this be done *as per* the regulations"). *As to*, which in bad writing precedes not only *why* but also *how, when, which, where* and *whether* is entirely redundant; *yet* does not require *as*; and *as per* belongs in a late Victorian lexicon of counting-house argot. Some writers also feel the need to place *as* pleonastically in front of certain phrases, exemplified by this extract from a magazine in January 2010: "In 1947 the Palestinians numbered 1.2 million as compared with 600,000 Jews."

One of the more promiscuous abuses of *as* is as a synonym for *because*: "I could not come as I was busy elsewhere". This should be regarded as a colloquialism and not suitable for formal writing.

It shares this problem with *since*, a word that is best kept for use in denoting a passage of time or in introducing a fact rather than attributing cause. Care must be taken when using *as* to introduce a clause. It is often a sloppy substitute for a more exact conjunction such as *since, because, on account of, for* or *while*, or even the more formal and archaic *whereas*, whose currency has not died out completely. *As* works in the following example, where it is used to introduce a statement consequent upon the meaning of the main clause: "she was pleased she had taken her macintosh, as it began to rain". However, were the sentence to read "she was pleased she had taken her macintosh, but later was annoyed, as it was stolen from the restaurant" it would be technically ungrammatical. The *as* should refer back to the main clause but does not: it refers to the subordinate one. Were the subordinate one removed it would read "she was pleased she had taken her macintosh as it was stolen from the restaurant", which would be nonsense. A recasting would avoid this problem, possibly just by removing *as* and replacing it with a colon. Better still, though, to be more precise with conjunctions, rather than use *as* as a catch-all.

Here are examples of how to increase precision:

"The girl cried *as* she had hurt herself." Use *because*.

"The woman slept *as* the house was burgled." Use *while*.

"*As* you are here, let's have a drink." Use *since*.

"They knew each other *as* they were related." Use *on account of their being*, or *because*.

"He sold everything he had to buy the house, *as* it was what he had always wanted." Use *for*, replacing the preceding comma with a colon.

As is not a relative pronoun and it is not a synonym for *such as*.

"The car as was coming down the hill" is a shocking vulgarism. "The standard of dress was superb, as was prevalent during the *belle époque*" is an illiteracy: it should be "such as was prevalent".

When using a well-known simile always retain the opening *as*, which colloquially is often omitted: be sure to write "that man is as rich as Croesus" rather than "that man is rich as Croesus". However, *as* is sometimes used redundantly; a person is not "*equally as entitled* to help as another", but just "*equally entitled* to help".

Partridge objected to the use of *so* as an intensifier, calling it slovenly: he preferred "it was very kind of you" to "it was so kind of you". That distinction appears now to have been lost, and the use of *so* in this context must now be considered a matter of taste. It has become idiomatic to intensify an adjective with *so*, as in "he was so wet you could shoot snipe off him" or "she was so ugly all the mirrors broke"; but in this case it has come to mean "of such intensity" rather than "very", and its usage seems defensible enough. One is on safer ground objecting to the use of *so* to mean *therefore*, rather as *as* has usurped the role of *because*. This makes sense because of the danger of ambiguity: "the man had walked miles in the hot sun, was parched, tired and *so* desperate for water" could mean he was *very* desperate for water, or, *therefore*, was desperate for water. A writer who does not misuse *so* in either way will be in no danger of misleading his readers.

So is also to be regarded as a colloquialism in a phrase such as "I went to the bar *so* I could see her", when *so* means "in order that" or "in order to". As with *as*, it runs the occasional risk of redundancy: "He had left the parcel behind, but not deliberately *so*". A phrase such as "I put on a hat so as not to catch cold" is heading out of colloquialism and into vulgarism. One would do better to say "I put on a hat in order not to catch cold", or better still, if subjunctively-minded, to say "I put on a hat that I might not catch cold"; though the latter may court accusations of archaism. In a construction such as "he worked so hard as to fall asleep", idiomatic usage prefers "he worked so hard that he fell asleep". One construction in which *so* is preferred by grammarians is "so admirable a child as she was", which is reckoned better that "such an admirable child". Also, use *so* as a comparator: "it is not so bad" is preferable to "it is not that bad".

Than is often to be found not far from *as* or *so*, and often being used wrongly. The most notorious is "twice as many visitors came to Britain than last year"; "as last year" is correct. *Than* has very limited legitimate usage: it is correct in a comparison (and in comparison-equivalents, such as *rather than* or *sooner than*), or in constructions with *other* ("other than Smith, they could not think of anyone to ask") and *otherwise* ("it was safer to do it that way than otherwise"). *Different than* is an abomination, and one does not prefer to do something *than* to do something else; one prefers to do something *rather than* to do something else. So "I prefer to swim than to ride" is wrong; "I prefer to swim rather than to ride" is correct but prolix. It is better, if possible, to use nouns: "I prefer swimming to riding".

Another word often misused for *as* – and indeed for other words – is the ubiquitous *like*. It is the filler of choice for current youth, which is its most abominable usage, in statements such as "he was, like, coming down the road". Its abuses far pre-date the early 21st century, however. *Like* is best regarded as a verb that expresses affection for something, or a means of making a direct comparison ("he looked like his father"). It has turned into an adverb under American influence, and has the meaning "in the manner of", which ought to be resisted in formal writing. "You cook it like my mother used to" should be "you cook it as my mother used to". "A strumpet like her" should be "a strumpet such as her" (it will be noted that, following Onions's precept, I am using the accusative case after *as* just as after *than*). Another vulgarism is *like that*, as in "why does she talk like that?" instead of "why does she talk in that way?" Similarly, do not write "she looked like she had been kicked in the teeth" or "it sounded like it was all over", write "she looked as if" or "it sounded as though". That last pair of examples also illustrates the distinction between *as if* and *as though*. The former is metaphorical; the latter literal. The woman has not actually been kicked in the teeth, she is reacting *as if* she had; but the event is real and it sounds *as though* it has ended.

Cause

Due to, ***owing to***, and ***because of*** are used by many writers as though they were interchangeable. They are not. *Due to* should not open a sentence: it should follow a noun or nominal clause that has introduced the fact or event that is *due to* something else's having happened, because *due to* has the function of an adjective. "The postponement of the start of Essex's match against Surrey, due to heavy overnight rain…" is correct. To say "due to heavy overnight rain, Essex's match against Surrey has been postponed…" is not, as the syntax demands that *due to* qualifies the cricket match and not the postponement. *Owing to* does not have these limitations and may be used to open a sentence. There should be no strict fetish banning the use of *because* at the start of a sentence, so that may be used instead. *Owing to* would be preferred by many, including me.

There is also the somewhat more rarified *for* ("I did not notice him, for he was in disguise"). This device may be used to introduce an expression that is confined to one of opinion, or to a statement of fact. Virginia Woolf was attached to it, and it makes a prominent appearance early on in *Mrs Dalloway*. The book begins: "Mrs Dalloway said she would buy the flowers herself. For Lucy had her work cut out for her." Two of the next four paragraphs open with the same formula ("For having lived in Westminster…one feels…a particular hush" and "For it was the middle of June").[33] Woolf's usage is largely rhetorical, for except in the first of the three times she engages in it the word *for* is unnecessary. It creates a sense of controlling, almost hectoring delivery of pronouncements that certainly indicates the insecure state of mind of Mrs Dalloway, and for that matter the character of the author herself. It can easily be overdone by the sane and stable. *For* cannot be used like *because* to introduce a sentence that details the consequences of a cause; in the sentence "because she was late, she missed the film" *because* cannot be replaced by *for*. However, one may just about write "she missed the film, for she was late"; a sort of sense is conveyed, but it is not idiomatic, and *because* here would be far more satisfactory. A Woolfish "she missed the film. For she was late" takes us back to the edges of sanity. Today, the idiomatic usage of *for* seems a little arch. It is best confined to prose where, in order to avoid repetition of *because*, it may provide a variation: "Because Smith had lost the key we had to stand outside. We became very cold, for it was the middle of January."

The other phrase routinely used to attribute cause is *on account of* – either with a gerund ("he had to buy a new tie on account of his other's being ruined") or suffixed by the phrase *the fact that*: "he had to buy a new tie on account of the fact that his other one was damaged"). The sheer prolixity of this construction, which has its roots in the worst sort of bureaucratic language, should itself indicate its lack of suitability for crisp, tight prose.

Ambiguity

"I considered this to be one of my better pieces of writing, if not one of the most informative." How often has one read a usage

33. *Mrs Dalloway*, by Virginia Woolf (Granada, 1976), pp5–6.

like this, and imagined one has grasped the writer's meaning, only to realise almost at once that one cannot be sure? In such cases the writer seems to mean that not only was it one of his better works, but, also, one of the most informative. Yet the construction he has used argues that it was certainly one of his better pieces of writing, but it was not in fact very informative: which invites consideration of just how good his better pieces are.

What he should have written was "I considered this to be one of my better pieces of writing, as well as one of the most informative". The construction he did use is, in logic, susceptible of only one meaning: which is to present the second clause as a negative consideration qualifying the first. This is but one example of how the choice of a certain phrase, in this case a familiar trope, can obscure or distort what a writer is trying to say. It is as if, in this context, the pursuit of elegance itself has trapped the writer into saying the opposite of what he meant. Had he avoided this slightly orotund construction, and stuck to plain words and forms, he would have caused no confusion at all. Another variant of this construction is found in a phrase such as "it was one of his more obscure, if more thoughtful, remarks", in which for perfect clarity the *if* should be replaced by a *though*.

It was reported that "a Tory MP left his wife for a woman while she was fighting cancer". Who was fighting cancer? Was it the wife or the mistress? The sentence demonstrates how easy it is when using pronouns to cause confusion. Choose a pronoun only when the noun it refers to is clear. If it is not, repeat a noun or a proper name rather than cause confusion; or use a formula such as *the former* or *the latter*. As I noted earlier, adverbs, if positioned wrongly, also have the power to confuse by creating ambiguity. Not only should they be chosen with care, they must also be positioned with care. Ambiguity will always be avoided if the word is not only chosen correctly, but placed in its best and most logical place in the sentence.

It also helps to avoid ambiguity if one keeps sentences simple. In her excellent and generally well-written book on the 1930s Juliet Gardiner, the social historian, perpetrates this: "The theatre had entered the blood of Terence Rattigan, the son of a diplomat whose career came to a premature end when he made Princess Elizabeth of Romania pregnant, at prep school, and as a member of Oxford University Dramatic Society (OUDS) he had a one-line part in *Romeo and Juliet* with Peggy Ashcroft and John Gielgud."[34] One hardly knows where to start in understanding what this means. Most obviously, Rattigan had a father who impregnated a princess while he (the father) was still at prep school; or possibly Rattigan himself achieved this remarkable feat. Either or both of them might also have done it again when at Oxford. We had better leave the complicity or otherwise of Dame Peggy and Sir John out of this.

Illogical, captain

As I wrote at the opening of this chapter, grammar is about logic. It may be well to include under this general heading some of the offences against logic that, if not strictly grammatical, are all syntactical and, like bad grammar, create the impression that the speaker or writer is not truly at home with the language.

One of the more obvious of these offences is **tautology**, a construction in which the same idea is repeated unintentionally and immediately, usually because of a failure to think about what the individual words in the statement mean. So one will read that someone was "frequently in the habit" or "often had a routine of" doing something. One hears reporters on television say that people

34. *The Thirties: An Intimate History*, by Juliet Gardiner (Harper Press, 2010), p654.

"continue to remain" in a certain condition. Many verbs that begin with *re-* invite a tautology if they are accompanied by *again* – such as "resume again", "repeat again" or "replenish again". "Revert back" is a tautology, as is "recoil back". Partridge has a long list of such offences, of which a few specimens may suffice here: "collaborate together", "descend down", "mingle together" and "refer back" all make the point that a meaning already contained in the verb does not need to be expressed immediately in a complement.[35] There are similar examples of nouns needing adjectives even less than is usually the case: "ugly monster", "savage brute" and "stupid fool" are some of the more obvious; there are many others. This afflic-tion may also affect verbs in the form of needless adverbs: it is hard to see the point of "she drank thirstily" or "he ate hungrily", because people normally do, just as they also "yell loudly", "rage angrily" and "stop completely". *Fully* can be a particular problem: when used with certain verbs it is meaningless, because the verbs themselves are absolute, and therefore *fully* is inevitably tautologi-cal. Verbs such as *abandon, convince, cede, close* and *stop* are but five examples: there are countless others.

Similarly illogical are incomparable adjectives. *Fuller* and *fullest* are the two most frequent offenders. If something is full, how can something else be fuller? Of several full things, how can some-thing be the fullest? The same is true of all **absolutes**, so watch out for the sense of an adjective before making it a comparative or superlative: *dead, more dead* and *most dead* is an extreme example. *Empty*, like *full*, is incomparable. So (to name but a few) are *black, round, square, alive, complete, closed, open, wet, dry, whole, unique, meaningless, pure, safe, chief, final* and, of course, *absolute* itself. Also, numerous adjectives beginning in *in-* and its counterparts *im-* and *ir-* are incomparable; such as *incomparable* itself, *innocuous, irre-proachable, immoral* and so on. So too are those that end in *-less*;

35. *Usage and Abusage*, pp325–6.

something cannot be *very harmless* or somebody *more thoughtless*. If in doubt, apply the "full" test to any adjective and if it fails, do not try to make a comparative or a superlative out of it.

One hears politicians say all the time that something is a "very real problem" or that the "more real question is...". Something is either real or it is not. Certain adjectives that already describe an advanced condition cannot be compared. The phrase *too premature* appeared in a newspaper. How can there be a correct degree of prematurity? Being premature is already too early. The adjective **unique** is a special case, because it is wrongly given both superlatives and diminutives by abusers. The point manifestly needs to be laboured. Something that is unique exists alone of its type. Each human being is unique. The Mona Lisa is unique. Table Mountain is unique, as is Sydney Harbour Bridge or the Empire State Building. Therefore, to argue that something is *more* unique, or that it is the most unique in the world is literally meaningless. Scarcely less vacuous are phrases like *almost unique* or *nearly unique*. Something is either unique or it is not.

An adverb such as *somewhat* or *rather* may be used to qualify certain adjectives, and indeed some adverbs; and when it qualifies incomparable adjectives the usage commits an offence against logic, which is to be avoided. Put either of those adverbs in front of any of the adjectives in the paragraph above and the point is made: something cannot be *somewhat wet*, *rather unique* or *somewhat incoherent*. *Somewhat large* or *rather ugly* are examples of legitimate usages. If the adjective you are about to qualify with such an adverb is an absolute then do not qualify it. If the sense of what you wish to say seems to demand it, then it may be a sign that you should choose a different, non-absolute adjective. If you find yourself about to write, for example, *rather innocuous* write instead *rather mild*, *mild* being an adjective susceptible to degree.

In the section on negation above I gave warning about the danger of the **double negative**, and in this section on logical matters

I must do so again. The obvious ones are not the problem, for all but the illiterate will spot them; it is those that come in longer sentences, usually including verbs that themselves have a negative import, that cause unexpected difficulties. Be especially alert to sentences such as "I cannot doubt that there may not be times when you feel like that", which will confound almost everyone who reads or hears it.

There is also scope for a fault of logic when two nouns – one singular, the other plural – appear in a sentence: let us call this the Red Herring error. It occurs in sentences such as these, all found in the press towards the end of 2009: "the potential for conflicts of interest are immense", "if the rise of new economic powers mean our capacity", "wide open spaces – indoors – is what we craved". As can be seen, it happens when the writer imagines the subject of the sentence he is writing has become the noun nearest the verb. It is a facile mistake and easily avoided, but remains promiscuous.

Do not use *if* in a sentence to introduce any idea that might not happen – "I don't know *if* I'll go" must be "I don't know *whether* I'll go", the test being whether the phrase *or not* may logically be appended to the statement. There is a subtle difference, which is worth noting, between two phrases such as "do let me know whether you can come" and "do let me know if you can come". In the former, the questioner is seeking to establish *whether or not* the person he is inviting is able to come. In the second, the answer has already been given that the person invited probably cannot come, but that may change: so the questioner is asking the potential guest to let him know *if* he can come – in other words, *if* the situation changes.

It is also a solecism to use *if* after the verb *doubt*. One either doubts *whether* something is so, or doubts *that* it is so. As before, the use of *whether* suggests an invisible *or not*. This conjunction is used in preference to *that* where the doubt is reasonable, as in

"I doubt whether the boy is clever enough to pass his examination". To say "I doubt that the boy is clever enough" means one is absolutely sure the boy is not clever enough. To put it another way: one would say "I doubt that there are fairies at the bottom of the garden" rather than "I doubt whether there are fairies". Used either after a negative, or rhetorically, the construction must be *doubt that*, as in "we cannot doubt that tomorrow is Tuesday" or "can you doubt that he is lying?"

Ensure always that there is a consistency of construction in a sentence. One such as "she welcomed her guests in order to make them feel at home, and giving them a sense of belonging there" is ugly. An infinitive should have been used in the second clause, not a participle. In long sentences, ensure that the subject remains consistent, and that no pronoun or participle can be interpreted as referring to anything else.

Some words themselves defy logical use, and their existence is so egregious that the problem requires a specific note of warning. Here, the offending tribe is usually business, in its attempts to communicate better (as it sees it) with its clientele. Some firms now offer services to their customers on a *pre-booked* basis. How else is one supposed to book? If one books at the time of use, or afterwards, one is not booking at all. This is an entirely illogical usage. Its cousins are *pre-used* and *pre-owned* and even *pre-loved*,[36] silly euphemisms for *second hand*. Something that is used or already owned can only have been done so beforehand. Indeed, it is a rule increasingly observed in life that almost anything with the prefix *pre-* can do without it. Can anything that is arranged be other than *pre-arranged*? Can a condition that is set in advance of some compact or agreement be anything other than a *pre-condition*? There are many other such shockers.

One also frequently hears someone say: "you have two choices".

36. I am indebted to Mr Robert Colvile for alerting me to this monstrosity.

You do not: you have a choice. A choice requires two (or more) options. A man may have two, five or a dozen ties to choose from. He still has only one choice, not two, five or twelve. Even worse is the statement "there are three alternatives". There are not. There can only ever be alternatives when there are two courses of action or items to choose from. There can be three options, or three courses of action, or even just a good old-fashioned choice. While we are on the subject of numbers, consider the depressing cliché "a game of two halves". How many other halves could the game have? The only context in which any other number makes sense is at Eton College, where the terms are known as halves, and there are three of them in each academic year. In a similar vein, one cannot have the best of two, nor can one of two objects be the most expensive, or most beautiful. To merit a superlative something has to be the best (or worst) of at least three. Where there are just two one is the better of them, the other the worse; one is more expensive, the other less so.

The wrong preposition also takes us into the waters of illogicality. Well-known is the phrase *centred around*, but recognition of it does not prevent people from perpetuating this absurdity. The centre is a fixed point, so something has to be *centred upon* it. A similar problem is found with *under the circumstances*. It must always be *in the circumstances*.

Logic in language is often damaged by negation. I have spotted in a newspaper the phrase *least unscathed* when of course the writer meant *least scathed* or *most unscathed*. The last of those would have been an absurdity, since if one is unscathed one cannot be more or less unscathed than any other unscathed person. This rule applies to all adjectives negated in this way.

Finally on the question of logic, when writing the conjunction *but* always pause and wonder how the sentence would read if you exchanged it for *and*. *But* should be used only when there is a definite contrast to be introduced, usually after a conditional clause:

"I would have given him some help, but he had been ungrateful in the past". Yet sometimes one reads it when the simple conjunction *and* would be correct: "I asked her to marry me but she said no" is better than "I asked her to marry me and she said no", because simply asking the question does not guarantee a positive answer, and a refusal is not necessarily surprising.

Mastering grammar requires practice and determination, especially if one has fallen into bad habits. Once one has mastered it, the next essential component of a good writing style or of correct speech is precision in one's choice of words: which is the subject of the next chapter.

CHAPTER FIVE

The wrong word

We write in order to communicate, and we communicate to convey information. Clarity is essential. If we are vague, obscure or hard to understand, what we are trying to say may be lost on our audience. In the next chapter I shall look at what makes a good writing style, and explain how the purpose of that style is not merely to give aesthetic pleasure to the reader but to communicate with him to the greatest effect. There are, however, various features of writing that one must consider in order to do this. None is perhaps so important as choosing the right word: or, more to the point, avoiding the wrong one.

What do you mean?

We need to choose the right word for reasons that seem obvious once we consider them, but often appear to elude certain writers. We always have a meaning to convey when we write, and it is important to convey that meaning accurately. That entails precision in our choice of words. The wrong noun, adjective or verb can leave a reader understanding something quite different from what the writer had in mind.

Adjectives are a minefield. We have already observed that these should be used sparingly. Highly adjectival prose can be satirical or humorous – the most justifiable use of the technique – but it is more usually a form that creates a feeling of sensationalism, insincerity and, paradoxically, vagueness, by reducing directness and clarity. There are two distinct types of adjective – those that describe matters of fact and those that describe matters of perception or opinion. The former are far less offensive than the latter, and therefore more excusable.

If you are going to use an adjective, take the trouble to choose one that reflects exactly the sense you wish to impart to your reader. This is especially important if you wish to use an adjective of perception. For example: you may be writing a letter to a friend describing someone you have just met. That person may have struck you as dull. There is little chance (unless you are being dishonest or exceptionally tactful) that you are going to describe this person as *sparkling, charismatic* or *lively*. A thesaurus will suggest adjectives of various degrees of harshness that you can choose to communicate the impression you had. Let us suppose *dull* does the job. *Boring* could do just as well. *Tiresome* is more negative, suggesting a more irritating effect on those who experience this person. *Shocking, ghastly, stupid, thick* and *revolting* take the description into hyperbole, and do a disservice to a person who, rather than being any of those things, is simply *dull*. Some people choose to exaggerate to provoke a laugh, or some other sort of reaction. If you simply wish to tell your friend the truth, think carefully before firing the adjective gun. The damage, whether to the dull man's reputation or to yours, may be hard to undo afterwards.

Equally, there are less potent adjectives that offer gradations of description, but which we tend to misuse. To take one example: *scarce* and *rare* do not mean the same thing. A rare stamp is one that was printed in small quantities and (pending the discovery of a cache of thousands of them) that will always be in short supply. A scarce stamp is one that has not always been in short supply, but which at this particular point is hard to find because the market lacks sellers of them. Rare objects are usually always valuable; the price of scarce ones rises with their scarcity, but falls when they become more plentiful. The terms are not synonymous or interchangeable. The same is true of certain nouns that writers often use indiscriminately. A *riddle* is not a *puzzle*. The dictionary defines a riddle as "a question or statement intentionally worded in a dark or puzzling manner, and propounded in order that it may be guessed or answered...an enigma, a dark saying". There is nothing so sinister about a puzzle, a term that may be applied to the most harmless toy for children, or a pastime for older people. A glance at a thesaurus will uncover numerous other examples of adjectives and nouns that appear to mean the same thing as each other but do not. Such is the level of imprecision now, however, that some writers use words as synonyms when they are not even close to being so. "The dress she wore was the same as mine" and "the dress she wore was similar to mine" are sentences that convey two entirely different meanings. If one is to write precisely, one needs to be aware of the degrees of meaning conveyed by these words.

It is harder to stray with more confined parts of speech such as nouns or verbs, though adverbs can be subject to the same dangers as adjectives and need to be treated with similar caution. Adverbs can be used to exaggerate, intentionally or otherwise. Before you say someone failed *badly*, ask yourself whether he merely failed. The verbs themselves can be loaded, so use them wisely. Think exactly what it is you wish to convey. If somebody is *walking briskly*, he is neither *running* nor *plodding*: that much should be obvious. However, if he *smacks* his dog lightly for stealing food, do not claim he is *beating* him or *thrashing* him. If a woman is a *flirt* it does not mean she is a *courtesan*; if a man is a *tramp* it does not mean he is a *criminal*. Exaggeration soon finds out the exaggerator. His currency as a writer is devalued once it is known he lacks precision. So think about every word that you use, and make sure it says what you want your reader to understand it to say.

It's not what you think

Even when armed with fine intentions, one can still fall into traps: for many words do not mean what one thinks they mean. I recall having an argument many years ago with one of my elders and betters who insisted, despite the evidence of the dictionary, that *prevaricate* meant to delay taking a decision. He had, in common with many other people who pretend to literacy, confused it with *procrastinate*, but he was not about to admit that. His Latin was not especially good, which is all I can offer as an excuse for his obtuseness. *Prevaricate* comes from the Latin verb *praevaricare*, to plough crookedly or (referring to lawyers) to collude. It means, as one would expect given that provenance, to deviate from straight-forwardness, or to speak or act in an evasive way. The latest edition of the *Oxford English Dictionary*, however, has run up the white flag on its meaning. Despite citing a usage in 2005 of the word in its strictly correct sense, it says that the usual sense now is to delay action: which it admits is because of the influence of *procrastinate*. It is an interesting policy for lexicographers to accept a word into the language with a new meaning purely because people confuse it with a word that begins with the same letter, has the same number of syllables, ends with the same suffix and generally sounds similar. It might be easier, more logical and more accurate to say that the frequent use of the word to mean "delay" is simply wrong. It is odd, given the promiscuous misuse of this word, that more newspapers are not sued by completely honest politicians, who find themselves accused of shiftiness when in fact all they are guilty of is the inability to take a decision.

In the interests of accuracy and precision, what follows is a reminder of the true meaning of some commonly misused words. A second list, in the next section, deals with words that are commonly confused with another. The lists are not exhaustive. They may be considered in places pedantic. Words do change their meaning over time: compare the way in which *naughty* was used 400 years ago and the way in which it is used now. As the dictionary confirms, between the 15th and the 17th centuries the adjective was used to mean "morally bad or wicked". It supplies the proof, from one of Barrow's sermons of 1678, by citing his phrase "a most vile, flagitious man, a sorry and naughty governor as could be". Now it is used largely satirically, or to describe the mild offences of a child. The question must always be asked whether it is a good reason for a word to change its meaning not because it starts to be applied to something else, but because people cannot be bothered to use it correctly, and the fashion of their ignorance catches on. In a sense that is a democratic decision, though one that can be validated by authorities such as lexicographers caving in to abuse. These are a few words on whose correct usage we should not, for the moment, choose to sign the act of surrender: not for reasons of pedantry, but because important distinctions will be lost to our language if we do.

Let us start with ***adultery***. This is not merely a term of convention; it is a term of law. The dictionary and the law are agreed on its meaning: it is "voluntary sexual intercourse by a married person with one of the opposite sex, whether unmarried, or married to another". It may be helpful to know that the former is technically single adultery, the latter double. In an age when marriage is no longer so common as once it was, but more people have "partners", adultery is a word that demands to be used with precision. Unmarried people who (to use two popular tabloidisms) "cheat on" or "betray" their partners with other unmarried people are not committing adultery. They are *fornicating*.

To ***aggravate*** something is to make it worse. It does not mean to aggress against someone or to irritate him. Those are slang usages, as is the misuse of the noun *aggravation* to mean irritation. The dictionary lists these slang usages, and the abbreviation of the term to *aggro*, and cites a reference that claims the term came from the London underworld's gang wars of the 1950s: however, the first misuse of it to mean irritation dates from the late 19th century. It has no place in respectable or serious writing.

Alibi – which in Latin means "elsewhere" – has become synonymous with the noun *excuse*. It is not: it means a plea of having been elsewhere at the time a crime was committed. It is a rare case of an adverb having become a noun: originally one would seek to prove oneself *alibi*. The diluted use of the noun, and indeed its development into a verb, is another thing for which we have to thank the Americans.

One of the better jokes among dry-as-dust grammarians is about the correct use of **anticipate**, in that "to anticipate marriage is not the same as to expect it". Yet this verb is frequently used, even by educated people, as a synonym for *expect*. We should take heart from the fact that, despite this, and despite the depressing example of *prevaricate*, the dictionary does not yet seem ready to concede to the ignorant on this word. It has for nearly 500 years meant to do something before the appointed time. In that sense it is exceptionally useful and worth preserving.

Appreciate means to form an estimate of the worth or quality of something. It does not mean to understand, or recognise, or admire, or even be aware of. When someone says "I appreciate that" in response to a criticism he means "I understand it" or, more usually, "I understand you". As an expression of gratitude – "I appreciate what you have done for me" – it is acceptable, since it means one is forming an estimate (probably a high one) of the value of the services rendered. However, when someone says "you will appreciate that we are unable to give any such undertaking" he means "whether you like it or not, we cannot promise that". One of the many abuses of this otherwise precise verb is in the service of aggressive euphemism.

Chronic, like *aggravate*, has suffered from its popularity as a

slang word expressing disapproval or irritation. *Chronic* illnesses
– and there the word is used in its correct sense, from the Greek,
as lasting a long time – often are dreadful and tiresome, but that
does not sanction the transference of this adjective to mean those
things.

One occasionally reads in newspapers about people who have
died or been injured in a car that has **collided** with a tree. This is
remarkable, because a *collision* requires both parties to it to be in
motion. The Latin verb *collidere* means to strike or clash together,
and the etymology is strict. So two moving vehicles may collide,
as may a car and a cyclist or even a car and a pedestrian, but not a
car and a tree. Like so much of our language this is a question of
logic based on the etymology; there is no perversity about it.

One should take care in using the verb **contradict**. For there to
be a *contradiction* there has to be a statement, for a contradiction
is a categorical statement in opposition to another. If one person
says "the dog is black" when it is obvious that the beast is white,
then to affirm its whiteness is a contradiction; and one may say
"I contradicted his assertion that the dog was black". However, if
what one is taking issue with is not a statement, but a suggestion,
or advice, or a conjecture, then one does not strictly *contradict* it:
one *rejects* it, *disputes* it, *contests* it, *ignores* it, *doubts* it.

A misunderstanding of musical terms leads to the misuse of
the term **crescendo**, which is a gradual rising of the dynamic in
a passage of music. Therefore nothing can "reach a crescendo".
Before using any musical term (*pianissimo, fortissimo, diminuendo*
and so on) in a metaphorical sense, be sure you have verified what
it means.

Another word that people insist on wrenching from its correct
etymology is **decimate**. As every schoolboy knows, this was a pun-
ishment meted out to Roman legions, in which every tenth man
was killed. Its correct sense in English, therefore, is the reduction
of the strength of a body of people by 10 per cent. It does not

mean more or less than that, though it is often used to describe the near elimination of a contingent, and has been wrongly used now for over 100 years. The greatest absurdity of all is a statement such as "the workforce was decimated by 20 per cent", followed closely by "the town was decimated completely".

To *deprecate* something is to seek deliverance from it by prayer. However, the dictionary lists a usage from as long ago as 1897 where it means to express disapproval of something, and this usage is now commonplace and widely accepted. The extension of the meaning of *deprecate* has been compounded by the term *self-deprecating*, when somebody (usually with a degree of cynicism) disparages himself in order to court popularity. Where one is minded to *deprecate* something it may sometimes be more exact to say that one *disapproves* of it, *regrets* it, or *cannot condone* it. To make matters worse *deprecate* is also confused by some with *depreciate*, which is what happens to an asset when it declines in value.

A *dilemma* can only be between two courses of action. It is from the Greek word meaning "two propositions". If somebody cannot decide between several options he may have a *problem*, or even a *quandary*, but he does not have the good fortune of merely having a *dilemma*. I am not clear why it should be thought that a *dilemma* has horns upon which one can be impaled, but at least that cliché serves to remind people that dilemmas, like horns, come in pairs: the unicorn being a mythical beast, and the rhinoceros an exception for this purpose.

As a nation we seem constitutionally incapable of using the phrase *eke out* correctly. Since the 13th century *eke* has meant to increase, lengthen or add to. Therefore, if one *ekes out* something, one extends it, or makes it last longer: so it would be correct to say that "she eked out her supply of water for five days" or "I eked out my salary for a month". Yet one constantly reads about a person "eking out his existence" to suggest a life of struggle or hardship.

It is easy to see why the mistake is made, but a mistake it is. If one is *eking out* an existence, one is making it last longer: which is not usually what is meant.

In his speech in Chicago in 2008 on the night he won the United States presidential election, Barack Obama spoke of the **enormity** of the task ahead of him. I am unclear whether this is now accepted American usage to describe something that is *enormous*. The word is used in such a fashion here, and appears to be one of those whose wrong usage has been accepted by some dictionaries (though not by the *OED*). An *enormity*, in its first current usage given by the dictionary, is a "deviation from moral or legal rectitude": though it does concede that, influenced by *enormous*, it can mean "extreme or monstrous wickedness". So an *enormity* is something bad, a transgression: it is not simply something big. One should speak not of the *enormity* of the task, but of its *enormousness*: even if one is President of the United States.

Forensic has the meaning of "pertaining to the courts of law", according to the dictionary: its etymology is traced back to the word *forum*. Even with its permissive attitude towards the misuse of words, the dictionary does not yet sanction its use to mean *detailed, rigorously examined* or *scrutinised*. One often hears that someone has made "a forensic speech" or has undertaken "a forensic examination" of something, or done "forensic research". In each case the adjective is abused, unless any of these activities is related to a court of law. The error no doubt stems from a misunderstanding of the term *forensic science*. Forensic science is highly detailed, because of the requirements of evidence needed to convict a criminal. That does not mean that everything else in life that is highly detailed or closely examined is *forensic*.

Educated writers will use the phrase "a **fraction** of the cost went towards overheads" without thinking of its logic. What such writers inevitably mean is a *small fraction*, which although still vague is a perfectly acceptable statement. However, they forget that nine-tenths is also a fraction, and so to use the noun without qualifying it with an adjective is almost meaningless.

We have all read the phrase about someone making a *fulsome* apology. Those who write it usually believe that the adjective means *full* or *plentiful*. It has not meant that since the early 16th century, and after 500 years of obsolescence we may legitimately consider that use redundant. It has since the 17th century meant something that is overdone or grotesquely flattering or obsequious, and therefore insincere. It was probably unnecessary to have this change of meaning at the time – *fulsome* served a useful purpose in its old sense and there are plenty of other adjectives to describe its new one – but such surrenders were common in the age before formal lexicography. We have less need to submit to them now.

For someone or something to be *immured* he or it must be walled in, as was the practice at one time with certain unfortunate nuns and monks. To be confined anywhere else is not to be *immured*, but *enclosed*: usages such as someone being "immured in a coffin" are plain wrong; though it is a verb that does admit of certain metaphorical usages, such as "she was immured by her work".

Involve literally means to wrap something up in something, or to entangle it. It has a legitimate (but limited) metaphorical usage, but is now used so widely that it has been rendered meaningless. Why say "two vehicles were involved in an accident" when one can say they *had* it. Why say, also, "would you like to be involved in planning our fete this year" when you can say "would you like to help?" The noun *involvement* is used with equal lack of precision. There is no need to write that "Smith's involvement in the crime was disputed" when one should say that his *part* was disputed. Both verb and noun are used by lazy writers to describe various forms of participation by people or objects in enterprises, activities, events or other specific contexts. If tempted to use it, think of a more precise synonym – which is likely to turn out not to be a synonym at all, but simply the right word.

Part of the problem with the interference of the state in our lives, and the apparent ubiquity of its bureaucrats, is that many of us find ourselves using – or misusing – the jargon of officials in our everyday language. We use the word **inquiry** when we mean *question* or *query*. An *inquiry* is really a formal investigation, usually conducted by a judge or senior official into some aspect of government activity or something for which the state has ultimate responsibility. Individuals should not say that they have an *inquiry*; they have a *question*, or a *query*.

Literally is one of the more abused words in our tongue. Should you find yourself about to write it, pause and consider whether it is really necessary; it almost never is. One hears people say "he literally jumped out of his skin", when we all know full well he did nothing of the sort. Yet *literally*, according to the dictionary in this sense, means "with exact fidelity of representation". One cannot say "he literally died" unless he is dead, and died as a result of the event being described; but people do say it when "he" still lives and breathes. To make matters worse, circumstances in which one could use the adverb accurately would almost always render its use tautological. If one has fallen down the stairs, nothing is added to the statement "I fell down the stairs" by extending it to "I literally fell down the stairs". So avoid this usually pointless, and often silly, word.

Mutual does not mean shared: it means reciprocated. The frequent misuse caused the Fowlers much agony a century ago, but the dictionary has surrendered, perhaps because the most notable offender was Charles Dickens. The Fowlers argued that "*our mutual friend* is nonsense…it takes two to make a friendship, as to make a quarrel; and therefore all friends are mutual friends, and *friends* alone means as much as *mutual friends*".[1] Dickens would have better called his book *Our Common Friend*,

1. *The King's English*, p65.

though the dictionary concedes that he and others avoid that adjective because of its ambiguity. A correct use of *mutual*, cited by Fowler, would be for two people to be *mutual* (that is, *common*) well-wishers of each other. Well-wishing does not require reciprocity in the way that friendship does, so the use of the adjective *mutual* in this instance is not tautological. It would, however, be wrong to say that if both people were well-wishers of a third they were necessarily *mutual* well-wishers: they would be *common* ones.

Many believe that for a person to be an **orphan** he must have neither parent alive. This is not so. An orphan is someone who has lost either parent; those who have lost both are double orphans. It is therefore quite correct to describe a child who has lost his mother or his father as an orphan. This was well understood in the past when charities ran widows' and orphans' funds: many of the orphans were in the care of their mothers, who were widows. It is also an adjective ("the orphan child" is correct: it does not need to be "the orphaned child"), and in explaining this the dictionary is guilty of an inconsistency. It says the adjective applies to a child or person who is fatherless or motherless or both, but in defining the noun it claims that that usage is usually applied to someone "both of whose parents are dead", citing the correct usage as something "rarely" found these days. That may be so, but if the dictionary is prepared to surrender on the noun then surely it must do so also on the adjective. Pedants will feel it should do so on neither.

If one **partakes** of something one consumes or experiences it: "he partakes of tea every morning at eight", or "she partakes of the sea air". It does not mean to take part, or to participate: when one hears a trade-union official say that he will not "partake in the negotiations" one must steel oneself not to mock the afflicted. The dictionary does claim that the verb has this meaning, but its only modern British English citation is about the young people of a nation "partaking of its culture and traditions", which seems to me clearly to be an example of the correct meaning, not of the incorrect one.

One of the more overworked adjectives of our time is ***prestigious***, used to describe anything of even the most humble eminence. It has become an almost meaningless word, not least because of the contexts in which it is applied ("this prestigious commemorative plate appears in a limited edition", etc). This is perhaps as well, because it is inevitably used wrongly. Its etymology, from the Latin *prestigiosus*, meaning deceitful or full of tricks, tells us exactly what it should mean. The French noun *prestidigitateur*, a conjuror, comes from the same root. The dictionary speculates that the word came to have its present, vulgar meaning (first cited in 1901) because of the "dazzling" or "magical" nature of objects with *prestige*. It is an adjective to be avoided on account of its emptiness and its misleading quality.

A ***profession*** is not synonymous with a *trade*. In an age of aspiration and self-improvement, it has become common for people in white-collar trades – such as journalism, for example – to speak of their *profession*. This is a solecism. By convention in Great Britain, professions require a specific learned qualification. Medicine, the law, the church and the officer class in the Army and Royal Navy constituted the original professions. The higher ranks of the civil service and the diplomatic corps, teaching, banking, stockbroking and accountancy all came to qualify as such because of the process of examination that was needed to enter any of them. Members of Parliament have also always, by courtesy, been regarded as professional men and women, irrespective of any evidence to the contrary. All other callings, even those of supposedly learned people such as writers or musicians, are trades. The dictionary noted as early as 1908 the tendency of anyone who regarded his occupation as "socially superior to a trade or handicraft" to call it a *profession*, but dismissed this as "vulgar" and "humorous". The movement towards blanket professionalism has continued in the last 100 years or so. Pedants or the legalistic may regard it still as vulgar, but this pursuit of *amour propre* is anything but humorous to those who undertake it. So-called *professional* sportsmen and women are termed such simply to distinguish them from amateurs. A *professional* footballer earns his living from the sport; an amateur does not.

A fight the Fowlers had a century ago in *The King's English* about the verb **quiet** may have been lost, but there is no harm in mentioning it here. They deplored the verb *quieten* since it was a longer, and ignorant, version of the verb *quiet*. We would now write without a second thought (or even a first one) "she quietened the child and he fell asleep". It would be more correct to write "she quieted the child", and be prepared to invite the quizzicality of one's readers.

Refute is a verb used by people who simply mean *contradict* or *deny*. *Contradiction* (discussed separately above) and *denial* are forms of assertion; they rely on the force of will of the gainsayer to press home his point, rather than upon any evidence contrary to whatever it is he is contradicting. *Refutation* requires proof. You may say that a painting is beautiful, I that it is ugly. Since it is a subjective exercise, neither of us can prove his point. We are merely contradicting each other, or denying the truth of the statement made by the other. I may say the train for London is scheduled to leave at 11.30. You may say it goes at 11.45. By recourse to the timetable, I can *refute* your claim.

Transpire is a verb that went from the literal to the metaphorical more than 250 years ago but has now taken a further step towards incoherence of meaning. In its literal sense it means to emit through the skin in the form of a vapour. The metaphorical meaning followed closely from this, meaning to become apparent or, as the dictionary puts it, "to pass from secrecy to notice". Yet it now seems to mean *happen* or *occur*, which is just silly – "it transpired on a Saturday afternoon". If you must use this in a metaphorical sense (and it is perhaps overdue for a rest), be sure to use it accurately.

Mistaken identity

Some people seem never quite to master the differences between very similar words whose distinctions require very little explanation and can be concisely defined. These distinctions can be just as easily learned and, once that is done, give a lifetime of pleasure.

An *acronym* is not an *abbreviation*. Nato, Aids and Unesco are acronyms: the EU, the UN and the UK are abbreviations.

Adverse is an adjective meaning antagonistic, hostile, or in opposition to. *Averse* is an adjective that signifies a disinclination to or an opposition to something. Compare "they were hampered by adverse weather conditions" with "she was averse to going out without a coat on in case she caught cold".

Affect is a verb with several distinct meanings, but *effect* is not one of them. A man who *affects* a bow tie likes to wear one. A woman who *affects* deep grief at the misfortune of another is being insincere. A mixture, it seems, of both meanings is when we hear of a man who *affects* an American accent; he is wearing it as some sort of imagined ornament, but it is a pretence. The most common meaning is "to have an effect on someone or something", and it is from this meaning that confusion with the verb *effect* comes about. To *effect* something is to make it happen, bring it about, or accomplish it.

To do something *alternately* is to do it by turns with doing something else. To do it *alternatively* is to have a choice in the matter of how it is done, or even to do it in a radically different way.

Something that is *ambiguous* is susceptible of two interpretations; someone who is *ambivalent* about something, by contrast, finds it hard to settle between two opinions on the question.

To *annex* means to add something on, usually by force. It can be used literally to add territory to a country, or to take over adjoining property. An *annexe* is a subsidiary part of a building.

The distinction between *assume* and *presume* seems to have been lost altogether. *Assume* retains its distinction in sentences such as "he assumed a new identity" or "the boy assumed the position". Yet few people now sense the difference between "I assume you will be joining us for dinner" and "I presume you will be joining us". More people instinctively understand the meaning of the noun *presumption*, and its inherent insolence and sense of improper entitlement: "he had the presumption to address me by my Christian name" makes it clear that the other party should have said "Mr Smith" rather than "John". That he *presumed* to do otherwise demonstrates the force of the verb. It is, as the dictionary defines it, "to take upon oneself; to undertake without adequate authority or permission". A subsequent definition uses an idiom that is popular today: "to take the liberty". *Presume* means that one takes it upon oneself to do something or to act in a way that one simply does not have the right to act in. So if one *presumes* another is coming to dinner it means that the host has absolutely no right to expect that person to accept the invitation, perhaps because the two of them are not even acquainted. If John Smith *assumes* someone is dining with him it is because he has issued the invitation to someone with whom he is on those terms, and has had no confirmation that the person is coming. It is to take something for granted, without any hint of presumption, because one has a right to take it for granted. *Assume* has other current meanings, as I have indicated above, and which the dictionary specifies – but it is only in this context that it and *presume* are confused.

Aural is an adjective of listening; *oral* an adjective of speaking. An *aural* test is when one has to listen; an *oral* test is when one has to speak.

Avert is not to be confused with *avoid*. *Avert* has two current meanings. It is something one does to one's own eyes or gaze, turning them or it from a spectacle; or it means to prevent or ward off, as in "avert disaster". Phrases such as "she averted his eyes" are solecistic, and should read "she avoided his eyes" or, better, "his gaze".

Bail out and *bale out* are ripe for confusion. The former is used to describe the act of scooping up water in a container and throwing it overboard to stop a boat from sinking; this, according to the dictionary, derives from the name of the buckets – *bails* – that were used for the purpose. It is often misspelt *bale out* in this context. *Bail out* is also used to describe the provision of financial assistance. This term became common during the banking crisis of 2008–09, but the dictionary cites a usage as early as 1916. Given that another use of the verb *bail* dates back to 1587, and means "to be security or pledge for, to secure, guarantee, protect", one could argue that this usage has a pedigree of over 400 years. *Bale out* is what RAF types did when their Lancaster bomber had been so badly hit by enemy fire that it would crash. In the case of the departing airman, the verb was spelt thus, according to the dictionary, "as if the action were that of letting a bundle through a trapdoor".

Biannual describes something happening twice a year: *biennial* describes something that happens every two years. They are easily and frequently mixed up. There can be a similar, but less promiscuous, problem with *triennial, quadrennial* and *quinquennial.*

A *chord* is a musical term. A *cord* is some sort of string, as in *whip cord.* Either spelling may be used for the vocal cords and the spinal cord.

A *compliment* is what one pays to an attractive woman; a *complement* is a number of people or objects, or something that adds to them. Therefore, a charming remark is *complimentary*; something that augments something else is *complementary.*

The use of *complimentary* to mean free of charge is a pompous euphemism.

A book may **comprise** 15 chapters, but is not *comprised of* them.

One who is **complacent** is satisfied about life or events, and does not easily see the potential for his complacency to be disturbed. One who is **complaisant** is eager to please or is compliant.

Whatever is **connoted** is indicated subsidiary to a main point. Something that is marked out as the main point is **denoted**.

Contemptible is an adjective describing a low or mean person who behaves in a way that excites contempt in others. **Contemptuous** describes the feeling those others have towards the *contemptible* one. However, it is a word whose main idiomatic usage now appears to describe insolence towards authority, with the undertone that the authority concerned is not worthy of respect.

A **continuous** noise is one that never stops. **Continual** noise is frequent, but with interruptions.

Convince and **persuade** are often used as if interchangeable: they are not. To *convince* someone of something is to make him admit the truth of a contention put to him thanks to the force of one's argument. To *persuade* someone of something means to induce him to believe something. The dictionary says that one can be convinced by persuasion, but that seems to me to undo the force of *convince* and to lose some of the nuance between the two verbs. If one is *convinced* of something one's conviction about it is much firmer than if one is merely *persuaded* of it, which seems to leave room for doubt and possibly even for persuasion back in the other direction. *Convince* carries with it an element of proof: *persuade*, an element of faith. Someone can *convince* me of his age by showing me his birth certificate. He can *persuade* me of the Christian miracles if I choose to believe him, but he can offer me no proof.

A **councillor** is a member of a council, of whatever description. A **counsellor** is an adviser or, in a modern sense, one who acts as a mentor. Confusion may arise with the Privy Council, whose members have long been designated *Privy Counsellors* (of the Sovereign).

In the course of one's reading one will find that **credible**, **creditable** and **credulous** all seem to end up in one another's place from time to time. *Credible* is an adjective applied to something or someone who is capable or worthy of being believed. *Creditable* is an adjective that from the early 16th to the late 18th century meant the same thing. Since then it has been applied to something that brings credit or honour to someone or something – "it was a creditable performance". *Credulous* is an adjective applied to someone who was "born yesterday": it means over-ready to believe, or ready to believe despite insufficient evidence.

A **curmudgeon** is not a bloody-minded old man. He is a miser and subject to avarice. That may make him difficult, but bloody-mindedness is not what defines him.

Deceased is a pompous term for *dead*, often misappropriated as a genteel euphemism. **Diseased** means sick.

Defuse is what one does to a bomb. **Diffuse** means to spread something out. The adjective *diffuse* means widespread.

Dependant is a noun. **Dependent** is an adjective. For example: "his dependants were dependent upon him".

Derisive describes something that projects derision, such as a *derisive* shout or a *derisive* article. **Derisory** describes something that should provoke derision, such as a *derisory* suggestion or a *derisory* offer.

Discreet and **discrete** sound the same, and are spelt almost the same, but mean two completely different things. Until 20 or 30 years ago there were few difficulties with these terms, because the latter was used only in learned journals. It has now become one of those academic terms that non-academics come across in everyday life and use: perhaps this is because of the large number of scientists who feed the appetite for expert commentary on television's 24-

hour news channels. *Discreet* means tactful, understated, restrained, lacking in vulgarity or advertisement; *discrete* means separate. *Discreet* service is service carried out without show or ostentation; a *discrete* service is one distinct or separate from something else.

At least one dictionary (I shall not embarrass its publishers by naming it) has put its hands up on the correct usage of **disinterested**. Once more, insistence on its correct usage is not a point of pedantry; it comes from the desire to retain an important adjective that indicates a not especially subtle distinction. If one is *disinterested* in a question one takes neither side in it. One can see both sides of the argument and is well placed to act impartially as an arbiter in the matter. If one could not care less about the point at issue, one is **uninterested** in it. One might attend a football match in which one supports neither side, or supports a team that is not one of the two playing, and one can be *disinterested* in the outcome. One could go to the match under sufferance, being bored by football itself, and be *uninterested* in the result. The dictionary still stigmatises the misuse of this word as a "loose use", even though the first person it can find to have been loose with it was John Donne in 1612. Most abusers are from the 20th century, and it is manifest from the contexts in which they employ the word that they have not realised it has a meaning different from *uninterested*.

Effective and **effectual** – and their negatives, *ineffective* and *ineffectual* – have shades of meaning now so close as to be almost identical. The dictionary defines *effective* as meaning "powerful in effect; producing a notable effect" but then, to complicate the issue, as also meaning "effectual". Under *effectual* the usage meaning "powerful in effect" is cited as "rare": *effectual*'s main meaning seems now to be "produces its intended effect". In the negative, *ineffectual* seems to be a shade beyond *ineffective*; someone who is *ineffective* does not produce the desired effect, but someone who is *ineffectual* is a failure.

Egoism and **egotism** are not interchangeable. *Egoism* is what Americans and psychologists would call "self-obsession" – the inability to consider any situation or question except in how it relates to oneself. *Egotism* is a different sort of objectionableness, and is about the projection of oneself; this usually manifests itself when one realises that somebody else is the favourite topic of his own conversation.

To **erupt** is to burst or break out; to **irrupt** is to burst or break in.

Especially and **specially** are both adverbs, but the former is the more emphatic. Compare "you will be in trouble, especially if you do that" with "he went to the shop specially to buy a bunch a flowers".

Something that is *flagrant* is glaringly obvious, but it has the necessary condition of being notorious or scandalous. Something that lacks those conditions is simply **blatant**.

A *ferment* is the process of leavening bread or brewing alcohol through yeast or other means and provides the verb *to ferment*. The verb *foment* means to encourage, foster, instigate or help spread, and is often used in the context of revolutions or revolutionary acts.

Flaunt and *flout* are frequently confused, usually with the former being used for the latter, as in "he was flaunting all the rules of good conduct". The dictionary does not surrender on this, pointing out under its entry for *flaunt* that it is sometimes used for *flout*: "erroneous", it says, and it is. To *flaunt* something means to display it ostentatiously or conspicuously; to *flout* something is to disregard it with contempt, the object normally being a law, rule or code.

Forgo means to forsake or refrain from. **Forego** means to go before or to precede.

There is no excuse, except the gravest lapse in concentration, for confusing *formerly* and *formally*. One was *formerly* a student; one is *formally* reprimanded for a misdemeanour.

To *haver* is not to be indecisive; it is to waffle.

Pictures and pheasants are *hung*. Men are *hanged*.

Two similar prefixes for English words that come from the Greek are a source of confusion. *Hyper* means over and *hypo* means under. Someone who dies of *hypothermia* has perished from the cold; of *hyperthermia*, from the heat. *Hypertension* and *hypotension* are two other terms often confused. Some writers, used only to hearing such words, have produced such terms as *hypomarket* and *hypoventilation* when they mean quite the opposite. Looking up unfamiliar words in the dictionary before committing them to print is always a good idea.

Infer and *imply* need to be taken together, because the former is too often used by mistake for the latter (it is seldom the other way round). You may say that someone you know is a blackguard and a scoundrel. From that I may *infer* that you do not like him. You are certainly *implying* that you don't. Yet time and again one reads that someone is *inferring* that someone is a scoundrel when in fact he is *implying* it. The entirely uneducated have no trouble with these words because they rarely use them. It is only once people have learned of their existence that they seem to have trouble with them.

Ingenious is an adjective applied to something clever in its invention or construction. *Ingenuous* is an adjective applied to a person who (as the dictionary has it) is "honourably straightforward; open, frank, candid". *Disingenuous* is therefore a rather disobliging negative of the word.

Into does exist, and has done for 1,000 years, to describe the movement that precedes the condition of being *in* somewhere. By association with it people have made the preposition *onto*. This, however, does not exist.

The rise of Muslim fundamentalism in recent years has given us cause to be more precise in our use of the terminology of that faith. An *Islamic* person is a follower of the Prophet Mohammed, and no extreme intent need be imputed to him. An *Islamist*, by contrast, expresses a fanatical devotion to his faith, sometimes to the point of violence, and inevitably adopts a fundamentalist approach.

Someone who is *laudable* deserves praise; something that is *laudatory* conveys it.

Lay is a transitive verb. *Lie* is an intransitive one (see Chapter Four).

To be *loath* to do something is a perfectly acceptable way of expressing reluctance. It does not require an *e* on the end of the adjective; that belongs only on the end of *loathe*, a verb that means to dislike extremely.

If something is *luxuriant* there is plenty of it: a woman may have *luxuriant* hair. If it is *luxurious* it is of high and sumptuous quality. One can avoid wrong usage by contemplating the absurdity of it. Should the woman have *luxurious* hair one could infer it was a wig, made to a high specification and bought at a high price, the adjective having no bearing on its quantity. A *luxuriant* fabric would be abundant, the adjective having no bearing on its quality.

It is strange that *masterful* and *masterly* cause terrible problems. Perhaps this is because some people think *masterly* is an adverb; it is not. Both words are adjectives meaning subtly different things. A *masterful* man is someone who, as Shelley put it, has "wrinkled lip, and sneer of cold command": he has qualities of dominance. *Masterly* describes an exceptional ability in something, such as a *masterly* command of the English tongue, a *masterly* cover-drive or a *masterly* way of baking a lemon meringue pie. If one behaves domineeringly, one behaves *masterfully*. If one does something exceptionally well, one does it *in a masterly fashion*. The last citation the dictionary has for *masterly* as an adverb is 1887, and it was not common before then.

Some writers and speakers also tend to confuse *mitigate* and *militate*, although their meanings are so distinct from each other that the dictionary has not followed the example of *prevaricate* and *procrastinate* and suggested that because they sound similar they may as well, these days, mean the same thing. If one *mitigates* something one lessens or alleviates its effects. A barrister pleading on behalf of his client in court before sentence is passed may ask the judge to award a lesser sentence than he may have considered handing down because the offence is *mitigated* by, for example, a plea of guilty. In turn the judge may *mitigate*, or lessen, the sentence. To *militate* means to strive, originally in the manner of a soldier, and in the last century of heightened political change it has come to mean to campaign for or against an idea or policy. The confusion of these two words is probably not provoked by ignorance of their meanings but by lack of concentration: it is almost a malapropism.

Nought is a number – o. *Naught* means nothing: "Say not the struggle naught availeth".

Onto does not exist (see *into*, above). The phrase is *on to*.

There are three spellings of a word that sound the same but have markedly different meanings: *palate*, *palette* and *pallet*. One only has to read (as one too frequently does) of a painter mixing colours on a *palate* to see the problem: painters do not usually mix colours on the roof of their mouth. *Palate* is how one spells that part of the anatomy, as well as the figurative usage to suggest a taste for food or drink. The mixing of paint happens on a *palette*. A *pallet* is a straw bed, something goods are stacked on or a piece of armour covering the head; in that third usage it is sometimes spelt *pallette*.

To do something *partly* is to do it incompletely. To do something *partially* is to do it by favouring one party in the matter over another; in other words, to do it with partiality.

A *peremptory* act is one that brooks no discussion. A *perfunctory* one is discharged as a matter of routine and without any enthusiasm.

Practical, practicable and their antonyms *impractical, unpractical* and *impracticable* are not always used literately. The dictionary says that something that is *practical* is something that occurs in practice or in action, as opposed to its being speculative or theoretical. An important secondary usage of the adjective is to describe something as suited to a particular purpose, or functional. *Practicable* is a near-synonym, but has the additional shade of meaning "able to be done or put into practice successfully; feasible". A *practical* solution is one that entails action; a *practicable* one can be executed without difficulty. Greater difficulty comes when trying to negate these terms. *Impractical* (which the dictionary cites as first having been used in 1865) is frowned on by pedants as a Johnny-come-lately, catch-all substitute for the much older terms *unpractical* (first cited in 1637) and *impracticable* (1677), and thus as lacking the precision of either. Those wishing to be precise should first judge whether they wish to use either *practical* or *practicable* and, if negating it, to do so by *unpractical* or *impracticable*; and leave *impractical* to the Americans, in whose land it seems to have found a happy home.

If something is happening *presently*, it is happening soon. It is not happening now, although that is the American understanding of the word.

Principle and **principal** have such a straightforward distinction from each other that it is remarkable anyone should confuse them. One has *principles*, or agrees to something *in principle*. If something is the most prominent feature of a large number of features, it is the *principal* feature; and if two people draw up a contract between themselves, they are the *principals* in that contract.

Pristine does not mean bright, shiny and new. It means original.

A **program** is something a computer runs. A **programme** is something one watches on television, or buys at the opera or the theatre.

A *proscription* is an instruction not to do something. A *prescription* is an instruction to do it.

A *radiographer* is a technician trained to operate radiographical equipment; a *radiologist* is a qualified physician who specialises in radiology, the branch of medicine that deals with the diagnosis of disease by use of X-rays.

Repetitious and *repetitive* are almost synonymous. The shade of difference between the two in British English usage is that the former has a strain of the pejorative about it, emphasising the tediousness and futility of the repeat; the latter is a neutral statement of fact. In American English the two words appear to have become interchangeable, with *repetitious* the more popular of the two.

Scotch is the adjective for whisky and is used in certain other formulaic phrases: *Scotch eggs*, *mist*, *ale* and *pines*, for example. The people and everything else have the adjective *Scottish*. As for nouns, there are *Scotsmen* and *Scotswomen*, or simply *Scots*.

Seasonal describes something that occurs at a particular time of year – strawberries in June, raspberries in July, apples in August, walnuts in September. *Seasonable* applies to something that is suitable for a certain time of year – it is *seasonable* to have snow in January, or hot sunshine in July, or to have gales around the equinoxes, or to wear an overcoat in winter.

A *solecism* is a grammatical error. *Solipsism* is the belief that the self is the only reference point of true knowledge.

Stationary is an adjective describing something that is not in motion; *stationery* is what one writes letters on.

A *strait* is a passage that is narrow; a *straight* is a part of a racecourse that has no bend on it. *Straitened* means confined or constrained; *straightened* means made straight. The two adjectives are often confused, usually the latter when the intention is the meaning of the former.

Terror is what one feels when one is terrorised; *terrorism* is the practice of inflicting it. A senior Scotland Yard anti-terrorist officer who finds himself described as a "terror chief" – as one occasionally reads in the newspapers – is manifestly nothing of the kind.

Something *tortuous* is either literally twisted or metaphorically devious. Something *torturous* is either literally or metaphorically excruciating or painful.

Treason is a particular act of treachery by a subject against the state towards which he owes allegiance. It breaks a law and carries with it severe penalties. *Treachery* may be used to describe treason, but may also be used (however histrionically) to describe the betrayal of one person by another in a private relationship. *Treason* cannot be so used.

A project or mission does not get *underway*, it gets *under way*.

If a person is *unresponsible* then he has no responsibility for a certain matter. Someone who is *irresponsible* is incapable of taking responsibility for anything.

Unsocial and *unsociable* have almost, but not quite, the same meaning. The first describes someone who is not fitted for society; the second one who may be fitted for it, but has no desire to participate in it.

Someone who is *venal* has a price. He is corrupt and can be influenced by money. A *venal* person will take a bribe and either have no principles to start with, or for a mercenary consideration will overlook them. This is not a *venial* fault; a *venial* offence is one that is trivial and easily pardonable.

Whisky is the Scottish drink. The Irish, and the Americans, make *whiskey*.

An extra syllable

There are several adjectives that appear to the untutored eye to be interchangeable but which, through the addition of an extra syllable, undergo a subtle change of meaning. They end in the first instance in *-ic*, and have an augmentation in *-ical*. The most obvious are *historic* and *historical*; *economic* and *economical*; *magic* and *magical*; and *comic* and *comical*. *Conic* and *conical* are less used. *Tragic* and *tragical*, and *psychic* and *psychical*, have become antique, the distinction between them lost except to the strictest pedant, and should not detain us. A variation on the theme, and worthy of note, is the pair *manic* and *maniacal*.

A moment's thought will appear to tell the intelligent writer what the difference is between each constituent of these pairs of adjectives. A ***magic*** moment is one where something illusory or supernatural appears to have happened. A ***magical*** moment is one where it is quite obvious that something illusory or supernatural has not happened, but the ambience of the occasion could cause one to think that it might. The adjective in *-ic* is literal; the one in *-ical* metaphorical, suggesting that something has the properties or likeness of magic. The dictionary defines *magical* as "of or relating to magic" in the first definition, but a second one, almost as old and now more idiomatic, is "resembling magic in action or effect; enchanting".

Yet the other pairs of adjectives have less straightforward distinctions. A ***historic*** event is one that will take its place in history; a ***historical*** one already has. If something is *historical* it is of the past; if something is *historic* it stands out, or will stand out, as a landmark in history. The dictionary notes the use of *historical* as a synonym for *historic* as an affectation of the Victorians, with no use cited since the 19th century. Therefore, we may accept that the idiomatic usages of these two words is settled, and as detailed above.

There is a greater distinction still between ***economic*** and ***economical***. *Economic* has evolved into an adjective describing financial affairs, usually on a national scale, or pertaining to the management of the political economy. Therefore we have phrases such as "*economic* policy", "*economic* crisis", "*economic* recovery" and "*economic* considerations". *Economical* is an adjective describing the frugal use of resources. If one has an *economical* meal, an *economical* holiday or an *economical* central heating system, one is spending as little money as possible on any of them. In the last 20 years the word has also taken on what was once an original and amusing metaphorical usage, after a senior civil servant admitted that he had been "economical with the truth". He made his point well at the time, and everyone immediately understood what he meant, but the phrase and its adaptations have become hackneyed, and are now best avoided by thoughtful writers.

By contrast with any of the above, **comic** – the adjective and not the noun – and **comical** appear to have lost almost all distinction in meaning when one is compared with the other. A *comic* situation has almost no perceptible difference from a *comical* one, other than in the minds of the strict. They will see the former as something intended to be funny, the latter as something in which the intention was anything but. For the most part this distinction is now lost, but that should not prevent the scrupulous from continuing to observe it.

The Fowlers took issue with the use of the suffix *-al* to make an adjective of anything other than a word of Latin origins (*-alis* is a common adjectival suffix in Latin, so they were holding to logic).[2] They mentioned adjectives such as *racial* and *coastal* that defied the rule, and made a case for the nouns *race* and *coast* to be used as adjectives instead. In the century since they made this proscription it is hard to say who has won the battle: we still speak of *coast roads* and *race riots*. There are nuances between *coast* and *coastal*, and indeed between *race* and *racial*: the adjectives ending in *-al* convey the sense of being in the area of the coast, or on the general subject of race, those without the suffix being more specific and

2. *The King's English*, p51.

direct. So little regard is given to strict etymology now that no-one would be likely to complain at the formation of an adjective from an Anglo-Saxon noun in this fashion – except on the grounds of instant redundancy, there already being a suitable alternative in the dictionary.

Getting difficult

Partridge has a long entry in *Usage and Abusage* on the word **got** – he could as easily have made the entry about the word **get** – but, if anything, this usually strict grammarian lets the promiscuous and often thoughtless use of this term off lightly.[3] Without detracting from Fowler's point that the Anglo-Saxon is to be preferred to the Romance at all times, the use of the verb *to get* in an increasing number of contexts is not merely "slovenly" (Partridge's word): it is downright confusing. If (and the point has repeatedly been made) one of the features of the best writing is that it avoids ambiguities, the ubiquity of *get* and its derivatives does more than most usages to undermine that. That is why it merits a section of this work to itself.

One abomination I shall mention in more detail in the next chapter – the Americanism "can I get a beer?" – has pointed the way to this problem. Its misuse long precedes the transatlantic influence, however. Partridge quotes a passage in which the word is used in these different senses: to mount ("I got on horseback"), to receive ("I got your letter"), to reach a destination ("I got to Canterbury"), to take a form of transport ("I got a chaise"), to change condition ("I got wet"), to catch a disease ("I have got such a cold"), to rid oneself of something ("I shall not be able to get rid of [it]"), as an auxiliary for the passive voice ("I got

3. *Usage and Abusage*, p136.

shaved"), to learn something ("I got into the secret"), to obtain or procure something ("getting a Memorial before the board"), to return ("I got back"), to fetch something ("I got my supper"), to travel physically ("I got to bed), to travel metaphysically ("I got to sleep"), to rise ("I got up"), as an auxiliary for a reflexive verb ("I got myself drest"), to exit ("I got out"), to enter ("I got into"), and to possess ("I have got nothing for you"). He could also have described certain other usages such as to be compelled to do something ("I've got to go") or simply to feel obliged ("I've got to help"), to be struck ("he got me in the ribs"), to recover ("she got over it"), to realise the truth ("get real") or to realise a sum of money ("they got £500,000 for the house"). I do not doubt there are many more.

It is desirable to use the short word rather than the long: but *get* and its relations are an example of obscuring meaning and repelling the interest of the reader by over-simplification – a charitable term for Partridge's "slovenliness". A lazy writer or speaker will use the word in these many contexts rather than make the effort to be precise. Other words, more definite, more evocative, more accurate and often not much longer, may be substituted. Many of them are, like *get* or *got*, but one syllable. "I *hired* a chaise," "I *reached* Canterbury", "I *caught* a cold", or "I *must* go" are far better English. Sometimes, the *get* is superfluous: as in "I dressed" rather than "I got myself drest". The verb *to be* works perfectly well in expressions of the passive – "I was shaved" for "I got shaved". It is especially egregious to say *have got*, when the simple *have* will do.

In a similar fashion, certain other verbs are used as maids-of-all-work in a way that suggests laziness on the part of the writer, or a lack of precision in his or thinking, or both. *Do* is an obvious offender, notably in the slang construction "do some ironing", "do some cooking", "do some painting", "do some gardening" when one verb (and a more precise verb at that) will serve in place of two. The verb *see* has been distorted in a different way, to allow inanimate objects or even concepts to "see" in a way of which they were previously thought incapable: "today sees the arrival of the new teacher", "the revised plan sees the demolition of the old buildings", "the road sees a new development in traffic calming" and so on. As with other overused verbs, this usage betokens a reluctance to think more energetically and specifically, and a failure (as discussed below in the passage on metaphor) to think logically about the feasibility of a verb taken out of its literal context.

Changing roles

In *Usage and Abusage*, Partridge is strict about the wrongness of the noun *mystery* becoming an adjective, arguing that no self-respecting writer would use the phrase "mystery murder".[4] Today we often hear the term *murder mystery*, which is little better, though the noun *murder* has become an adjective in such contexts as *murder suspect*, *murder inquiry*, *murder squad*, *murder trial* and so on. Just as I deal elsewhere with nouns that have become verbs, so we must accept that they can become adjectives too. It is interesting that the *OED* does not seem to accept this, but lists phrases such as *murder charge* as compound nouns – two nouns used together where one takes the role of an adjective to describe the other. It has a similar set of compounds for *mystery*, such as *mystery novel*. Perhaps in this way order can be preserved, and words kept in their categories. However, some nouns have and do become adjectives in a way that stretches the notion of compounding. It is hard to be sure whether *champagne moment* or *champagne socialist* are proper compound nouns, or whether it is now the case that the noun *champagne* can be applied to any other noun to convey a

4. *Usage and Abusage*, p190.

sense of celebration or luxury. If one has to do such a thing with an adjective, it is probably best to do it frivolously, and therefore to avoid it in serious writing, or in writing that one wishes to be taken seriously. This use (or abuse) of language has become more frequent in recent decades, for which we can probably blame the media.

Modern usage also appropriates adjectives as nouns. One of the most common is *homosexual* and its popular slang counterpart *gay*. *Homosexual* is an adjective. One can describe *a homosexual man, a homosexual encounter, a homosexual inclination*, but *a homosexual* is as wrong as saying *a handsome, an ugly* or *a tall*. The late journalist Auberon Waugh used to make much of this, and frequently used the somewhat bizarre, but not incorrect, term *homosexualist*. The dictionary cites the first usage of that term at 1931, but cites the first misuse of the adjective as 1912, only 20 years after the first adjectival use. Pedants would always write *a homosexual man* or, for that matter, *a lesbian woman* or *a heterosexual man/woman/ couple*. Another example, identified by Kingsley Amis, is *classic*, which began as an adjective and has become a noun – one that, as Amis pointed out, has come to mean not something classical, but merely something that is "standard or ideal".[5]

Sometimes even a participle becomes a noun. One of the vogue preoccupations of this era is environmentalism, and it has had an effect on language. What we used to call "material for recycling" – and what some of us still call it – has simply become *recycling*; however, it is not a noun, it is a participle. It has also become fashionable to put a definite article in front of the noun *science* when a speaker or writer is referring to a particular branch of it, such as that examining global warming. From the tone of voice used by those who do so, it seems they feel that to speak of *the*

5. *The King's English: A Guide to Modern Usage*, by Kingsley Amis (HarperCollins, 1997), p34.

science adds extra authority to their pronouncements. Instead of saying "the science supports our view" they should say "scientific analysis" or "the results of scientific research". *The science* sounds pompous and silly to that large portion of mankind who are not scientists.

The most promiscuous mutation of words today is of nouns into verbs. This has always happened, as the dictionary confirms. However, in recent times this seems to have become an especially American habit that, like so many of them, has caught on here. Gowers reflected on it decades ago in *The Complete Plain Words*, citing nouns that had become verbs that few of us now would blink at – "feature, glimpse, position, sense" – but he also adds "signature" which, if it was prevalent in the 1950s and 1960s, has died a welcome death by now.[6] Therefore, we read of books being *authored* instead of written; money being *gifted* rather than donated; objects being *loaned* rather than lent; something being *impacted* upon rather than suffering the impact of or, more simply, being hit; a person's being *partnered* by someone else instead of accompanied by him; and so on. The strong contemporary American influence causing this mutation is clear from even a cursory encounter with one of that country's television programmes – a common example these days is when one hears someone has been *tasked* to do something. However, such changes have happened throughout the evolution of the language: the dictionary gives the first use of the noun *battle* as a verb in 1330, though suggests *fight* is now more usual. The first use in British English of the verb *partner*, however, is given as 2000. Many will embrace this renewed enthusiasm for turning nouns into verbs as enriching the language; pedants will argue that perfectly good words already exist for the actions described. Rather than causing the

6. *The Complete Plain Words*, by Sir Ernest Gowers, revised by Sir Bruce Fraser (Pelican, 1973), p47.

language to expand, such terms will only shunt perfectly serviceable ones out of the way and into desuetude.

A reasonable exception to this stricture is when a new
technology, or technological process, requires a new vocabulary to
describe it. Until the late 1990s nobody would have thought that
the English language needed a verb *text*. Then the text message
was invented, possibly also inventing an adjective in the process
(or, at the very least, a new compound noun). One may send a text
message, or one may *text* someone. The new verb, coined from
the noun, has the advantages of clarity and concision: it is a new,
logically-derived, usage to describe a new phenomenon. There
can be no feasible objection to it.

American English had a strong influence in the last century in
minting verbs by taking nouns and adding the suffix *-ise* (or, as the
Americans spelt it, *-ize*) to them. This also happened with adjectives.
However, there was a long pedigree of both in British English.
Standardise appears in the late 19th century; but *particularise* in
the late 16th. However, *digitise* was coined in 1953; the Americans
gave us *monetise* in 1867 (and again, in a subtly different sense, in
1954), *corporatise* in the 1940s and *privatise* in the 1950s. Some of
these words usefully described something in one word that would
otherwise have required several. *Privatise* was itself a preferred
shorter term for *denationalise* and meant "sell off state-owned
assets to private corporations or individuals". *Digitise* succinctly
puts a complex electronic procedure into one word. Perhaps it is
the efficacious way that the *-ise* suffix makes a verb that has made
it so popular: but not all such uses may be judged so necessary.
Some will always struggle to be persuaded that *conceptualise* is any
better a word than *imagine* or *conceive*. Before minting such a word
in this way, think carefully about whether a feasible alternative
already exists.

Some unnecessary words, however, put up a fight for centuries.
The dictionary gives the first use of *repairable* as dating from 1489,

of *reparable* from 60 years later: both seem to be current, though pedants prefer the idiomatic usage of the latter, citing its Latin antecedents (via the French) as the justification. What, though, about *explicable*, which dates from 1556, and *explainable*, which comes from 1610? *Explicable* has the upper hand, with the citations in the dictionary for the alternative much scarcer, and used, it seems, rather by accident: the second most recent is from 1842, and in a letter from Charles Dickens. Yet one often hears, even in the broadcast media, this term being used, presumably in ignorance by speakers who do not know that *explicable* exists. As Latin dies out in all but the most exclusive schools one may expect such abusage to become more common, as writers and speakers conclude that something to be explained must be *explainable*. Although *treatable* pre-dates *tractable* by nearly 200 years, pedants prefer the latter to the former since both come from the Latin *tractabilis*; the former came into the language from upstart mediaeval French, though the word *traitable* survives in that tongue to this day. The best guide for using, or choosing not to use, any changing word today is whether or not a perfectly good alternative exists. Such a rule, sternly applied, would have done for *tractable* in the early 16th century.

Branching out

New metaphors or similes are coined daily, despite what we consider to be the lack of originality of thought encouraged by our education system. The problem with new metaphors or similes is that they quickly become old. They tend to be overworked by those in search of a quick thrill, or who wish to propagate a sense of sensationalism. The principal culprits, therefore, are to be found in the mass media. Words that had a literal use were, one day, seized upon by a writer and given a metaphorical one.

A random example is that almost everything that comes about now *transpires*, as we have already noted. In a similar vein, only ships used to be *launched*. Now books, initiatives, plans, schemes, even people find this verb being applied to them. There is nothing wrong with such usages if the writer using them is convinced that he is doing so for the first time; or, if he knows very well he is not, if he believes that their staleness will not repel his readers or cause them not to compute properly what he is telling them; or if he does not mind being branded as a lazy or second-rate writer.

There are many other examples of words whose literal meaning has been complemented or supplanted by another, and whose branching out in this way has long since delighted us enough. A cursory perusal of a tabloid newspaper will quickly turn up plenty of them. Birds, and later aeroplanes and rockets, used to be the only things that *soared*. Now prices, stocks and shares, reputations, deficits, averages and all manner of other things do it too. By contrast, so too do they *plunge*, something that was once restricted to divers or swimmers, or to dishes being washed up. *Searing* used to be a process applied to meat, wounds and flesh in general. Now anyone written about in the newspapers who has had an even remotely unpleasant experience can usually be relied upon to have found it *searing* too. There are many more of these colourful, but tired, usages. Should you ever find yourself about to write anything metaphorical that you have picked up from elsewhere, don't.

In choosing words carefully one can play one's part in maintaining the intellectual rigour of the language. I observed in Chapter Two that there are perfectly good reasons why language changes, such as in order to become more precise and to eliminate ambiguities, or to amplify and enrich meaning and understanding. What no serious writer should have any part in doing is debasing the language. This requires a simple understanding that usages change sometimes for those good reasons, but at others for no better reason than loose thinking or ignorance. That is when language is debased and becomes either imprecise or illogical. The battle is almost lost, for example, on the use of *warn* as a transitive verb, with supposedly intelligent people now wilfully using it without an object.

Emerge, to take another example, is now used so ubiquitously that it has come to act as a synonym for *happen, derive from, come out of* or even just for the verb *to be*. Often, when one reads that something has *emerged* it is simply that it *is*. A verb once used to evoke the appearance of a sea monster from Stygian waters, or an ogre from pitch darkness, is now used to try to convey a sense of excitement about the occurrence of the most banal of facts. The dictionary defines *emerge* as to come out of a liquid or out of darkness and, either way, to become visible. It is easy to see how the word acquired a figurative meaning from this sense, and it has had it for 300 years; but that figurative meaning has now been debased to the point where the verb covers anything that comes to one's attention. There are many other examples of such exhausted words.

As I describe at greater length in the next chapter, a good writer understands that a good style depends to an extent on choosing words that are precise and, if used figuratively, fresh. If more people are educated to take such care, our language will remain sharp and logical. We all have our part to play; we are all in this together. The prize at the end of the process of mastering grammar and the meaning of words is that we have a chance of writing well. However, like all accomplishments, that of the power of expression may be used to corrupt ends, so I must close with a word of warning.

Dishonesty

Orwell, as I have observed elsewhere, had something of an obsession with the dishonest use of words: words used to convey an idea that was not quite, or in some cases anything like, what it seemed. He saw this as a form of political manipulation engaged in by cynical and over-mighty states. It is still the case. It has been popular for politicians to speak in recent years of *modernising* aspects of our lives, when they simply mean *changing* them, and quite often changing them for their own convenience. The same is true of *progress, freedom, liberty* and other words that suggest some sort of utopian achievement: they are used to dress up something that is far less than the word suggests, or to obfuscate something that is in fact the very opposite of the word. *Democracy* is an especially abused term, used at election times by political parties who will be glad to put it in abeyance for up to the following five years while they engage in elective dictatorship. Politicians also go on about *values* when they mean *prejudices*. If a politician has *vision* it merely means that he has managed to devise an idea of what to do that is different from that of his opponents.

Public and private corporations engage in this manipulation of language too. How often has one travelled on the London Underground and been told by a smug announcer that a *good* service is operating? He means a *scheduled* or a *normal* service, or something approaching it; unwittingly, he is using the adjective of value to draw an oblique comparison with the normal bad service, which does not live up the promise of the schedule. There is a fine line between euphemism and downright misrepresentation. Any retailer conducting a *special offer* is merely concealing the fact that he has goods he cannot sell at the price he was originally asking for them. A performer of any description who is described as *brilliant* almost certainly isn't. When touring the English countryside, one notices that food advertised as *farmhouse cooking* often has been cooked, but has never been near a farmhouse. If one hears a broadcasting outlet engage in an act of self-reference in describing itself as *impartial* or *unbiased*, one should be aware that this may depend on a quite radical definition of either partiality or bias. *Fact* is often used when the writer or speaker means *assertion*.

Almost any adjective contained in advertisements by estate agents, used-car salesmen or political parties should be treated as specious.

CHAPTER SIX

The wrong tone

Language does change, and some think there is no point trying to fix it, or becoming upset over the failures of others to stick to accepted conventions. This is especially true of a language such as English, which is spoken in so many discrete communities around the world. Although most of the grammatical rules in this book hold good for wherever English is spoken, the educated standard of British English from which they are taken is not identical to the standard as spoken in America, or indeed in other Anglophone nations. The decline in rigour in education in Britain itself means, indeed, that many who think themselves to be speakers and writers of the British standard will in fact be some way from it; and, as I have noted in my Prologue, there are many more (often with a fine grasp of the tongue) who believe that the notion of such a standard is a bourgeois or anti-intellectual conceit.

It is my view that, for ease of communication and the avoidance of ambiguity, there should be a grammatical standard and, indeed, there is one in most formal means of communication. Individual words are a different matter. They come in to (and drop out of) English from all sorts of sources: we freshly mint them, or the Americans (or Australians, or Indians, or any other of the large groups and civilisations that use the language) do and we borrow them, or they come in from a completely alien tongue. Sometimes they grow from classical roots. Many of the words we now use, and have used for centuries, came from Germanic and Norse languages before the Conquest, or French after it. We then borrowed widely from Latin and Greek during the Renaissance, when it became popular to explore again those dead or decaying languages, or from Persian, Turkish, Arabic or the Indian tongues during the age of imperial expansion in the 18th and 19th centuries. For years, maybe decades, a foreign word is italicised when we write it as a sign that it is still a stranger to our language; then one day it will be quietly accepted as naturalised, and the italicisation will end.

However there are, and in the interests of comprehensibility there need to be, limits to the freelance activities of an established language such as ours when it comes to defining any sort of standard. In the era before either mass education or mass media, and before lexicographers attempted to settle the orthography of the English language, there was room for debate about how the content, form and structure of the living language could or should change. This is less so now, when effective mass communication requires a consistent set of standards: schools, perhaps, should strive to teach those standards. Although new words are constantly coming into the language, and for the very good reason that technological and social changes require new precision in expression, the spelling is settled and the conventions of grammar widely accepted. Where they are breached it is not because there is a less ambiguous, or more convenient, or more logical way of doing things; it is usually out of a laziness or an ignorance that it is deemed impolite to mention.

There are tribes within British English who speak the tongue in various distinct ways. Not all of them are "correct". I do not mean by that that they fail to conform to the rules of the language as spoken by a certain caste: I mean they fail to conform to the standards that would be accepted by an averagely intelligent newspaper, for example, and its averagely intelligent readers. In this chapter I want to look at some of the more obvious influences on contemporary English, and work out not so much where they fit in to the way the language is spoken, but how those who wish to speak it or write it in a conformist fashion should deal with these sometimes alien forces.

Over there, over there

Although English is spoken in numerous communities around the world, none of these at present has such an influence on British English as the United States of America. It is hard not to note a strong strain of anti-Americanism in our culture these days. Sadly, from the place where this prejudice might best be applied – in matters of language – it seems for the most part to be conspicuously absent. More and more of us visit America, but that seems unlikely (unless we are instantly impressionable) to be the source of the contamination. The ubiquity of American television programmes, American films and American popular music has ensured that the Americans' way of speaking English constantly impinges upon, or at times seeks to usurp, our own. It seems not to matter how much some of us may affect to despise the Americans for their imperial adventures in the Middle East, their resistance to the notion of man-made global warming, or their determination to set the cause of international cuisine back by several decades; we still seem to be unable to avoid being seduced by aspects of their language.

Just looking at a page of American prose, we can soon tell that this is not English quite as we know it. I do not only mean the interesting typefaces that we and the Americans seem not to have in common: I mean their spelling. This is an aspect of American English that we have so far avoided imitating, at least consciously. None of us, unless illiterate, would dream of writing *honor, neighbor* or *color*, or *tire* in reference to a car, or have a *favorite* thing, or think that in Britain we had a Ministry of *Defense*, or imagine that there was such a verb as *practicing*. American orthography departed from ours before either of our nations had properly codified spelling: neither of us is "right", except in the context of our own cultures. Spelling has continued to develop in different ways on different sides of the Atlantic; despite a flirtation with the American form here, Americans tend to end some of their verbs and adjectives in *-ize* and *-ized*, whereas we tend to end ours in *-ise* and *-ised*. Some American spellings do slip in accidentally these days, however: on both sides of the ocean we *curb* our enthusiasm, but here we step off the *kerb*; in America, and with alarming frequency here, it is the *curb*. *Carcass* may be exactly how it sounds, and is indeed how most people spell it; but over here *carcase* is an acceptable alternative spelling.

These separate spellings are what happens when societies with a common language live so separately from each other and have long-standing, independent cultures. It is why some verb forms are different in America from here. The Americans say *gotten* where we say *got* not out of perversity, but because at the time of Pilgrim Fathers we all said it. America has stuck conservatively to this form, and we have not. Americans also use *dove* as the past participle of the verb *dive*, something that has died out here even in the dialects where grammarians like Partridge felt they detected it during the middle of the last century.[1] They are more careful about use of the subjunctive – as in "I order that he be punished", whereas we would these days more usually add the auxiliary verb *should* after the *he*. Our physical separation is why some words come to mean different things in our two countries: it is not advisable to go around America telling people to "keep your pecker up", as they will imagine you are referring to a penis. We have *lifts* and Americans have *elevators*; we have *bills* and they have *checks*; we fill forms *in*, they fill them *out*. Perhaps most

1. *Usage and Abusage*, p100.

important of all, no Briton should seek out a *rest room* to have a lie down; it is where Americans empty their bladders or have bowel movements. (Something comparably confusing for Americans must be the English's propensity to *wash* when they wish to go to the lavatory; one of our more retentive euphemisms and, oddly, one that originates from further up the ladder than the genteel middle classes.) Americans have *movies* where we have *films*; *cookies* where we have *biscuits*; *automobiles* where we have cars; *faucets* where we have *taps*; and so on. They have also created words to replace ones that we shared, and that have remained perfectly serviceable on this side of the Atlantic: such as *normalcy* for our *normality*, or *specialty* for our *speciality*; though the medical profession in Britain uses the jargon word *specialty* to describe a doctor's particular field of practice. To use such Americanisms in America at least ensures one is not misunderstood; to use them in Britain sounds pretentious or just silly.

Under the influence of films, television shows and pop records we have started to adopt certain American phrases in popular or demotic usage even though we have perfectly good English ones already. In restaurants one may hear people in the early stages of Americanisation asking if they may *get* a beer, a glass of wine or a plate of spaghetti when they really mean may they *have* one. In our usage, asking a waiter whether we may *get* a fillet steak implies that we are seeking permission to go into the kitchen and fetch it ourselves. One also hears people say that they will do something *momentarily*. This adverb, used in English since the 17th century, has been deployed to indicate that whatever is being done is being done fleetingly. The Americans, and now we, use it to indicate that it will be done "in a moment". This is a loss to British English, since the original usage is valuable – it is clear what "he paused momentarily before moving on" means. In Britain one starts again or has a fresh start; one does not *start over*, though the influence of American popular culture has caused this phrase to insinuate itself into many people's language.

Another newly-popular British usage, borrowed from America, is *meet with*. The preposition is unnecessary, but we can see why the Americans use it. They do so for the creditable reason of avoiding what they consider to be an ambiguity. If you say "I met him last week" in American English you imply that you met someone for the first time. If you say you "met with him" you imply that you knew him already – you had met him before – and this was but the latest of a series of encounters. To the educated ear on this side of the Atlantic, *met with* sounds wrong. We simply *meet* each other. We may qualify the phrase, if there is a danger of a misunderstanding, with a detail such as its having been for the first time, or that it happened last week as opposed to earlier or later. In British usage, if someone says "I met the policeman last Thursday" the listener or reader instinctively knows what happened, without the help of a preposition.

More and more, by contrast, one hears the use of certain American phrases with a missing preposition. In America, the aggrieved are always *protesting the decision*. Here, we require a preposition (and they usually come at no extra cost) so that we may protest *against* the decision. There is a similar problem with the verb *appeal*. When someone has been sentenced to 99 years in jail in an American drama, his attorney will spring up and announce that he is going to *appeal the verdict*. A British barrister would appeal *against* it. The popularity of American police and courtroom dramas on British television has had a subversive effect on this area of the language. As well as these improper usages, we have witnesses in our own courts *taking the stand* instead of, as is traditional, giving evidence. Their barrister or lawyer may even be called an *attorney*, a usage that ceased to be common here in the 19th century, though it lives on in the title of the government's second most senior law officer, the attorney-general. A lawyer may be accused of working in a *law firm* when, unless he is a solicitor, he will be in *chambers*. A trial may take place in a *court-room*, within a *courthouse*. All these are to be avoided. A common American usage that seems to the British ear and eye to lack a preposition is that of the verb *write*. A Briton *writes to* his family; an American simply *writes* his family.

Other Americanisms that change the idioms of our language to no apparent purpose include *on the weekend*, whereas the British have always done things *at the weekend*, and *in school* rather than *at school*. Despite the long pedigree of the word *obliged*, which the *OED* first records as being used in 1325, we now have the term *obligated*, as in "he felt obligated to improve his English". *Comedic* is entirely unnecessary so long as the adjective *comic* lives and breathes; as is *filmic* when we have *cinematic*. The English term *railway station* has functioned perfectly well for nearly 180 years and does not need to be shunted aside by *train station*; nor does *railway* need to be derailed by *railroad*. It is hard to see why we should ever need to say or to write *parking lot* when we all know what we mean by the phrase *car park*. A different political system also gives rise to different idioms that we thoughtlessly import into our own. Americans *run* for office; we *stand* for it. If they are sacked or defeated it is an *ouster*. We may be ousted, but losing or being defeated is more like it. The word *raise*, both as a noun and a verb, has crept into English too. Britons have, or ask for, a *pay rise* rather than a *raise*; and their children are *brought up* rather than *raised*. Also, the usage *alright* is ubiquitous in America, though educated Americans avoid it as fervently as we should. *All right* remains all right.

No Americanism, though, has registered more strongly in recent years than the vogue for answering the polite question "how do you do?" or "how are you?" with the rejoinder "I'm good". To many Anglo-Saxon ears this still sounds like a profession of one's moral condition rather than an observation about one's physical well-being. Such things are silly in speech; they should be avoided in writing of any degree of formality, or in any communication where one does not wish to be thought semi-literate. People are far more forgiving of an alien idiom in speech than when they see it in writing, simply because one has more time to reflect on what one is committing to paper before one does so. Those Britons who attain a decent level of bilingualism may show it off when they get to Manhattan or Palm Beach, but they would be well-advised not to try it at home.

Vulgar, vulgar, vulgar

Britain is an old country with what passes in the modern world for a free market economy. It therefore has a class system. Each class will speak with its own argot. There is no guarantee that because someone is from a higher social class he will speak English better than someone from a lower one. The private schools, patronised for the most part by the higher classes, are just as capable of inadequately teaching their charges as those at the bottom of the pile. If we divide society into those who have had the good fortune of a rigorous education and those who have not we are better able to predict how well a person will use English. Vulgarisms are not just found in the poor use of grammar ("what was you doing?") or in punctuation errors such as the grocer's apostrophe ("egg's £1 a dozen") but in idiomatic phrases that fail because they simply defy logic.

One much beloved of the tabloid press is *falling pregnant*. Consider, for a moment, the politics of this phrase. It is intended as a parallel to *falling ill* rather than to *falling from grace*. It is not intended to signal any moral failing or impropriety, as it is often applied to perfectly respectable married women who have been impregnated by their husbands. When one falls ill the event has seldom been within one's control. A germ or an infection has been in the air and one has become the unwitting, and unwilling, victim of it. One does not need to have a degree in biology to understand that becoming pregnant is not accomplished in quite the same way. Yet to say that one has *fallen pregnant* is almost a Pontius Pilate moment. It is as if the condition has been achieved without any conscious act on the part of the mother. It is nothing to do with her and she can – pending further developments – wash her hands of it. This sort of absurdity should not be indulged by this phrase's being used by intelligent people.

Another modern abomination that has crept into the language of supposedly educated people is the expression *sorted*. For some generations it has been a popular pastime of the more affluent classes to imitate the speech of their supposed social inferiors. In the 1920s even the heir to the throne affected a cockney drawl from time to time, and public schoolboys have enjoyed speaking something called "mockney". As well as engaging in the patronising pursuit of imitating accents, those who wish to mint themselves anew as self-made proles have always sought to use the slang of the class they wish to imitate. *Sorted*, which appears to have come into vogue after a rash of violent British gangster films in the 1990s, is the latest word to make this journey. When something is *sorted*, in the current usage, it is *sorted out* in the language of civilised people. The term, used in those gangster films with an undercurrent of menace or smug satisfaction that asserts the moral (and quite often physical) superiority of the sorter, is used now by those who wish to impress upon others that a serious difficulty has been overcome; and that it has been reflects some credit on the person who did so.

In fact, something can only be sorted if it is a multiplicity. It is a verb used to indicate that order has been imposed on a confusion of objects. Mail is sorted; buttons in a box are sorted; so are seeds for planting. Adding the word *out* requires little effort, but by doing so the speaker loses the allegedly witty imitation of a cinematic hard man. We all use slang in speech; but there has always been a dividing line between speech and formal written prose. Even today most of us understand what slang is, and how slang usages create a poor impression if used in a formal piece of writing. We therefore avoid them. It is only because I have seen the expressions *fell pregnant* and *sorted* in print rather too often in the last few years that I use them as examples of where, through carelessness or ignorance, slang is drifting across into formal English usage. It is unfortunate not because it is vulgar, and not even because it is wrong, but because the existing richness of our language makes it completely unnecessary.

The same point applies to the misuse of the verb *to sit*. One often sees the solecism "people were sat". This is grammatically impossible. What a writer who abuses the verb in this way means is "people were sitting", or "people were seated". Best of all – since we should always prefer the active voice to the passive – he would have written "people sat". There is a similar fault with the verb *to stand*. It is wrong, too, to say "he was stood". "He was standing" or, better, "he stood". An inanimate object can be stood somewhere – it would be correct to say "the clothes horse was stood in front of the fire" – but beings with the power of locomotion do not require another to place them in this way.

Another common mistake among poor speakers of English is that "something can't be beat". This, too, is sliding into polite speech. The correct participle is *beaten*. Some writers seem to have been obstructed in their thought by the widespread vulgar misuse of these common verbs. As with *sorted*, resistance is not necessarily futile. Vulgar usage also invents and abuses its own verbs, such as taking the adjective or noun *front* and creating the verbal phrase *front up* or simply *front*. We hear this as in "he fronted up the bid for the Olympics" or "she fronts her own band". We also hear that people "front up a television show". In the first example the vulgarism could be avoided by the verb *lead*, or *direct*; in the second by *lead* again; in the third by the verb *present*.

Sport creates its own argot and usages that almost never have a place in respectable writing. It has coined verbs for those lucky enough to win prizes – we hear of them *podiuming* or *medalling*. Another abomination that is moving outside sport and into the rest of life is when a person has to *commit* to something. This always requires the reflexive pronoun and almost never has it: a player *commits himself* to the team.

We also seem to be reaching the end of the period in our history when the adjective *well* is widely used as an attempted witticism by educated people to mean *very*: the rash of films about cockney gangsters has left this as another legacy. Individual gangsters were *well hard*, and if they carried a firearm (or *shooter*) they were considered *well tasty*. The vogue for sounding like an East End thug transmuted into sounding like a black musician, and the highest term of approbation became *well wicked*. Even more frequent is the application of the noun *rubbish* as an adjective – a *rubbish* football team, a *rubbish* film, a *rubbish* pop group. It is not as though the English language lacks terms to describe low quality or inadequacy. I should not have to stress that these absurdities have no place in serious writing, but I shall.

The use of the terminology of weights and measures is often wrong in vulgar speech, and should not be translated into the written word. A man may be described as being "six foot tall" and weighing "13 stone". In both cases the plurals should be used. Liquid measurements seem to be immune to this sort of solecism: no-one would ask for "three pint of beer" but such a customer would happily speak of "two foot of snow". Adjectival uses do not need to be plural: a *ten-gallon* hat, a *five-pint* jug and a *three-foot* rule are all correct.

Chapter Four deals specifically with grammatical errors. There are some that are so widely perpetrated in vulgar speech that they seem to have crossed the divide into the speech of civilised people; though they are used only when concentration slips, and it is worth noting that here. One is the commonly heard "he would of done that" instead of "he would have done that". One only has to look at the error to sense the enormity[2] it represents, and one need say no more. The same is true of the use of *ought* with an auxiliary verb, as in "I *didn't ought* to have drunk that" or "she *shouldn't ought* to have said that to me". *Ought* never requires an auxiliary verb. Another popular vulgarism is found in a sentence such as: "she had twice as many as what I did" or, still worse, "she had twice as many than what I did". The *what* is superfluous; the *than* in the second example is simply wrong. To describe something obtainable that carries no cost as being *free* is to use another vulgarism. It is better to say that the item is *free of charge*. The notionally free-of-charge item is today often described in a particularly saccharine euphemism as *complimentary*, even when it is clear that its availability is a cynical exercise by which no compliment is intended.

Finally, the double negative (dealt with at greater length in Chapter Four) is a common feature of vulgar usage – "I ain't got no money", and so on. So too is tautology ("and you can also stop doing that too"). Unless needed for satirical purposes, or in dialogue in the writing of fiction, such forms can safely be regarded as already outside the lexicon of those aiming to write correct English, so we need not trouble ourselves further with them.

Upstairs, downstairs

In 1956 Nancy Mitford made waves with an essay, in a collection called *Noblesse Oblige*, that described the usages of her class (she

2. Given this word is almost inevitably misused, I have devoted a paragraph to it in Chapter Five.

was the daughter of a peer) and compared them with terms used to describe the same items or abstracts by people in lower social classes. It is hard to determine whether this was an exercise in rampant snobbery or in sociology. Whatever its intention, it has stuck. She did not invent the terms "U" and "Non-U" to describe these two forms of usage – that had been done two years earlier by Alan Ross, a linguistics professor. However, once Ross had had the idea, Mitford went off with it. There is no need for an exhaustive list, not least because some of the usages were archaic even then, and have disappeared almost entirely now: even duchesses today say *mirror* and *ice cream* rather than *looking-glass* and *ice*. Some have stuck and continue to be indicators of the class of the speaker or writer. If the writer and his audience do not mind being looked down upon by pedantic aristocrats and members of the *haute bourgeoisie*, then none of this really matters. If one does mind, then one had better take care. Partridge gives a superb example of the problem in *Usage and Abusage*, and the entry on the word *lady*. He says it "should not be used as a synonym for *woman*, any more than *gentleman* should be used as a synonym for *man*". He then strikes the killer blow: "Only those men who are not gentlemen speak of their women friends as *lady friends*, and only those women who are not ladies speak of themselves as *charladies* and their men friends as *gentlemen friends*." His point, perhaps less visible in what we are told is a classless society, was about the ghastliness, not to say ludicrousness, of mock gentility. One suspects that was part of Mitford's intention too.

Writing is about communication, and if the writer and his readers know exactly what a *cycle* is, then there is no need to affect the U term *bicycle*. However, all writers need to know their audience, especially if they are writing commercially, because they wish to retain that audience for the future: and writing in a language that is common to the audience, even if it means the writer himself inching up the social scale a notch or two, is at times useful.

For that reason I advise my colleagues on *The Daily Telegraph* to bear in mind the sensitivities of the readers, because we would like them to continue to buy the newspaper and not feel alienated by its diction. So our readers communicate with each other on *writing paper*, not notepaper. They will eat their turkey or roast beef for *Christmas lunch*, not *Christmas dinner*, unless the meal is specified as taking place in the evening. If it is, the men may wear a *dinner jacket*, not a *dress suit*. *Evening dress* is white tie, a white waistcoat and a tailcoat. Their lunches or dinners include a *pudding*, not a *sweet*; a *dessert* would be taken after the pudding and the cheese and would consist of nuts, fruit and fortified wines. They use *napkins* and not *serviettes*. They go to the *lavatory*, never the *toilet*, though they use *toilet paper* because the stuff is part of their toilet. In their *houses* (never *homes*) they have a *drawing room* or a *sitting room*, never a *lounge*. In those rooms there are *sofas*, not *settees*. If they are *sick* they are vomiting; if they are *ill* they are laid up. I must stress that there is nothing inherently wrong with the non-U alternatives to these usages. However, I repeat, we are an old country with a class system, and in our society what we say inevitably stands as a badge of who we are. Our reaction to what we read says it just as clearly to ourselves, which is why writers with a certain audience that they wish to propitiate need to speak the same language as their readers do.

Some misuse of terms does stem from ignorance, which does not necessarily depend on one's position in the class system. One should never use the definite article before *Last Post* or *Magna Carta*, but many do. A *ship* of the Royal Navy is never a *boat*; and its sailors are *in* it, not *on* it. It is the tomb of the *Unknown Warrior*, not of the *Unknown Soldier*. The Cambridge college Peterhouse is never *Peterhouse College*; it is *St Peter's College*, and *house* is a synonym for *college*. At Eton the school has *halves*, not *terms*. A *bullock* is a castrated bull, not a small one that will one day grow into a bull. A *crescendo* is not a climax, but a rising dynamic. The day between Good Friday and Easter Sunday is not *Easter Saturday*. It is *Easter Eve*. *Easter Saturday* is the Saturday after Easter Sunday. A *head of state* is not always the same as a *head of government*; in France and America, for example, it is, but in Britain the head of state is the monarch, the head of government the prime minister. For that reason one does not write "Mr Cameron's government" but "Her Majesty's government". The *line of fire* is where one is in danger of being hit; the *firing line* is from where one does the shooting. A *leading question* is not necessarily a prominent one nor a difficult one, but one that contains a strong indication of the answer desired in the way it is framed. *Great Britain* comprises England, Scotland and Wales. *The British Isles* are Great Britain, Ireland and their associated islands. The *United Kingdom* comprises Great Britain and Northern Ireland. The *Union Flag* is correctly described as the *Union Jack* only when on the jackstaff of a British warship at anchor or alongside the jetty. *Wedding* and *marriage* are not interchangeable terms: *wedding* is the ceremony, but each of its principals undergoes a *marriage*.

Slang

In a category of its own is slang. These are not always vulgar usages: the Bright Young Things of the aristocracy and upper-middle class in the 1920s had their own argot. Just because it was used by apparently educated people did not mean it was correct. What we understand to be slang has shifted over the centuries. The dictionary begins by defining it as "the special vocabulary used by any set of persons of a low or disreputable character; language of a low and vulgar type". However, it says this has now "merged" into a later definition (the first citation given of the first usage is 1756; the first of the second 1818), which is "language of a highly colloquial type, considered as below the level of standard

educated speech, and consisting either of new words or of current words employed in some special sense". This makes it clear
that slang is no longer the exclusive province of the submerged
tenth, that it has a blurred border with what we used to call colloquialism, and that it covers, for example, the vogue for public
schoolboys to describe something of which they approve as "well
wicked". Slang tends to distinguish itself from colloquialism by
being the argot of a distinct group, except when it tips over into
obscenity. Colloquial speech is more widespread and less exclusive. The difficulty with slang in written English is that readers
who are not part of the group may not understand it. Colloquialism often fails in formal writing because it seems out of place,
and alters the desired tone: it may only, in such writing, be used
self-consciously, notably for comic effect.

Good non-fiction writing will sometimes feature slang, but
this will usually be for comic or satirical purposes. In these contexts it is usually obvious, and clear to the reader that the writer
knows it is slang and is using it for effect. (The question of how
tiresome that effect may be, and how it detracts sometimes from
good style, is a different matter, but worth considering.) Do not
draw attention to it by the arch device of putting it in quotation
marks. If one is going to use it, one should use it out in the open.
This is not least because the act of trying to do so may be all the
deterrent one needs from the crime itself. Should one be writing
fiction, however, it is likely to be impossible to portray a remotely
realistic character without recourse to slang in any dialogue.

Some slang has invaded and corrupted correct usage. For example: *fine* is an adjective and not an adverb. It should not therefore
be used as one. The verb *to be*, which is a law unto itself, takes an
adjective, so one may say "I am fine" or "she is fine" just as one may
say "he is ugly", "they are slow" or "we are tiresome". Verbs such as
look (in its meaning of *seem*), *seem* itself, *smell*, *taste*, *sound* and all
other verbs that link with an adjective or a noun – "it looks fine,

tastes fine, sounds fine, seems fine" and so on – are other exceptions. However, one should not use *fine* with any other verb in this way. To say "it went fine" or "she's doing fine" are slang usages with no place in formal speech.

Other slang comes from regional dialects into the mainstream of colloquial English. One such word that has become more ubiquitous in recent years, especially among inadequately educated writers and speakers, is the adjective *picky* to describe the state of mind of someone who in formal writing would be described as *discriminating* or *fastidious*. This is an odd development, for our slang already had a word to fulfil this function, *choosy*. *Choosy* now takes on an air of formality, promoted to that rank by the invasion of *picky*. *Picky* is heard frequently in American usage, a survival no doubt from the dialects of those from the English provinces who migrated there centuries ago. It may have pushed its way into mainstream English slang from American television and films, and not necessarily from the influence of English dialect. Cockney rhyming slang is a peculiar form of dialect and has passed into mainstream slang too, in some cases. People far from London know what *having a butchers* is (*butcher's hook*: look), or what the *apples and pears* are (stairs). Perhaps more recondite is what someone means when he is having trouble with his *chalfonts* (*Chalfont St Giles*: piles) or when he considers another man to be an *iron* or a *ginger* (*iron hoof*: poof, and *ginger beer*: queer). These are rare examples of double slang, and examples of how slang often passes straight into the realms of the politically incorrect. I deal with the effect of political correctness on language later in this chapter.

Slang or colloquialism – as the boundaries are blurred these days it is hard to tell which is which – has particularly potent force in describing physical or mental characteristics of our fellow man. Think of someone who has *got the hump*, or is *potty*, or even *randy*, or *saucy*, or *fly*, or *bent*, or *tasty* (an adjective susceptible of more than one slang usage), or has been *poleaxed*, or *flattened*, or *shafted*, and one begins to realise how widespread such usages are.

Various trades have their own slang; so too does mainstream slang have its descriptions of those trades. A carpenter may be known as a *chippy*, an electrician as a *sparks*. A *chippy* is also a popular haunt of the British, for it is where their fish and chips, a form of *grub*, come from; just as their beer, or *booze*, comes from a *pub*, a *boozer* or even an *offie*. Much slang concerns bodily functions and sexual activity, and perhaps better comes under the heading of vulgarity: though what I class as vulgar usage is more defined by its grammatical accuracy than necessarily by its vocabulary. It is possible to talk in slang almost entirely while remaining grammatically correct.

One of the problems of slang is that it often removes the freedom from ambiguity that correct language has. Take Mrs Thatcher's memorable phrase during her political assassination that "it's a funny old world". Her audience knew that the adjective *funny* meant odd or peculiar, and that she was using it satirically. In good writing, use *funny* to mean something that makes one laugh. If you mean odd, peculiar, strange or weird, say so. Slang also has the habit of taking a word that is accurate in certain contexts and making in inaccurate in others. Partridge offers a good example of this with the word *gang*.[3] It is correct to use it of workmen or criminals; to use it about "a set, a clique, a fortuitous assemblage of idle or harmless persons is to fall into slang". There are numerous other examples, few of which any but the most thoughtless would be tempted to use in formal writing or speech. It is one thing to describe a male person of 90 as an "old man"; quite another to use the term to signify a woman's husband or someone's father. On the subject of family members, it can never be acceptable to refer to children as *kids* except in dialogue. This word began as an

3. *Usage and Abusage*, p128.

Americanism and has now been properly anglicised as part of our own slang. Like many such demotic usages it does not grate in parts of the tabloid press or in certain advertisements, but its use in anything approaching formal writing is to be abhorred.

Great is another word that has legitimate usages (though in this age of hyperbole, its currency has been debased); but it does not mean much. If one wishes to express that *much* thought has been given to a subject, say so: do not say that *great* thought has been given to it. This implies (albeit ungrammatically) that a profound philosophical mind has been at work on the matter, which may not be the case. In slang parlance, almost anything that merits approbation or esteem is *great*, and that alone should be reason enough to avoid the word. Another term of approbation that has been manufactured is *quite*, as in "she's quite a girl" or "that was quite a bottle of wine". This is a slang usage and it, too, has no place in formal writing: *quite* has a correct usage with adjectives or adverbs, as in "she was quite beautiful" or "they went quite quickly", and should be confined to those realms.

At the time that the Fowlers were seeking to codify English usage a century ago one of the changes in progress was the compounding of words beginning with *any-*. By 1926 H W Fowler had decreed that "anybody, anything, anyhow, anywhere, anywhen, anywhither are already single words", as was the adverb *anywise*. There was, he pointed out, no such word as *anyrate* and we should be compelled to agree with him. Fowler essentially conceded that *anyway* had become one word, except in the sense that one would use it as two words today ("I cannot see any way out of this problem"). A similar rule applies to *anyone*. What, though, are we to make of *anymore*? This word is not listed in the dictionary. It is slang and not suitable for formal writing. "I do not want any more cabbage" shows the correct usage as two words. The colloquial phrases "I don't live there anymore" or "she isn't my friend anymore" would in formal English be "I no longer live there" or "she

is no longer my girlfriend". *Now* is also an acceptable alternative
– "I don't live there now".

Some slang creeps into polite speech because it sounds almost
formal. Partridge (the acknowledged expert on slang in English)
dismisses the usage of "you have been much too previous" to mean
someone has acted hastily or pre-emptively. He is right to do so.
One suspects that *previous* has attained this level of usage because
by being polysyllabic it does not sound as though it might be
slang. Also, it is an adjective associated in the mind with legal
procedure, as in "previous convictions". None of this is any excuse
for using it in this coarse way, but these may be some of the reasons that explain it. Like much slang, its origin might also have
been in humour. However, such jokes quickly wear thin, and never
bear repeating in serious writing.

Beating about the bush

One of the prime targets for Orwell in *Politics and the English
Language* is the use of **euphemism**. To make his point he uses,
quite understandably, an extreme example. He says that an English professor defending Russian totalitarianism "cannot say outright, 'I believe in killing off your opponents when you can get
good results by doing so.'" Instead, Orwell puts into the professor's mouth a 65-word circumlocution that disguises the matter.
I have already noted, in the previous chapter, how both politicians and marketing men use individual words in a downright
dishonest way, sometimes in the form of euphemism, sometimes
not. In Chapter Eight, where I deal with the components of a
good writing style, I emphasise the need to eliminate unnecessary
words. This is a fundamental point made by all the prescriptive
writers on English, as it must be: superfluity of words obscures
meaning. Orwell's point about euphemism is that it helps those

with sinister political intentions to conceal them while claiming to support democracy. The trade of spin doctor has grown out of this perversion.

Yet Mitford also stigmatised euphemism as a tool of the lower or less educated classes, painting it as part of the sentimentality shunned by more hard-minded people such as her: like Orwell, she saw its use as tribal, though she singled out a different tribe. Death is the best example. The lower classes have all sorts of euphemisms for this inevitable event. A *loved one* (a term that seems only to be used posthumously, or when the reaper is heaving into view or into one's consciousness) may *pass away*, or *pass on*, his bereaved family and friends may *lose* him, he may *lose his life*, or if they are feeling especially Bunyanesque he may even *pass over to the other side*, where he becomes *deceased* or *departed*. (The last two terms are reminders of how the aspiring, under-educated person passes through a phase in which he feels it is right to imitate the language of bureaucrats, few of whom know how to speak or write English properly.) *Joining the heavenly choir* is simply Monty Python. To Mitford and her class the person simply *dies*, and thereafter is *dead*.

Her class made a point, during the rise of the middle class in the period between the end of the Great War and the end of Mrs Thatcher, of mocking the faux-gentility they felt they detected in such people, and the careful avoidance of directness that they discerned to be part of it. Death may be the best example, but there are plenty of others. Anything to do with bodily functions, be they digestive, excremental or carnal, was ripe for attention. So too were references to psychological or physical illnesses or handicaps. Whatever the upper classes would say, they would not *spend a penny* or *wash their hands*, nor would they *go courting* or have a *young man*. They would know no-one who was *simple* or *soft in the head*, but they would know people who were *mad* or *lunatics*. The invention of political correctness, which takes euphemism into a different stratum of paranoid art form, seems a standing rebuke to the likes of Mitford, and to their determination to call a spade a spade.

PC plodding

The phenomenon now called **political correctness** may well have had its roots in the habit of a certain section of society to use language as directly as possible, and the determination of those distressed on behalf of the victims of their tactlessness to do something about it. However, it is mainly the product of the sensibilities of privileged and educated liberals who wished to remove disadvantage or even the dispassionate perception of disadvantage, wherever possible, from those less fortunate than or different from themselves. Given the potency of language as a labelling device, it is inevitable that the way words are used, and indeed which words are used, should be affected by this political mass movement. Language has always changed because of fashion; and because fashion has changed language, it has often changed it needlessly. Much of what happens to language because of political correctness is, in fact, simply the exercise of good manners: it has never been especially polite to use terms of abuse towards minorities, even if some black people choose to call themselves *niggers*, or some homosexual men and women are happy to refer to themselves as *queers*. However, we should not forget that until quite recently it was acceptable to use terms that shock today. One example of the speed with which sensibilities change can be gauged by Partridge's entry on *nigger*. What he had to say was thought acceptable not merely when *Usage and Abusage* was published in 1947, but in the 1973 revised edition. This term, he said, "belongs only, and then only in contempt or fun, to the dark-skinned African races and their descendants in America and the West Indies. Its application to the native peoples of India is ignorant and offensive."[4] Perhaps in 1947 a black man would have found it rib-tickling to be addressed in such terms by a jester, though I doubt it; I doubt it even more about 1973. It is clear it is now a term of gross offensiveness: but I doubt very much that a polite person would have attempted to make a joke of the term even in 1947.

Terms to describe sufferers from certain illnesses or handicaps are now deemed to be callous, and have changed. They are thought callous, perhaps, because what were once considered neutral terms to describe a condition (such as *spastic*, or *cripple*, or *idiot*, or *lunatic*) have become pejorative because of their adoption by unfeeling people as terms of abuse for others. Those with Down's syndrome are no longer described as *mongols*, mainly because of the irrelevant unpleasantness of so labelling those with the Asiatic features typical of this affliction; and also because of racist overtones. These sensitivities appear humane and natural, and reflect the fact that we live in times where these afflictions are better understood and seen to have no stigma attached to them. However, there is always someone seeking to ratchet up the mechanism of sensitivity, or looking for offence where it is often very hard to find it.

No handicapped person was aware, until recently, that he was supposed to be offended by his group of disabled people being termed *the blind*, *the deaf* or *the disabled* (the dumb, for reasons outlined above – that term having become one of abuse – had every reason not to be happy with that word being applied to them). Yet many groups working with the public are now informed, by those who make it their business to set the standard for such things, that the references have to be to *blind people*, *deaf people* or *disabled people*. There are euphemisms for each of these too, though these are so clunking they have hardly caught on – *sight impaired*,

4. *Usage and Abusage*, p203.

hard of hearing, people of restricted mobility. Any suggestion that not to use these terms implies heartlessness or lack of sympathy for those so afflicted drives a pointless change in the language. As with all elements of usage the application of logic is valuable. It is one thing to stop using words that have been made offensive, and that are generally accepted as being so. It is quite another to invent a whole new vocabulary to replace words that serve their purpose effectively, clearly and well, and offend only those who (often not being afflicted themselves) seek to define the offence.

Much of what has been done to the language by political correctness is, however, absurd. Gender is a particular problem. It is right that writers should be aware that for the most part they are addressing an audience comprising women as well as men. The old rule that the male is to be taken to include the female at all times, and which, as I have already remarked, I have reluctantly adopted in writing this book, may begin to grate. What, however, is the alternative? Writing a sentence such as "anyone may swim if he or she has a costume" is long-winded, but is probably the best option if those hearing or reading such a thing are likely to be offended. "Anyone may swim if they have a costume" is simply illiterate, and "anyone may swim if he has a costume" seems to suggest that women may swim under no circumstances at all. In popular usage the non-gender-specific *they* is greatly favoured, but that is no reason to use it. Rules in language are made by logic, not by a democratic vote. In the sentence just quoted, the best option would be to recast the sentence: "anyone wearing a costume may swim". My own reasons for taking the course I have, in the absence of third person pronouns common to both genders, have worked very well for generations. That course may have to serve a little longer in circumstances where the highest standards of grammatical accuracy are required.

The apostles of political correctness have gone to lengths to try to ensure that gender discrimination is eliminated from the

English tongue. It is up to the educated user of the language to decide whether he (or she) wishes to award them an easy victory, or to stand and fight. The most egregious example of the absurdities brought by such a victory is that a word used for centuries to describe a piece of furniture – *chair* – is now routinely used, except in some reactionary institutions like the Conservative party, to describe the person who leads a board, committee or some similar body or institution. This word has been arrived at because of the impossibility (in the eyes of the politically correct or, rather, politically correct people) of the perpetuation of the word *chairman*, an understandable dislike of the word *chairwoman* and the sheer preposterousness of the term *chairperson*. Yet it has never been satisfactorily explained why, given the nature of the label (and label is all it is), a woman cannot be a *chairman*.

The dictionary is helpful on this vexatious point. Its first definition of the noun *man* is "a human being, irrespective of sex or age". As a gloss for our politically correct times, it adds a note saying that "Man was considered until the 20th century to include women by implication, though referring primarily to males. It is now frequently understood to exclude women, and is therefore avoided by many people." Just as beauty is in the eye of the beholder, perhaps it is so that understanding is in the mind of the understander. The word is thought to have Sanskrit origins, preceding its Germanic ones, that are to do with the roots of our word *mind*, "on the basis that thought is a distinctive characteristic of human beings". Ironically, the male is now increasingly used to include the female, despite this being the age of equality. It is now the fashion (and this started in America, the home of political correctness) to refer to actresses as *actors*, a word no less masculine than *chairman*. Like most prescriptive grammarians of the past, I would argue that in all these circumstances, common sense should apply. Unfortunately, there is precious little of that in the cult of political correctness, where the main concern appears to be peer pressure, grandstanding and a different sort of prejudice to the ones that are occasionally being countered. America (which gave the world *affirmative action* and other euphemisms that become more generally offensive and patronising the more they are contemplated) continues to make the most significant contribution to the English lexicon of political correctness. A correspondent in *The New Yorker* (4 January 2010), writing about disabled athletes, used the phrase *a challenged runner*. It appears that *disabled* itself is now considered offensive. How long will it be before *challenged* is too?

Some corner of a foreign language

Read any book in English for long enough (especially if it was written more than about 50 years ago) and you will come across a **foreign phrase**. There is nothing especially wrong with using foreign phrases, provided they have no exact English equivalent. The Fowlers deplored the attempt to translate phrases such as *demimonde* and *esprit d'escalier* literally as "half-world" and "spirit of the staircase" when those translations ignored the idiomatic sense of the French and seemed, as a consequence, absurd in translation.[5] The first phrase refers to high-class prostitutes or kept women; the second to that ability to think of a devastatingly witty rejoinder only after the event. As one can see from the translations of the idioms, the French phrases really are superior and deserve to penetrate English usage. There are many other French phrases, or words, that have no equivalent in English and for which a case may thus be made. One is always, however, up against the fact that so few Anglophones speak French in any degree today, let alone in one that allows them command of idiom.

5. *The King's English*, pp41–42.

Some authors drop French in to show off the fact that, after a fashion, they speak it. The show-offs are the ones who use phrases or words that do have perfectly acceptable English equivalents: there is no need to write that a steak was served *à point* when, by expending fewer words and letters, one can write that it was served "rare". However, no English phrase that does not require several more words can quite convey the meaning of the Italian style of cooking pasta *al dente*. Sometimes a foreign language will do better than English: one of the superscriptions of this book, indeed, is in French for no better reason than I had found no piece of English that conveyed the point nearly so well. In some cases the use of another tongue is pointless, and merely rubs the reader's nose in the fact that he doesn't understand it. When we can say that the law takes no account of trifles, why say *de minimis non curat lex*?

However, if you are going to use foreign phrases, for heaven's sake use them correctly. There will always be somebody reading what you have written who will speak the language better than you do, or understand it better, and you risk humiliation if you are careless or go off piste (and "piste", like many other foreign words, is one that is now anglicised). Those who write *nom de plume* or *bon viveur* show themselves at once to be charlatans: a Frenchman would write *nom de guerre* or *bon vivant*. The first of those terms is merely a flashy way of saying "pseudonym", or the perfectly harmless "pen-name": the second is something that English cannot quite match. "Gourmet" has passed into English as one who is a connoisseur (ditto) of food; yet some think it is interchangeable with *gourmand*, which has not passed into our language, and means someone who is greedy. "Confidant" is a useful borrowing from the French, but if we wish to use it about a woman then we must call her a "confidante", as the French would. The Americans do not observe this nicety, but we have already learned that there is little to be gained by imitating them. They have "blonds" of both genders, whereas our women are "blondes".

Because of the leanings – or "penchants", if you prefer – of our education system many of the foreign phrases we use in English are from Latin or French, for decades the two most popular languages taught in our schools once Greek fell into decline. Greek supplies many of our words, or parts of our words, but they have long since been transliterated and anglicised and only a scholar would know their origins. Most of the Latin that is now around has itself been anglicised – "in camera", "sine die", "et cetera" – and there is only the odd phrase that retains a meaning so distinct as to be used in its original form without yet having become English – such as when we speak of an *ex cathedra* pronouncement, or something being not *de jure* but *de facto*. Engaging in activities *pro bono* could yet go either way, but I would still italicise it. "Hoi polloi" is a rare survival of raw Greek, to describe the masses. Should you use it, remember two things: first, that "hoi" is the definite article, so you don't need another one – "the hoi polloi" is wrong. Second, it is plural, so hoi polloi *do* something, not *does* something. If you are writing a French phrase, use accents where they are required: there is no point in trying to burnish your image by dropping a wry *chacun à son goût* in a frightfully *décontracté* way if you omit the grave and the circumflex accents. German, from which the odd phrase has been known to turn up, also has the occasional accent: and nouns all begin with a capital letter unless they have been anglicised. It is probably the case that "schadenfreude" is now English enough not to require either the initial capital or italicisation. This is not yet true of *Weltanschauung*, or other terms beloved of those who talk about philosophy.

The danger area for users of foreign words is when they are plurals, or when some concession has to be made to gender. This is especially true of Latin words. The word "alumnus" has passed into English – via America, it seems – and is now routinely used to describe graduates of universities. More than one of these are "alumni"; a woman is an "alumna", and more than one are "alumnae". "Larvae", "data", "media" and "genitalia" are all plural, though this does not prevent some writers (especially in the journalistic trade) from using them with singular verbs. It remains the convention in British English that if one is using a noun anglicised from the French one still respects its gender. Therefore, as with "confidant" above, a noun like "savant" would become "savante" if referring to a woman. Inevitably, this is true when using terms that have not been properly anglicised. It is one thing to use the correct term *bon vivant* for a man, but it is imperative not to foul up by failing to use *bonne vivante* for a woman who enjoys the finer things in life. The process, as you will note from that example, applies to adjectives too. Except in America (as noted above) one sees a "blond man", but a "blonde woman".

It is perhaps easier to make a fool of oneself in writing English prose by using a foreign phrase than by any other means. I recall reading some years ago in a newspaper a writer who, deciding to show off, had inverted *rus in urbe* as *urbe in rus*, which had former Latin masters and many of their pupils writing in their legions to the newspaper concerned. If in doubt, leave it out. There is usually an English substitute the use of which will not betray a lack of grounding in foreign tongues.

New words, and old words used newly

New words enter our language all the time. The *OED* regularly publishes supplements to its main work listing them and, as I have already noted, a third edition of the great work is in preparation. Often, necessity is the mother of invention. A new product, procedure or discovery comes into being and requires a name. Sometimes, a new idea requires a name too. Partridge, writing in 1947 in *Usage and Abusage*, described the shades of meaning of *unmoral, amoral, non-moral* and *immoral*.[6] He argues that the first three are synonymous, whereas only the fourth has a positive meaning ("evil, corrupt, depraved"). *Amoral* he says describes the sense "not to be judged by a moral criterion; not connected with moral considerations". Many, and I am among them, will consider that the meaning of this word has subtly altered over the last six decades or so, to describe a person who has no morals. It is often used not of the evil, corrupt or depraved (though those to whom it is applied may be all those) so much as of those who themselves choose not to be judged by moral criteria. In Partridge's idea, it was another who made the judgements. *Amoral* is today often used of people who, for example, spurn conventional sexual morality, or who will try any ploy short (usually) of downright criminality to advance their careers or prosperity. The dictionary sticks close to Partridge's understanding of the term, but the last revision of the definition is 1989, and I suspect the meaning has altered since then.

Two related words that are used carelessly, rather than in a new sense for which there was a legitimate need, are *obscene* and *obscenity*. The dictionary is straightforward: *obscene* means "offensively or grossly indecent; lewd". It is "grossly indecent" and "lewd" that reflect the true meaning of this word. Many things are offensive, but not all of them in a way that has a sexual ramification, or pertains to the propriety of sexual behaviour. During the 2000s one often heard that it was *obscene* for the West to go to war in Iraq, or that poverty was an *obscenity* in the modern world. There may well have been strong objections to either, but to use *obscene* as an adjective or *obscenity* as a noun to describe them was simply wrong. The dictionary acknowledges the mutation of *obscene*, however, going back to Shakespeare in 1597, and defines it as being fit to describe anything "offending

6. *Usage and Abusage*, p342.

against moral principles, repugnant; repulsive, foul, loathsome". It notes especially its use to describe a very large amount of money being demanded in return for something. For all its four centuries' heritage, and the estimable provenance of the misuse, it still smells of carelessness and seems to betray an ignorance of the real, and valuable, meaning of the word; as does the misuse of *obscenity*. A thesaurus will supply plenty of words to describe a shockingly large amount of money, or an unjust war, or the shocking nature of poverty, without having to take one that still means something quite different, and quite specific.

It is interesting, however, to note just how many words whose misuse is still being berated have endured that fate for hundreds of years. Kingsley Amis, in his lively polemic against bad English, correctly laments the illogicality of using the verb *execute* in the sense of putting a criminal to death. "By rights," he observes, "the sentence, not the criminal, is executed."[7] This is so: but the dictionary discloses that the barbarous abuse of this verb was first noted in 1483, so the battle is probably lost. Nevertheless, try to be sure that when you use a word, you use it correctly. Do not make nouns into verbs ("he *authored* the book", "she *sources* her ingredients from organic farmers") when there is a perfectly serviceable verb available to you. The dictionary cites the first use of *source* as a verb in 1972, in America. It is perhaps of more interest that it finds a lone use of *authored* in Chapman's Homer (Keats's beloved book) in 1596, after which it becomes obsolete until resurrected in America in the mid-20th century (the dictionary still does not believe it is used over here, but that, I fear, will have to change). We on this side of the Atlantic must therefore decide whether we wish to engage in this American habit, or not. Since there appear to be perfectly good existing verbs for the new ones minted by our American cousins (what is wrong, in the two instances I have

7. *The King's English: A Guide to Modern Usage*, p64.

given, with *written* and *obtained?*), I feel we can continue to resist. Do not make adjectives into nouns either, despite the long tradition of doing so ("the area was popular with *ethnics*").

In recent decades there has been a rash of mintages of words (many of them pointless or, where not pointless, illogical) ending in the suffix *-ee*. The prevalent view, indeed, seems to be that anybody who does something is a person ending in *-ee*. Someone who goes to a meeting is an *attendee*; someone who gets out of a jail is an *escapee*. There is little sense to this. Someone who goes to a meeting is an *attender*. Someone who escapes from somewhere is an *escaper*. Subjects of verbs are usually people whose titles end in *-er*, such as *trainer, examiner, interviewer, employer*. In logic, the suffix *-ee* should describe not someone who does something but someone to whom something is done, or for whom something is made to happen, such as *trainee, examinee, interviewee* and *employee*. A *referee*, for example, is someone to whom some matter is referred. Some usages defy this logic but seem to make perfect sense, such as *absentee* (unless one interprets the word as being not one who is absent, but one who by circumstances is made absent). The point about some new *-ee* nouns that one sees is that they are not necessary; there are words already in the language to do their job.

The worst tribe of all is multifarious, and consists of vested interests with their own private languages. I look more closely at these in Chapter Seven. Each sub-tribe perpetuates its own jargon, which is always a handicap to widespread communication. Jargon is a word that originally meant "the inarticulate utterance of birds, or a vocal sound resembling it". It has come metaphorically to be "applied contemptuously to any mode of speech abounding in unfamiliar terms, or peculiar to a particular set of persons". One has an insight into this when overhearing the conversation of members of the medical profession or the Bar, or when reading their learned journals; or, at another extreme, when listening to conversation between members of the army of former professional sportsmen who now act as commentators on television. Some jargon, however, in time passes into everyday use thanks to the layman's exposure to it through media such as television and the press.

Sir Ernest Gowers, a senior civil servant and therefore a man exposed regularly to jargon of a peculiar sort, raised objections to elements of it in his book *Plain Words*: yet his dissatisfaction with words such as *multilateral, bilateral* and *unilateral* cannot now hold. It is not just that they are ubiquitous, for that does not make them right: it is that they are in fact clear, and serve a comprehensible function. Equally, just as some words change over time from being abstruse to being common, others change from being terms of abuse to badges of honour (as both *Whig* and *Tory* did), and one needs to decide at what stage in their development some words are before one uses them. Writing is all about judgement, and if one wishes to remain formal, one will know by experience and often by instinct what vocabulary, or argot, has a place in such writing and what does not. As well as exercising judgement about formality, one should also exercise it about the plain sense of a word. One vogue expression in recent years has been that of the word *community*: we no longer have *authors*, we have "the writing community", and presumably also "the reading community", and so on. This sort of thing is just silly: it represents the cloying desire by people in the public sector or in marketing to seek to develop a jargon to make more human groups of people about whom they are talking, or to whom they are trying to "reach out". By lapsing, often unwittingly, into absurdity, they achieve the opposite. Their jargon alienates them from intelligent people, not just by its ludicrousness but also by its capacity to patronise. In non-fiction writing, unless one wishes to be deliberately satirical, sticking to the mainstream is always the best policy.

CHAPTER SEVEN

Three sinners

Some groups of people – state officials, academics, lawyers, certain breeds of scientist – talk to each other in a private language. Some official documents make little sense to lay people because they have to be couched in an argot that combines avoidance of the politically incorrect with obeisance to the contemporary jargon of the profession. Some articles written by academics in particular are almost incomprehensible to those outside their circle. This is not because the outsiders are stupid. It is because the academics feel they have to write in a certain stilted, dense way in order to be taken seriously by their peers.

Many officials seem to have lost the knack of communicating with people outside their closed world. Some academics, however, are bilingual. If asked to write for a publication outside the circle – such as a newspaper – they can rediscover the knack of writing reasonably plain English. They do not indulge themselves in such a fashion when they write for learned journals. There are certain phrases that they feel obliged to use: *positing a thesis* always goes down well, for example, where most of us would simply *assert* or *argue* or, in a radical move, *say*. One example of this will suffice to make the point. It is from an American psychology journal:

> Human behavior is a product both of our innate human nature and of our individual experience and environment. In this article, however, we emphasize biological influences on human behavior, because most social scientists explain human behavior as if evolution

stops at the neck and as if our behavior is a product almost entirely of environment and socialization. In contrast, evolutionary psychologists see human nature as a collection of psychological adaptations that often operate beneath conscious thinking to solve problems of survival and reproduction by predisposing us to think or feel in certain ways.[1]

It is almost as though the purpose of such writing is not to be clear: that the writer is recording research in order to prove to peers or superiors that he has discovered something. It does not seem to bother such people that their style is considered ugly and barbaric by anyone of discernment. It is repetitious, long-winded, abstract and abstruse. Those who write in such a way probably will not easily be discouraged, unless the prevailing standards of their disciplines change. What is important is that others do not think it is somehow clever to emulate them. Academia – however clever its inhabitants are supposed to be – seems the constituency most resistant to the notion of clarity's being the most desirable aspect of writing. The example above is not unusual or extreme. Its long words, scarcity of punctuation, abundance of abstracts and even the odd tautology ("innate human nature") suggest to me that little care was taken in trying to communicate what we must be sure are important ideas. Were I the sub-editor on whose desk this piece of prose landed, and it was my job to turn it into comprehensible English, I should need a stiff drink and a lie down before even trying.

This obscurity is not a vice confined to academics. Creative types tend to have their own private languages too, which help add to the aura of pretentiousness and self-regard that such people are reputed to have around them. I found the following on the

---

1. *Ten Politically Incorrect Truths About Human Nature*, by Alan S Miller and Satoshi Kanazawa, *Psychology Today*, 1 July 2007.

website of Daniel Libeskind, the celebrated architect, about his designs to extend the Military History Museum in Dresden:

> The wedge cuts through the structural order of the arsenal, giving the museum a place for reflection about organized conflict and violence. This creates an objective view to the continuity of military conflicts and opens up vistas to central anthropological questioning.[2]

Few people will have any idea what much of that means. The ideal style is one comprehensible to any intelligent person. If you make a conscious decision to communicate with a select (or self-selecting) group, so be it: but in trying to appeal to a large audience, or even a small one that you wish to be sure will understand your meaning, writing of the sort exemplified here just will not do. This sort of writing used to be kept from the general public thanks to the need to find someone to publish it. The advent of the internet means that one is no longer so shielded from its pernicious effects as one used to be; and such accessibility and ubiquity threaten to have a pervasive effect on the soundness of the language and its suscepti-bility to corruption. It is estimated that 80 per cent of pages on the worldwide web are in a language purporting to be English.

The examples above are only by way of an hors d'oeuvre: now for three more extensive passages that show much that is wrong with modern prose. Gowers published *Plain Words*, and a sequel, more than 60 years ago in an attempt to drive bad practices in English usage out of the British civil service. For a time it seemed he had succeeded. The application of his classically-trained mind to the problem infected many of his colleagues with the same determination to clean up official English. The classically-

---

2. www.daniel.libeskind.com/media/single-view/browse/2/article366/topping-out

educated civil servant is no longer so apparent as he used to be, as this extract from the proposals for the Research Excellence Framework, published in October 2009 by the Higher Education Funding Council for England, makes clear. I apologise for its length, but the "impact", as the drafter would no doubt have put it, needs to be clear:

> The REF will provide significant additional recognition where institutions and researchers have built on excellent research to deliver demonstrable benefits to the economy, society, public policy, culture or quality of life. To assess impact, we **propose** that:
>
> * A rounded assessment should be made of the impact of the submitting unit as a whole, not the impact of individual researchers. Submissions should provide examples of research-driven impact that arose from the unit's broad portfolio of work.
>
> * The impacts must have been underpinned by high-quality research. The focus of REF is to identify research excellence, with additional recognition for strong impact built on that excellence.
>
> * Because of time-lags, especially with blue-skies research, the impact must be evident during the REF assessment period, but the research may have been undertaken earlier (we suggest up to 10-15 years earlier).
>
> * The assessment will be based on qualitative information informed by appropriate indicators. Submissions should include the following evidence of impact:
>
>   – An **impact statement**, using a generic template, for the submitted unit as a whole. This will describe the breadth of interactions with research users and an overview of positive impacts that became evident during the assessment period.

- A number of **case studies**, using a generic template, to illustrate specific examples of impact and how the unit contributed to them. We propose one case study should be submitted for every five to 10 members of staff.

- The case studies and the impact statement should include appropriate indicators of impact, to support the narrative evidence.

• The assessment will be made by the REF expert sub-panels, comprising people who understand research in the discipline and its wider use and benefits. Panels will be supplemented with members who are research users, to assess impacts.

• Sub-panels should assess impact against criteria of **reach** (how widely the impacts have been felt) and **significance** (how transformative the impacts have been). They will form a sub-profile showing the proportion of impacts meeting each level on the five-point scale. To achieve a four-star ('exceptional') rating, an impact would need to be 'ground-breaking, transformative or of major value, relevant to a range of situations'.[3]

The usual vices are there. The reader is saturated by abstracts. There is a torrent of jargon ("blue-skies research" and "the breadth of interactions"). It is repetitious. When it seeks to explain (as in the three examples of "evidence of impact") it merely introduces more jargon ("a generic template" and "qualitative information") that serves only to deepen the confusion. Seldom have the injunctions of the Fowlers and Orwell against using long words and in favour of using short ones, which I discuss in the next chapter, been proved to have more substance.

---

3. *The Research Excellence Framework Consultation: a Brief Guide to the Proposals,* pp4–5 (found at http://www.hefce.ac.uk/Research/ref/).

Research into efficiencies to be obtained by the better use of English would, we must assume, not attract promises of funding.

Local government publications and websites are a goldmine of solecisms and catachreses. The frequency and velocity with which they have to communicate with the public has been matched by a decline in the ability of those charged to communicate to do so effectively and in accurate English. This is from the Essex County Council website in the spring of 2010:

> Following the harshest winter in decades, Essex County Council in partnership with the Local Government Association is holding a national Snow Summit to assess the performance of Local Authorities this winter, and to find new and innovative ways forward for the future.
>
> The Snow Summit, which has a string of top speakers from industry, government, service users and even the Swiss highways division, will provide a forum for discussion and debate which will feed into new policy decisions.
>
> Delegates will assess delivery across the UK this winter and will have the chance to question the Government's policy of centralising salt supplies and rationing it to local authorities, known as Salt Cell. John Dowie, the Chair of the Department for Transport's Salt Cell will defend the Government's record.
>
> Schools, road users and businesses will all get the chance to argue their case, and the Automobile Association will challenge delegates with their recent survey findings taken from 20,000 of their members who used the roads this winter.
>
> The debates and technical sessions will contribute to the LGA's review process, meaning the Snow Summit will feed directly into future policy.
>
> Councillor Norman Hume, Essex County Council's Cabinet Member for Highways and Transportation said, "This winter has

been a challenge for us all and one that we have worked hard to meet.

"The Snow Summit provides the whole country with an opportunity to look at what practices have worked during the recent adverse weather and analyse what could have been improved upon, as well as encouraging us all to look towards future preparations.

"We're trying to enable the development of future UK winter services based on best practice gleaned from operations across the UK and the rest of Europe. This will provide a better foundation to shape the way in which both local and national government can work together with their partners to keep the country moving."

Councillor David Sparks, Local Government Association said, "Councils have a crucial role to play when it comes to winter weather and keeping the country moving. The LGA will be conducting a review to learn lessons from this winter, looking at what was done well and what can be done better.

"The LGA is pleased to be associated with this event, organised by Essex County Council as an important part of that process. Councils and their staff have worked tirelessly to keep the country moving this winter but it is only right to see where we can improve preparedness for bad weather."

Let us note first of all the eccentric command of punctuation. Then let us note how the official who has written this has a grasp of cliché ("way forward" and "worked tirelessly") that perfectly complements that of the people he is quoting. Jargon is everywhere: "feed directly into future policy", "assess delivery across the UK" and the now inevitable "best practice". All that appears to be missing – and one cannot easily tell why – is the equally familiar "fit for purpose".

That example looks like fine writing compared with our third sinner. The combination of earnest and politically-correct trade unionism and the lower echelons of academia has produced this nearly incomprehensible piece of prose, on the undeniably serious topic of stamping out the bullying of members of ethnic minorities in the workplace:

> Although some advancements have been made of late with research on the significance of gender as a factor in the perception and experience of bullying, for example issues relating to gender harassment, unwanted sexual attention and sexual coercion (Pryor and Fitzgerald, 2003), much of the initial focus of bullying research has firmly concentrated on wide-ranging population groups rather than minority groups. Notwithstanding an appreciation within bullying research that individuals may continue to be treated inequitably due to their minority status, the possible impact of ethnicity has been afforded little attention, with most studies seemingly overlooking the issue altogether. Furthermore, the limited number of studies carried out on ethnicity and bullying have proved to be inconclusive due to methodological constraints, sector-specific focus, limitations with sample sizes and varying experiences across different BME groups ...
>
> Utilising the growing evidence base from this relatively new field of research, this study aims to report on the extent of BME employee experiences of workplace bullying and the implications these experiences have on individual employees and organisations, employee representatives, industry in general, and policy makers, as they move into a new era of a single equalities and human rights framework through the Equality and Human Rights Commission (EHRC).

1.1 Aims and objectives

The aims and objectives of this study are to use wide-ranging secondary data sources to:

1. Highlight the extent of BME employee experiences of bullying in comparison to the general workforce;
2. Identify the causes of BME employee perceptions of unfairness in the workplace, with a particular focus on sectoral issues and leadership style.
3. Develop the business case for tackling workplace bullying from a Black and Minority Ethnic Employee perspective.

1.2 Methodology

This 35-day research project has been carried out over a six-month period. In order to maximise the potential of this study, we adopted a multi-dimensional methodological approach including a literature review, consultation with experts, and planning / review meetings with Dignity at Work Partnership Steering Group representatives.

Utilising extensive University of Bradford electronic and library resources, we conducted a comprehensive review of scientific journals, policy documents, statistics, and national and international reports in order to explore previously published data on workplace bullying with a particular focus on BME employees and the impact negative experiences have on individuals and organisations. In addition to a review of the published literature, this research has benefited from the inclusion of on-going or unpublished grey literature obtained by attending an international work psychology conference during the early stages of the project, and then partway through the study, hosting an experts conference to review interim findings.

Aside from the obligatory jargon with which this extract drips ("sector-specific focus", "on-going or unpublished grey literature" and "a multi-dimensional methodological approach"), what strikes one most of all about it is its sheer pomposity and self-importance. What is all this *utilising* when most people would be *using*? Why are we *commencing* when we could be *starting*? Where did the adjective *sectoral* come from? We are even treated to a *notwithstanding*. It is as if the writer is being paid by the syllable: no short word seems to be used where a long one will do. Since the piece is about bullying, that everyday word (in its inevitably frequent use) stands out in a sea of Latinity like a good deed in a naughty world. On top of that there are the contortions brought about by the coercion, or fascism, of political correctness. The entirely inoffensive term *ethnic minority*, still widely used and widely comprehensible outside the race relations industry, has been supplanted by the apparently more acceptable *minority ethnic*. I am sure there is a point to this private language, but it is hard to fathom.

The stylistic problems of this piece are also evident in its structure. Its paragraphs, in the early part of the extract, are long and dense. There is no variation in tone, which creates a sense of monotony. The long words mean that even the occasional attempt to keep sentences short pays no dividends. It is a clear example of a private language: written by the same sort of people, with the same cast of mind, as those for whom it was intended. It is a means of erecting a barrier against the outside world. In that – whether or not it was the actual intention – it appears to be entirely successful.

PART THREE

GOOD ENGLISH

CHAPTER EIGHT

The essence of good style

As literacy became more widespread after the expansion of the middle classes from the time of the English Civil War onwards, and especially after the 1870 Education Act in Great Britain brought reading and writing to the children of the working classes, so a language whose form had been agreed by educated people began to mutate in a fashion that lay outside that agreement. Two types of offence provoked hostility – or snobbery, depending upon one's point of view – to this mutation. The first was the sheer misuse of words, and the abuse of grammar. The second, related to the first, was the difficulty in communicating effectively that these catachreses and solecisms caused. Some people were now being educated to a point where they learned not only how to use words that would once have been above their station, but to use them with something approaching grammatical propriety. However, they were often nonetheless verbose, particularly if they worked in any sort of petty officialdom. It was the sight of these offences that caused various learned men (and, at that point, they were almost exclusively men) to begin to write manuals telling the newly literate that, if they wished to use these precision tools of language, they had better use them according to the rules that those more experienced in them had always adopted.

The brothers Fowler, in 1906, opened their magisterial work *The King's English* with five rules about a writer's choice of words. To generations of users of English these became a holy writ of literary fundamentalism. We should therefore note them here:

Prefer the familiar word to the far-fetched.
Prefer the concrete word to the abstract.
Prefer the single word to the circumlocution.
Prefer the short word to the long.
Prefer the Saxon word to the Romance.

The Fowlers add that "these rules are given roughly in order of merit", which one assumes is how *circumlocution* came to survive beyond the proof stage. The rules are the codification of the book's first sentence, codified, one assumes, for the benefit of the hard of understanding: "Any one who wishes to become a good writer should endeavour, before he allows himself to be tempted by the more showy qualities, to be direct, simple, brief, vigorous and lucid."[1] *Endeavour* is a synonym for *try*.

The Fowlers' book is still in print more than 100 years after its first appearance and has sold hundreds of thousands of copies. Yet the message remained, and still remains, slow to sink in. That was why George Orwell, in *Politics and the English Language*, also set some rules for the struggling communicator:

i. Never use a metaphor, simile or other figure of speech which you are used to seeing in print.
ii. Never use a long word where a short one will do.
iii. If it is possible to cut a word out, always cut it out.
iv. Never use the passive where you can use the active.
v. Never use a foreign phrase, a scientific word or a jargon word if you can think of an everyday English equivalent.
vi. Break any of these rules sooner than say anything outright barbarous.[2]

---

1. *The King's English*, p11.
2. *Politics and the English Language*, in *Why I Write*, by George Orwell (Penguin Books, 2004), p119.

Another way of making the last of those points is Winston Churchill's celebrated line about "this is the sort of English up with which I will not put".

Everyone who writes a book about English usage will have his own rules, and presume to inflict them on his readers. I am no different. The Fowler/Orwell rules seem serviceable to me, given the importance of a writer's being understood and communicating a message or idea. Rather than outline rules, perhaps I may be allowed to outline the bones of a philosophy with which I approach English as a professional writer.

First, I see no reason for orthography to be varied, since we have had a completed standard dictionary for over 80 years. Second, I see no reason for grammar to be varied, since there has been general agreement among educated people about how it should work for even longer than we have had a dictionary. That agreement has been based on sound logical and historical principles. The grammar agreed upon is one that allows such a high degree of precision that it eliminates almost all ambiguities and is easily comprehensible. Perhaps the last important development in our grammar (as opposed to a change's being caused by deliberate neglect or abuse, as with the very useful subjunctive mood) was that of the passive voice as we now recognise it in the early 19th century. Jane Austen writes that "the house was building". Within a few decades this had become "the house was being built". This change in grammar seems to me defensible in that it imposed greater precision and removed scope for ambiguity. These must be the aims of any system of grammar.

Third, given that we have (according to the latest edition of the *Oxford English Dictionary*) over 171,000 words in our language, plus another 47,000 classed as obsolete and 9,500 derived from existing words, I see no reason for a word to be used in other than its etymologically correct sense. I have given plenty of evidence for this in Chapter Five. This is not to be construed as an objection to new words' entering the language: only a fool would take such a view, since new concepts, objects and experiences occur all the time and a new word may be required to describe them accurately. Usually, those words will come about by a logical means, often by reference to a classical antecedent: it is why an era of invention gave us telephone, television, refrigerator and video. However, wilful misuse of a word to describe something for which plenty of other words already exist seems to me to be unpardonable, even if in some instances the dictionary has capitulated and admitted to a new meaning. It can also be confusing to those readers who have a careful appreciation of the meaning of words. I would refer readers who still harbour doubts about this to the observations I have made in Chapter Five with regard to words such as *prevaricate* and *flout*, and to many others. We live in a harsh world, and one of its harshnesses is that we are sometimes judged by the way we use our language. One who uses a word wrongly may go undetected among his peers only to be snared at a crucial moment by someone he may be trying to impress. It is better, if one seeks to be taken seriously, not to run the risk of such humiliation.

My fourth and final prejudice, having expressed my strictness about grammar, spelling and vocabulary, is about concision in expression. There is little point in spelling correctly, having immaculate grammar and using each word in its correct sense if one is verbose. Most of us, when we read verbose writing, think of it as flannel. We lose respect for the writer and discount his opinions. One should strive not to have that effect on one's readers. Therefore, use the minimum number of words to say whatever you have to say.

Playing by the rules

The five rules of the Fowlers, or the six of Orwell, are the essence of how to develop a good style. What follows in this chapter amplifies and expands them, and reflects the prejudices of my own that I have just outlined. You may have noticed that the prescriptions of the Fowlers and Orwell to an extent overlap. That is hardly surprising, because there is relatively little to the art of writing well. It requires adherence to the rules of grammar and punctuation set out already; thoughtful and precise choice of words; brevity; and, in the use of imagery and metaphor, the pursuit of the original. Should you feel daunted by this, remember that, like anything, excellence comes with practice. Since you speak and possibly write English every day, the opportunity for practice is large. Seize it greedily, think about what you say or write so that you apply the rules, and your style will quickly improve.

I write books when I have the time and the opportunity, but I have earned my living for almost 30 years writing for newspapers and periodicals. One cannot overstate the discipline attached to such work. The marketplace in which these publications operate has always been fiercely competitive. If a writer acquires a reputation for complexity or obscurity – in other words, for being hard for the reader to understand – then he will quickly be out of work. Those who wish to maintain a career in this line of business must communicate effectively. That entails doing precisely what is detailed above. Readers distracted by poor grammar, or confused by ambiguity, or estranged by pompous vocabulary, or bored by prolixity, or puzzled by vagueness, or who come to hold a writer in contempt for the use of cliché will be readers who do not come back. Journalism is, or tries to be, a precise trade for that reason. It is, perhaps, because readers expect high standards of writing in journalism that they complain with such ferocity when they find the opposite.

A good style is not one that shows off the vocabulary or the extensive reading of the writer. It is one that combines clarity of expression with ease of reading while conveying the maximum information, with every word essential to the task and used in the correct grammatical framework. Anyone unclear about what that is should re-read Chapter Four. Good style also includes words that are used in their accurate sense, such as described in Chapter Five. As has been noted before, the expansion of the literate class from the mid-19th to the mid-20th centuries resulted in many more people who knew how to read and write, but not necessarily how to write well. Achieving stylistic excellence was a matter for the individual's further study and application. Few could be bothered to do this, but many had jobs in which they had to communicate with the public – perhaps as minor functionaries in central or local government, or in other parts of the bureaucracy, or in clerical roles for great corporations. The ready availability of bad English in wide circulation that was the result helped provoke Orwell's statement that a "mixture of vagueness and sheer incompetence is the most marked characteristic of modern English prose".[3]

Economy is the best policy

The most basic rule, put in different ways by the Fowlers, Orwell and almost every other commentator on the use of language, is to be brief. This does not just mean shorter documents. It means the most concise use of expression within those documents. Why say "he fell asleep on the majority of occasions he went to work" when one can say "he fell asleep most times he went to work"? Why say (to use a popular horror) "at this moment in time" when one can

3. *Politics and the English Language*, in *Why I Write*, p104.

say "now"? Why say "it is possible to go there" when one can say "I can go there"? Why say (to use another popular horror) "when all is said and done" when probably one need say nothing at all? Our speech tends to be full of fillers such as that. They become verbal tics, or they allow us a moment to mark time in our speech and think what we really want to say. They are tiresome in that context, but unpardonable in a considered piece of writing. Concision is the writer's weapon against obscurity, and precision his shield against incomprehension. If a word is unnecessary, do not use it. Clarity of expression reflects clarity of thought, and helps a reader not just to understand, but to take seriously, what the writer is saying to him.

Some writers seem unaware of their use of redundant words. Why should someone say "the painting we bought was the best one in the gallery", when the *one* is redundant? Another example of this pointlessness is "the restaurant we ate in was one known around the world". There was a time when grammarians were united in their ridicule for the construction "prepared to..." as in "I am prepared to vouch for the fact that...". The verbal construction is unnecessary and verbose: the test for this is that if the construction "to be prepared to" is removed and replaced by *will* or *shall*, the sense of the sentence remains unchanged. This, indeed, is the test for all writing; if a word or phrase can be removed from a clause or sentence without altering its meaning or rendering it more obscure, remove it. Our language, written and spoken, is littered with pointless words that are verbal tics or fillers: words and phrases such as *actually*, *really*, *in fact* or, perhaps most vacuous of all, *in actual fact*. Some people appear incapable of eliminating these in speech; it ought to be far easier to do so in writing.

Even apparently sharp writing may contain redundancies. One can often express things more concisely by using a verb instead of a noun. Why write "both examples are illustrations of the depravity of politicians" when you can write "both examples illustrate the depravity"? Depending upon the context, one might not even need the word *examples*. One cannot always do entirely without abstract nouns: but the fewer abstracts, the better. Another such is "these things are reminders of..." when one could without impairing the sense write "these remind us"; *things* is also all too often a word with no point to it. Nouns (notably, again, abstract ones) in verbose constructions also sometimes take the place of simple adjectives. The teacher who says "there is too much noise in this class" would better say "this class is too noisy".

Beware, too, of the pleonastic introductory phrase. How often does one read *it is obvious that, by and large, for the most part* or *as a matter of fact*, or some other piece of padding before a phrase such as "the economy is not getting any better", when the sentence could just as easily start with that phrase itself. Another such phrase that also invites itself into the middle of sentences is *of course*. This is rarely necessary, because if something is *of course* one hardly needs to say so. Get straight to the point: most readers do not need an introduction to allow them time to collect their thoughts, even if the writer appears to.

When one hears verbose language, one may conclude that the verbosity is a way of killing time while the thought-processes of the speaker light up: or, it may be an indication that they are never going to light up. Whatever the reason, some people get into the habit of speaking badly, and then write badly. This applies as much to those who appear to be educated as to those with no such pretension. How often has one heard a senior bureaucrat, interviewed in the broadcast media, talk of something happening "on a daily basis"? What is the point of the words *on*, *a* and *basis* in that phrase? When one hears phrases such as "it was of an unfortunate character" or "it was not of a very agreeable nature", one learns no more than if one had been told "it was unfortunate" or "it was disagreeable". When somebody introduces a statement with the filler "at the end of the day", is it ever necessary? Would it even be necessary if the statement were being made as the sun was setting, or midnight approaching, let alone if it were just after breakfast?

Gowers was also strict about abstract nouns such as *position* and *situation* being used to remove clarity from statements, and he was right to be so.[4] A desire for euphemism seems to trigger both usages. If someone is seriously ill one may as well say so, rather than observe that "the situation is serious". If a company is broke it is better to say so, rather than to claim that "its position is serious". In each example, the abstract nouns create distance; they are used to divorce the reality from the entity. No serious writer, unless briefed to deceive, should seek to do that. These terms are used sometimes where there is no attempt at euphemism. "I am writing to enquire about your situation" can be paraphrased as "what are you doing?" just as "could you inform me as to your position on this matter" is "what do you think about it?" Jespersen, writing in his *Philosophy of Grammar*, demonstrated for other reasons the difference between the sentences "I doubt the Doctor's cleverness" and "I doubt that the doctor is clever".[5] One can see immediately that the former is euphemistic, the second more direct to the point of being insulting. While being rude is not always going to be the intention of a writer, avoiding the abstract wherever possible will always lead to the writer's communicating his meaning more directly.

Even when one uses only one word rather than several, it may be an unnecessarily long word. One such example that the Fowlers railed against was *provided*. "*Provided* is a small district in the kingdom of if," they wrote, in one of those entertaining observations that show the considerable charm of their supposedly pedantic book. "It can never be wrong to write *if*

4. *The Complete Plain Words*, p135.
5. *The Philosophy of Grammar*, by Otto Jespersen (George Allen and Unwin, 1924), p129.

instead of *provided*; to write *provided* instead of *if* will generally be wrong, but now and then an improvement in precision."[6] A contemporary example shows the eternal truth of this rule. "You won't be caught for speeding provided you don't break the speed limit" loses nothing by having *provided* removed and replaced by *if*. Sometimes, however, as even the Fowlers conceded, *provided* is necessary, not least to avoid giving the wrong impression. I would re-frame their rule as follows: where *provided* describes a straightforward option or condition (as it normally will), replace it with *if*; yet on the rare occasions that it describes an indispensable or essential condition, retain it. So "provided it is nice this afternoon, we shall go for a swim" becomes "if it is nice…"; but "I told him that I would look after him provided he resolved to mend his ways" is preferable to "…if he resolved" since the use of *provided* establishes that his mending his ways is not a casual option, but an important and indispensable condition of his being looked after.

There are some clichéd phrases including prepositions that have become tired and are verbose. They exemplify the failure of writers to think about the words they are using, and they radiate pomposity: "in respect of your letter of…" or "with regard to your letter". The officialese of these should be obvious at once; they have no place in humane communication, and may usually be cut out altogether. This is usually also true of the phrase *the case*; or, as I might just have written, "this is usually also the case with the phrase *the case*". The phrase has become a filler and is used at the expense of a more precise word – *true* will often suffice.

When writing in reported speech about events destined for the future, use the form "after his successful debut, Smith would go on to open the batting for England" rather than "Smith was to go on to open the batting". Paring down one's sentences to the bare

6. *The King's English*, p23.

minimum is never a wasted exercise, for it gives the maximum help to readers.

In speech and writing to which too little thought has been given, too many words and phrases are simply padding or verbal tics, and inexact phrases often replace precise words. This was illustrated in Chapter Six by the example of *get* and *got* and it is also true of *do*. Some words seem to exist purely to provide a breathing space for both writer and reader. When, for example, you next read the word *overall*, note how you may almost always remove it from its sentence without affecting the meaning: such as in "he was in overall charge" (a tautology as well as a pleonasm), "overall, it made no difference", "there was an overall view that it shouldn't happen", "the overall case was made for keeping the rule" and so on. *Overall* has a legitimate function when describing something that really is over all: such as in politics, when to use the phrase *overall majority* conveys concisely and accurately the fact that in a legislature one party has more seats than all other parties combined, rather than just more than any individual party. It takes little time to weigh every word; and the need to weigh every word makes an important point about reading what one has written before letting anyone else see it.

Short, sharp sentences

Orwell, like most commentators on the language, makes the point that adherence to conventions is not reactionary: it is about maintaining clarity. What had passed for progress in some people's estimate of the language was, in his view, simply sloppiness of speech or of writing that betokened sloppiness of thought. It is axiomatic that if one doesn't know what one is trying to say, one will say it badly. This is most often revealed in the seemingly interminable sentence.

Fashion has changed on this point in the last century. In *The King's English* the Fowlers asserted that too much "full stopping", even when used correctly, was a "discomfort inflicted upon readers, who are perpetually being checked like a horse with a fidgety driver".[7] They added, for the avoidance of doubt, that "no sentence is to be condemned for mere length; a really skilful writer can fill a page with one and not tire his reader."[8] Even they conceded, however, that "a succession of long sentences without the relief of short ones interspersed is almost sure to be forbidding". It is not causing tiredness or being forbidding that seems to be the problem: it is preventing the sense of what is being communicated from being clearly received by the reader.

For those like the Fowlers who grew up in the Victorian age and were well-educated, the long sentence, upholstered with commas, semicolons and colons, was a delight. They luxuriated in its elegant phrasing and the juxtaposition of its clauses. It is now viewed as a barrier to clarity, in my view quite rightly. The change in fashion is almost certainly the fault of the rise of the mass media. It is not only broadcasters who speak concisely in order that their listeners may not lose the thread. Newspaper writers and those who write for the internet need to convey detail as quickly as possible, to prevent losing the attention of the reader and having him move on somewhere else. The more truncated style of sentence structure was taken up by such writers as Graham Greene (who had been a journalist), Evelyn Waugh and Aldous Huxley, all of whom came to prominence in the generation after the Fowlers. Modernists attacked the earlier style, as they did much that lingered on from Victorian times; Joyce parodied it extensively in *Ulysses*. The fashion shows no sign of altering again.

A mass of clauses, not always punctuated with the precision

7. *The King's English*, p234.
8. *The King's English*, p309.

the Fowlers would have hoped for, helps the reader lose the point: that is, if he has found one in the first place. If one considers properly what one wants to say, one will think of a way of saying it concisely. Even the most complex ideas benefit from being broken down into constituent units. Commas or conjunctions can be replaced by full stops without very much – indeed, any – harm being caused. Having written a sentence, read it again and judge whether it needs to be the length it is. Is it easily divisible into smaller sentences? May conjunctions be removed and replaced by a fresh start? May a full stop be substituted for a semicolon?

One hesitates to imagine one could improve on the prose of such a master as Smollett, but this extract from *Roderick Random*, while clear in so many respects, is rather taxing for the reader:

> I rose and sat down, covered and uncovered my head twenty times between the acts; pulled out my watch, clapped it to my ear, wound it up, set it, gave it the hearing again; displayed my snuff-box, affected to take snuff, that I might have an opportunity of showing my brilliant, and wiped my nose with a perfumed hand-kerchief; then dangled my cane, and adjusted my sword-knot, and acted many more fooleries of the same kind, in hopes of obtaining the character of a pretty fellow, in the acquiring of which I found two considerable obstructions in my disposition, namely, a natural reserve and jealous sensibility.[9]

It is fine prose, its clarity not least guaranteed by the scarcity of adjectives, hardly any of which appear until the very end of this 106-word sentence. It is comic writing, so we may forgive Smollett this construction. It also well conveys the agitation and restlessness of the narrator, who is desperate to be noticed. However, such

9. *The Adventures of Roderick Random*, by Tobias Smollett (Hutchinson, date unknown), p310.

a framework, in the hands of an amateur, would be an invitation to disaster. Compare it with this passage from Orwell, the master of the short sentence, in which as much vividness is created, but of which any imitation would carry fewer dangers:

> He went on picking bluebells. It was the best thing to do. It might be the girl, or he might have been followed after all. To look round was to show guilt. He picked another and another. A hand fell lightly on his shoulder.
> He looked up. It was the girl.[10]

The Georgians and Victorians were hard put to understand the limits of comprehension of even the educated reader when faced with a sentence a hundred or so words long, or a paragraph that went over several pages. This could cause confusion where there were numerous subordinate clauses, where pronouns were used with increasing ambiguity, and where prepositions were sometimes lost altogether. Even where the writer's grasp of grammar was precise, a long sentence with numerous clauses could exhaust the reader before it reached its end. Hallam, writing in 1827 in his *Constitutional History* about the work of Hooker, presented this to the reader:

> He enquired into the nature and foundation of law itself as the rule of operation to all created beings, yielding thereto obedience by unconscious necessity, or sensitive appetite, or reasonable choice; reviewing especially those laws that regulate human agency, as they arise out of moral relations, common to our species, or the institutions of politic societies, or the inter-community of independent nations; and having thoroughly established the fundamental distinction between laws natural and positive, eternal and temporary,

10. *Nineteen Eighty-Four*, by George Orwell (Penguin, 1954), p97.

immutable and variable, he came with all this strength of moral philosophy to discriminate by the same criterion the various rules and precepts contained in the scriptures.[11]

A 104-word long sentence (by no means unusual or excessive for this writer, or for others of his era) might have been considered exemplary by the grammarians of the 19th century, but it looks abominable now.

Style is often about the reinforcement and observation of logic. For this reason, one sort of sentence that is always to be broken in two is the sort combining a statement and a question. This will usually occur only in rhetoric or first-person writing. "You must stop speaking to me in that tone, can't you see it is hurtful?" is such an example. The question mark violates the sense of the first clause.

Breaking things up

Even short sentences can comprise two or three clauses; and where there are two or three clauses, or even just one, there is scope for ambiguity. In Chapter Three I considered the technical aspects of punctuation. Here I consider the stylistic ones. There are many simple examples of how a comma here or there can change the meaning of a sentence, and of the how a supreme stylist will position his punctuation with the greatest care to ensure that the right information is communicated to the reader. Take this sentence: "she hit the thief who was escaping with her umbrella". Now look at the various ways of punctuating it. "She hit the thief, who was escaping with her umbrella", suggests that

11. *The Constitutional History of England from Henry VII to George II* (Vol I), by Henry Hallam (J M Dent and Sons, 1925), p202.

the thief was escaping with her umbrella, and she hit him. "She hit the thief, who was escaping, with her umbrella" suggests that as the thief was escaping (without her umbrella) she hit him with it. One could even have "she hit the thief who was escaping, with her umbrella". That last sentence, which is eccentrically punctuated, has the same meaning as the one before it, but it opens up a different array of meanings. It suggests there was more than one thief; that there was one thief among them who was escaping; that she managed to hit that particular thief; and that it was worthy of note that she hit him with her umbrella. So, depending on the information one wants to convey, one punctuates accordingly.

It is clear from these simple examples that the wrong punctuation can and will convey quite the wrong meaning. It is also important to note that the first, unpunctuated sentence is susceptible of so many different meanings that it is a stylistic abomination. It defeats the first rule of writing, which is that one's meaning should always be clear. It is also true that the final example should, to avoid any doubt, and to eliminate the bizarre punctuation and make its meaning precise, be recast as "she hit with her umbrella the thief who was escaping". For reasons of emphasis that, too, can be punctuated in various ways, but no form of punctuation will alter this clear meaning. It may be punctuated as "she hit, with her umbrella, the thief who was escaping", in which the writer feels that the important part of the sentence – the part that needs to be emphasised – is the part that refers to the weapon she used. Or, it may be punctuated "she hit with her umbrella the thief, who was escaping", which emphasises not the weapon but the action the thief was taking. Finally, it may be punctuated "she hit, with her umbrella, the thief, who was escaping", which emphasises both the weapon and the thief's action. It also looks cluttered: the good stylist will want to stress only one part of any sentence.

Punctuation may also be used to create certain effects. A semi-colon or colon will slow down a sentence more than a comma will, and writers use these punctuation marks to draw attention to clauses within sentences. Butler does this to great effect in *The Way of All Flesh* when he is describing the plans Miss Pontifex has for distributing her estate: "She wanted those to have it who would be most likely to use it genially and sensibly, and whom it would thus be likely to make most happy; if she could find one such among her nephews and nieces, so much the better; it was worth taking a great deal of pains to see whether she could or could not; but if she failed, she must find an heir who was not related to her by blood."[12] Modern writers would divide that up into several sentences. Butler would have considered, rightly at the time, that the use of one sentence was correct for one idea; and that its division by semicolons was radical at a time when the comma was so frequently used to break up long sentences.

The placement of commas in routine sentences is something many writers find difficult. There are five fundamental rules that solve most problems. The first is that commas should be used sparingly and logically. Some writers have a temptation to insert them after every few words, irrespective of the need for them or of the sense this punctuation then conveys. Commas are only required where to spare them would create problems of ambiguity or comprehension. In prose they are not respiratory guides.

Second, where commas are parenthetical, be sure to remember to end the parenthesis. One occasionally reads sentences such as "they went to the beach, which was crowded so they returned to the hotel". A comma is required after *crowded* to separate that statement – an adjectival clause, for it describes the beach to us – from the rest of the sentence by completing the parenthesis. Remember, also, to use the correct relative pronoun when using a

12. *The Way of All Flesh*, by Samuel Butler (Penguin, 1966), p165.

parenthesis: it will be *which* rather than *that* for abstracts or inanimate objects, as discussed in Chapter Four. Parentheses are often seen in sentences with adverbial phrases in them, such as in this example: "she closed the curtains and, with the deftest of movements, got into bed". One can see the offences to logic and style of omitting the second comma and therefore of failing to complete the parenthesis, just as in adjectival clauses. The same applies to rhetorical parentheses, which often appear in dialogue or in oratory: the parenthesis must be completed. Therefore logic and style require "I ask you, members of the jury, to acquit my client", and "where, I ask you, is my fountain pen?" The application of logic should be sufficient to avoid making mistakes with any sort of parenthesis, as the removal of the second comma from each of the examples just given will show. Another rhetorical (though unparenthetical) use will normally only be found in dialogue – as in "I shall kill you, you swine", or "I shall never leave you, not for a second", where the comma is used to introduce a rhetorical emphasis.

The third rule is that in a list no comma is required before a final conjunction. When one reads "his wife was wearing a blue dress, necklace, high-heeled shoes, and a hat" one should see at once that the comma after *shoes* is superfluous. A comma may however be used in this position to remove an ambiguity, such as in this example: "he went to the bar and ordered three pints of beer, a sherry, a whisky, and water", which indicates that the water was a separate drink from the whisky. Had the drink been mixed, the correct way to cast the sentence would have been "three pints of beer, a sherry and a whisky and water", though a comma could for the same reasons of clarity be added after "sherry". It is also correct to use commas in lists of adjectives – not that one seeks to encourage adjectival writing. "The room was dark, ugly, smelly, damp and filthy" requires commas in precisely those places. Where only two things or qualities are listed a conjunction and not a comma is needed: as in "the boy was clean and tidy" or "he resigned with dignity and good grace, and left the office". The comma in that last example is required for reasons of good style, clarity and the avoidance of ambiguity; however, another after *dignity* would be redundant and confusing.

The fourth rule is that a comma should not separate a verb from its subject or object, unless that comma be the first of two forming a parenthesis. When one sees a sentence such as "the man knows, that his son will get a bad report", or "the vicar said, we should all pray for deliverance" we can see the superfluity of the punctuation mark. Were the first sentence to read "the man knows, whatever his wife may tell him, that his son will get a bad report", that use of the parenthetical commas would be entirely proper. The fifth, and final, rule is that in good style no comma is required before quotation marks. One either has no punctuation at all or the formality of a colon, but not a comma. "Smith said: 'I have no intention of leaving'" is correct. So is "Smith said 'I have no intention of leaving'". However, "Smith said, 'I have no intention of leaving'" is not. The fundamental point is this: the shorter one's sentences, the harder it is to make mistakes with commas and other forms of punctuation.

In this sentence, published in 2009 in a newspaper and already mentioned in the section on word order in Chapter Four, one can see how the simple insertion of a comma will help stave off ambiguity, even if it cannot provide elegance (that could come only by recasting the sentence in the way suggested in Chapter Four; but for the purposes of showing what a difference a correctly-placed comma may make, this exercise is instructive). It was reported that "the Queen sent a letter of condolence to a pensioner whose dog died after he wrote to Buckingham Palace about the death". First, to be correct reported speech the auxiliary *had* needs to be inserted after *dog*; but then a comma needs to be inserted after *died*. Otherwise, it appears that the dog itself achieved the remarkable feat of writing to the Sovereign about its own demise before it happened, dying shortly thereafter. As remarkable was this sentence (also analysed in Chapter Four) about how "the body of a 45-year-old darts fan was recovered from beneath ice in a frozen lake in Frimley Green, Surrey, where he had been watching the darts world championships". The unfortunate man had not been watching the darts match under water. A comma would not be enough to save this statement from absurdity. One either changes the word order as suggested in Chapter Four, or divides the statement into two sentences such as: "The body of a 45-year-old darts fan was recovered from beneath ice in a frozen lake in Frimley Green, Surrey. He had been watching the darts world championships nearby."

In a more complex sentence commas must be used to avoid the danger of ambiguity or downright error. In a sentence such as "the chief executive, invited by the chairman to address the board, having arranged his notes did so", only one meaning is possible given this punctuation. Were the comma to move from after *board* to after *notes* the meaning would change. The chief executive would still be addressing the board, but the invitation would have come from the chairman to do so only once the notes were arranged: and there would be some doubt about who (either the chief executive or the chairman) was arranging the notes. Better still to divide up the sentence: "The chief executive was invited by the chairman to address the board. Having arranged his notes, he did so." This is also an instance where the use of the passive voice is excusable, since the *he* in the second sentence clearly refers to the chief executive in the first. Had the active voice been used – "the chairman invited the chief executive" – the pronoun would seem to refer back to the main subject, which would be wrong.

One could also end the first sentence with a colon, and make the second sentence a separate clause. The prejudice of this book (and of much modern English writing) in favour of short sentences does not sound the death knell for colons and semicolons, but it makes them rare species. Both punctuation marks continue to serve a purpose of allowing a distinct expression in a visibly separate clause to be presented without a main verb. This has rhetorical uses, notably when presenting a list of similar thoughts, where the items on the list are separated by semicolons. Churchill gave us a most memorable example: "In war, resolution; in defeat, defiance; in victory, magnanimity; in peace, goodwill." In another speech he exhibited the ideal rhetorical use of the colon, in presenting a paratactic conclusion to a sentence: "Success is not final, failure is not fatal: it is the courage to continue that counts." There is nothing wrong with using colons and semicolons provided they are used correctly, in the ways specified in Chapter Three. The 19th century deployment, of carving up into chunks sentences that would now be several paragraphs long, would now be considered unacceptable unless used by a parodist.

I also touched in Chapter Three on the occasional interchangeability of colons with dashes, and gave examples. From a stylistic point of view, the dash is likely to be more prevalent in dialogue or rhetoric. The colon will be more frequent in formal writing. The dash is by its nature dramatic and exclamatory and therefore will be an infrequent visitor to serious prose. I also explained earlier how, used parenthetically, it varies from the use of brackets. For stylistic reasons it is important to use these devices sparingly. They give prose the appearance of being cluttered, they can cause ambiguities and they can distract. Since the writer's aim at all times should be to be understood precisely, these effects are undesirable. When a single dash is used for emphasis it may sometimes be almost an instruction to the reader to find what follows it either shocking, funny or remarkable. This too may be overdone, and suggests a lack of self-confidence on the part of the writer. It can also become bathetic if what follows the dash is something of an anti-climax. Take this sentence from Galsworthy: "All very well to determine that she would not torture Tony, would keep away from him and spare his senses, but without him – she would be dull and lonely."[13] The sentence would also be improved if it contained a main verb.

As indicated in Chapter Three, only when making a parenthesis (which we may define as matter which, if removed, would not alter the meaning of the sentence) should two dashes appear in the same sentence. A sentence that flouts this rule is stylistically difficult because it offends logic. For example: "neither of the men was prepared to admit the problem – that they had run out of money – entirely" is a mess. Remove what the reader initially takes to be the parenthetical matter and what is left is gibberish. Such a sentence always has to be recast.

It used to be deemed that paragraphs were scarce commodities, and a new one should only be opened to indicate a profound change in subject matter. That is why in the writings of some of the early Victorians one can find paragraphs that are several hundreds of words long, if not longer. Today, just as sentences have become shorter, so have paragraphs. The subject matter may, and usually does, remain the same. Each development in an argument on the same subject may command a new paragraph, and no harm is done for all that. It is the method used in writing this book.

The killer noun is better than the adjective

Adjectives get in the way. They are not always necessary. Enoch Powell, a stylist of Orwellian abilities, would call adjectives "very *Daily Mail*", which he did not mean as a compliment to that great newspaper. Gowers makes the essential point about them when he

---

13. *Over the River*, by John Galsworthy (Heinemann, 1933), p149.

writes: "Cultivate the habit of reserving adjectives and adverbs to make your meaning more precise, and suspect those that you find yourself using to make it more emphatic."[14] A well-chosen noun can do away with the need for an adjective to precede it. They are, as descriptive words, sometimes loaded, and can distract from the clarity of the message rather than enhancing it. Reputable newspapers will often ban all but the most functional of adjectives from their news reporting, since they may wreck the objectivity that is supposed to be inherent in that genre of journalism. Adjectives fall into two categories in this respect. There are those that state facts – the *elderly* man, the *disabled* woman, the *fat* dog, the *large* majority, the *sick* child. These add value to a noun by giving the reader more information about the condition of the person or thing nominated.

The other class of adjectives does nothing of the sort. It expresses an opinion held by the writer. Adjectives from this class must be deployed with care. So an editor of a newspaper does not expect to see one of his reporters writing in the news pages about a *disgusting* man, a *beautiful* woman, a *smelly* dog, a *loathsome* politician or a *brilliant* child. It is for the reader to make such judgements according to the facts presented to him. If such sentiments appear in a piece of reporting, they should be in quotation marks as the opinions of a third party whom the reporter has interviewed. If they appear in a piece that is clearly in a newspaper's opinion pages, that is a different matter; such as it is if they appear in a work of fiction. Even in those contexts they can be overdone; for, as I said at the beginning, adjectives get in the way.

Some adjectives are instantly redundant. Consider the sentence: "he had slept with three different women". The women were *different* from what, or whom? *Different* is unnecessary; the sentence conveys just as much information without it. Adjectives

14. *The Complete Plain Words*, p82.

may be a statement of the obvious – the *old* man, the *deep* river, the *cold* day. However, when they are expressions of opinion it is their subjectivity that makes them dangerous. The *stupid* child may be nothing of the sort. Nor may the *plain* woman (beauty being in the eye of the beholder), or the *sincere* man. Adjectives may often be avoided either because they are incipiently inaccurate, or because they add nothing to the meaning of the phrase, or because one chooses a noun with sufficient care to render them tautological or in some other way unnecessary. They do however exist, and exist far more in some sorts of writing than in others. It is well to be alert to their potency, their power to deceive, and to their dangers. Not the least of those dangers is that so many of them do not so much inform the reader as distract him.

One measure of bad writing is that it distracts rather than informs, which it will often do if it is laden with adjectives. Some writers, recognising this, choose their nouns in a way that removes the need for adjectives. An obvious case is the vocabulary of abuse or denigration. Of the nouns that do not cross the line into coarseness or vulgarity, those such as *idiot, shocker, lunatic, crook, whore, scum, imbecile, strumpet, filth, rat* and so on hardly require an adjective to amplify them, so loaded are the nouns themselves. Even away from such emotive subjects, a proper choice of noun renders an adjective pointless. Why call something a carefully-crafted and characterful object when you can call it a *gem*? Why say something is one of one's prized possessions when one can call it a *jewel*? Notice that both the substitute nouns are metaphorical (and similar metaphors at that); some nouns used singly and metaphorically can be exceptionally powerful, but such powerful usages do not have to be metaphorical. A street of squalid houses may be accurately and evocatively described as a *slum*. A property at the opposite end of the scale may be vividly described as a *palace*. Who needs an adjective? When seeking to describe anything, do not immediately reach for the adjective: ask yourself whether the noun could be improved upon. It is, however, important not to be so vivid when choosing a noun that one exaggerates: a minor accident is not a *catastrophe*, a heavy fall of rain is not necessarily a *deluge* and a difference of opinion is not always a *row*. Nor is a sportsman who wins one important prize a *titan*. I deal with this sort of hyperbole below in the section on the language of the tabloid press.

Even without highly descriptive nouns, adjectives may be pointless because they are tautological. There is no point in saying an *established* convention or an *earlier* precedent, because all conventions are established and all precedents are earlier. Similarly, one need not talk of a *convicted* criminal – the libel laws of our country make it clear that to describe someone as a criminal without his having been convicted as such is to invite a demand for substantial damages – or of a *pair* of twins, since twins always are. *Global pandemic* is another example, and a newspaper article recently talked of *live* vivisection. Nor is tautology confined to adjectives and nouns. The solecism *revert back* is a tautology because *back* is the only way one can *revert*. There are other examples, not least *advance forward*, *dive down* and *mount up*.

One adjectival usage to be deployed with care is that of interposing the indefinite article between adjective and noun. There are certain, limited idioms in which this is permissible. They are mostly rhetorical and will therefore be rare in formal writing. "How appalling an injury!" and other such exclamatory uses are one. "She had never seen so appalling an injury" and other comparative uses are another. It can also be evaluative, as in "that depends upon how big a piece you want". A use such as "I believe he had no different an experience from that of his friends" is ugly and unnecessary. The gravest offence of all with adjectives is to lard them with an adverb; many such usages have become clichés: *severely beaten*, *heavily veiled*, *viciously attacked* and *supremely confident* are all familiar from the columns of the poorer newspapers, and should be avoided by careful and sensitive writers. However, one should also be alert to usages that are not clichés but in which the adverb is rather more than is required. Sometimes these may be tautological (*badly damaged*, for example; it is hard to see how something can be *well* damaged, so if you wish to indicate a high degree of damage, use *very*).

Even if the phrase is not tautological, the adjective would do the job quite as well on its own ("a fully functioning car", for example – the adverb can be taken for granted in the adjective). It becomes apparent that just as nouns may be chosen with such precision that they require no adjective, so may verbs be chosen that require no adverb. If somebody *races* or *speeds* somewhere we hardly need be told that he did it *quickly* or *fast*; if somebody *gorges* on food or *binges* on drink we know already that he has consumed much of either commodity without needing a further expression of degree in an adverb such as *greedily* or *voraciously*; and so on.

A careful writer never forgets that the currency of potent words is devalued by overusing them.

Fewer repeats

One of the essentials of good style is a large vocabulary. This does not merely enable the writer to choose the word that exactly suits his purpose, it also gives him the discrimination to reject those that do not. There is a further use of a large vocabulary, and that is to help avoid **repetition**. A piece of writing that includes the same words or phrases over and over again is tedious to the reader. Words have a musical quality, even when not read aloud, and too many of the same note will jar. Repetition retards the process of communicating meaning and causes the reader to doubt the clarity of thought, and therefore intelligence, of the writer. In some writing it is impossible to avoid repeating certain words or phrases. A report may well require the frequent mention of a person's name. If that person has a job title, then his post may be varied with his name – "Mr Smith" or "the minister", for example. Personal pronouns may also be used, but this may lead to vagueness or confusion if the report is about more than one person of the same gender.

There is no excuse, however, for repeating nouns, adjectives, verbs or adverbs that have synonyms. It is also wise to be sparing with conjunctions. A phrase such as "he argued that it was important that politicians should remember that their policies had a widespread effect that was not always obvious" is just shocking and thoughtless. The sentence should be recast, perhaps as follows: "he argued the importance of politicians' remembering that their policies had a widespread, and not always obvious, effect". The surviving *that* is important for the avoidance of ambiguity. It is not their policies that the politicians should remember, but the effect they have.

There will be some phrases in any piece of writing where it is legitimate to repeat a phrase not merely for emphasis, but for clarity. Such a device is common in speech-making: remember Churchill's "we shall go on to the end, we shall fight in France, we shall fight on the seas and oceans, we shall fight with growing confidence and growing strength in the air, we shall defend our Island, whatever the cost may be, we shall fight on the beaches, we shall fight on the landing grounds, we shall fight in the fields and in the streets, we shall fight in the hills; we shall never surrender".[15] However, it also has its uses in normal prose-writing. Without repeating more than one word – the preposition *in* – Ruskin in this extract from *The Poetry of Architecture* repeats the form of a phrase but builds up a clear picture of an aspect of design that offends him: "…and the whole system becomes utterly and absolutely absurd, ugly in

15. Speech in the House of Commons, 4 June 1940.

outline, worse than useless in application, unmeaning in design, and incongruous in association".[16]

The most common form of repetition is of a substantive word, repeated for emphasis: "The satires are savage – perhaps satires should be; but Pope's satires are sometimes what satires should never be – shrill." This only just works, and one imagines that *satires* is repeated, and not replaced by a pronoun in a couple of instances, not for the avoidance of ambiguity, but to impress upon the reader that Pope's works under that name are not what the writer nor the reader understands by the term.[17] Sometimes, humour is advanced by repeating whole phrases, as in this extract from *Martin Chuzzlewit* by Dickens: "These injuries having been comforted externally, with patches of pickled brown paper, and Mr Pecksniff having been comforted internally, with some stiff brandy-and-water, the eldest Miss Pecksniff sat down to make the tea…."[18] As with any form of joke, joke by repetition can wear thin, so be sparing. The main stylistic argument against repetition is that it may be distracting to the reader. So too, however, may be the use of increasingly florid synonyms, so be thoughtful when using them.

A logical order of words

I have already dealt with this question at length in Chapter Four. I concentrated there on marshalling the order of words to convey the correct sense in a phrase or sentence, and stressed the care that must be taken with the positioning of adverbs. Here

16. *The Poetry of Architecture*, by John Ruskin (Routledge, 1907), pp105–106.
17. *Obiter Dicta*, by Augustine Birrell (Duckworth, 1910), p187.
18. *Martin Chuzzlewit*, by Charles Dickens (Chapman and Hall, Popular Edition, 1907), p11.

I am concerned not so much with sense as with what constitutes the best style – what it will be most pleasing for another to read, and what will make a piece of prose not just comprehensible, but most comprehensible. It is essential to put the words of any sentence into a logical order, to avoid ambiguity and also any charge of pretentiousness in diction: Keats might have been able to get away with "Much have I travelled in the realms of gold/ And many goodly states and kingdoms seen…" but those writing prose should not attempt such a word order unless they wish to become objects of curiosity. There is an archaic, or pretentious, ring these days to sentences with inverted word order. Conventionally, a sentence proceeds as follows: subject, verb, object. So we say "the boy ate the pie" and not "eating the pie was the boy" or "the boy the pie ate".

As can be seen from the last example, in our uninflected language there is scope for ambiguity when the word order is inverted. It could be that the pie ate the boy, but that is unlikely. In an inflected language such as Latin or Greek it would be obvious who was doing the eating, and what was eaten, because of different endings for nouns that are nominative and those that are accusative. English does not have that luxury except when certain pronouns are used. Some inversions of word order are more acceptable than others, and these are where the inversion helps provide an emphasis deemed necessary by the writer: such as "in my class at school were Smith, Jones and Brown" rather than "Smith, Jones and Brown were in my class at school". In that example, the writer has chosen to emphasise the common educational experience that he had with the three other men, rather than making the three other men the most important feature of his statement.

The Fowlers also illustrate the different principles of inversion in paratactic and syntactic clauses.[19] A paratactic clause, as

19. *The King's English*, p197.

I described in Chapter Two, is one that follows another without any connecting word that indicates the relation of the two clauses, or whether the second is co-ordinate with or subordinate to its predecessor. An example of parataxis is found in "his crimes were terrible: chief among them was the murder of Smith", compared with "his crimes were terrible, chief among which was the murder of Smith", the second part of the latter being a relative clause. The inverted word order of the paratactic clause is unnecessary: it could as easily read "the murder of Smith was chief among them". However, where there clearly is a subordinate clause, the relative pronoun needs to precede the subject for the sentence to make sense.

It is also common to invert word order in sentences featuring negation. For the sake of emphasis one might write "never had I been so insulted" rather than "I had never been so insulted". In some statements inversion is essential if they are to make sense: "by no measure can he be said to be the best batsman in their team" must be right, since "he can be said to be the best batsman in their team by no measure" sounds bizarre. The most frequent form of inversion is seen when asking questions: "would you help me?" is used as opposed to "you would help me".

The importance in other contexts of using the right word order can be seen in this example, from a contemporary news-paper article: "a shop assistant was stabbed to death 11 times at a store in Thurmaston, Leics". However, even altering the order of that sentence will not redeem it. It has to be rewritten as "a shop assistant at a store in Thurmaston, Leics, has died as a result of being stabbed 11 times". It was also announced that "wisps of hair from Charles Darwin's beard are to go on public display 200 years after he was born in a Natural History Museum exhibition". In that case, simply altering the order of words would have resolved a doubt about the great evolutionist's place of birth. It was also reported that a farmer had been out "shooting dead rabbits". This seems a pointless exercise, until one realises that he had in fact been shooting rabbits dead.

As mentioned earlier in this book, accurate use of punctuation may, as much as word order, help avoid ambiguity in a sentence. However, in some cases of ellipsis in sentences – the leaving out of words that, if included, might remove any hint of ambiguity, but which are left out for imagined reasons of elegance or felicity – punctuation is not enough. In a sentence such as "the boy ate the beefburger with relish" are we to suppose he ate it enthusiastically, or with the complement of some sauce? A comma after *beefburger* would lead most readers to suppose the former, but even that is not certain. Sentences such as that, where phrases may be either adjectival or adverbial, are better recast. "The boy ate the beefburger and relish" may mean only one thing; as may "with relish, the boy ate the beefburger".

The placement of adverbs in phrases with auxiliary verbs used to cause grammarians great debate and worry. Some held that one should no more split an auxiliary from its verb than one would split an infinitive. So one would always write "never had I seen such a sight" rather than "I had never seen such a sight" or "I never had seen such a sight". At this stage in the development of our language, the only remotely sane advice must be to do what appears most naturally idiomatic, and what best serves the purpose of the writer. It may be that in certain contexts to write "she had particularly wanted a diamond necklace" would be inadequately emphatic; and that the sense the writer wishes to convey would be better represented by "particularly, she had wanted a diamond necklace". This would make sense had this sentence been preceded by one or several that listed this woman's desires. The only rule in this matter is comprehensibility.

No showing off

Few things turn the stomach more when reading a passage of prose than detecting that the writer is showing off. Elaborate metaphors, flowery language, archaisms, the use of foreign tags where English phrases will serve the same purpose and be at once comprehensible, pretentious diction, coy little phrases – all of these, unless they are being used as part of some sustained parody or satire, prevent the reader from receiving a serious message (if there be one). Perhaps our most fundamental objection to such language is that it is unnatural: people simply do not speak like that in real life. When they write in that fashion, therefore, their readers find them lacking credibility.

The Fowlers, and 40 years after them Orwell, touched on this when they argued in favour of the Anglo-Saxon word rather than the Romance or classical. Some people feel they have to use a long word where a short one will do. We have all seen writers do this out of a sense of insecurity: they feel that by saying *masticate* rather than *chew* they are confirming a superior intellect or status. The odd long word never harmed anyone: but if one uses a string of them, or lards one's prose with them from beginning to end, one becomes tiresome – even if the words are all so well-known that the reader does not need to pause after each one and look it up in a dictionary. If a writer has to send his readers – and they are intelligent readers – to the dictionary more than very occasionally, then he has failed. The journey should be necessary only if the prose is dealing with a specialist subject, and one is reading it specifically with a view to being educated in that subject. If the topic is of everyday interest, there is no excuse for dragging out words that even sophisticates will have to look up, other than that the writer has decided to try to draw attention to himself.

Most plain monosyllables have polysyllables longing to step

into their shoes. Poor stylists cannot bear to use verbs such as *walk, try, wash, eat, tell, say, ask, see, use, start* or *show* when they may (at no extra cost except to their credibility) use *perambulate, essay, ablute, consume, communicate, demand, perceive, utilise, commence* or *demonstrate*. It is useful to have a store of synonyms to avoid repeating words within a few sentences of each other; but if there is no risk of repetition, stick to simple words. Some elaborate usages can also be confusing. If one hears a man say to his wife "I understand you are ill", is he telling her that he comprehends the nature of her predicament, or is he simply using the long word as a substitute for *hear*? It is probably the latter, but other instances of the use of the verb may be more deeply ambiguous.

It can never be right to use a long word where there is a perfectly legitimate short one crying out to be used instead. Take this example, from *The Sunday Times* of 27 December 2009, quoting Ed Balls, the Children's Secretary: "One of the big signifiers of whether children do well is if there are strong adult relationships in the home." Why did Mr Balls feel he had to say *signifier* when he could more easily have said *sign*? Is there a difference between a sign and signifier, other than that the latter is a typically pompous word used unnecessarily by bureaucrats and politicians?

Show-offs also like foreign words, phrases or abbreviations. Even if used correctly, these alienate readers who do not have these rarities at their command. It is important for writers to know their audiences. The same applies to allusion. If one is alluding to books, events or people in one's writing, one risks confining understanding of one's meaning to those who have read the same books, experienced the same events or know the same people. Sometimes allusion is valuable and illuminating, but it may have to be explained. A balance must be struck, for if an allusion requires such explanation that outweighs the insight it conveys, then it is not worth alluding. If one is confining allusion to quotation, be sure to quote accurately and that the quotation means what you think it means. Milton did not, for example, write in *Lycidas* about "fresh fields and pastures new", nor Shakespeare that "all that glistens is not gold": though many subsequently have. "The exception that proves the rule" does not mean what most who use it think it means. It means a rule is only proved to be so by leaving out or ignoring something that might normally be held to be subject to it – that is what *exception* means in this case.

There are other dangers to the writer of showing off, notably using a word to mean something it does not, or using a phrase wrongly. Many examples of the former are given in Chapter Five. An egregious example of the latter is the phrase *begging the question*. Most people who use this term seem to think it means "inviting the question". It does nothing of the sort. Fowler gives a summary of the problem that cannot be bettered: he defines it as "the fallacy of founding a conclusion on a basis that as much needs to be proved as the conclusion itself".[20] So if one were to say "it is good to smoke because tobacco has health-giving properties", that would beg the question about the health-giving properties of tobacco. However, if one were to say in response to an assertion by another that all French men are philanderers that it "begged the question about the philandering of French men" it would in fact do nothing of the sort, since no other conclusion is being based on that questionable statement.

Certain spellings are now archaic, but so easily lapsed into that one should not condemn as show-offs those who use them. *Amongst* and *whilst* are relatively harmless. *The Times* used the spelling *connexion* until the 1980s, but that really has had its day.

---

20. *A Dictionary of Modern English Usage*, p614.

Evening, all!

It is perhaps unfair of me to use the catchphrase of Dixon of Dock Green to illustrate the vice of **prolixity**, as it is not peculiar solely to policemen. Almost anyone working in the public sector can easily catch the disease – that is, after all, why Sir Ernest Gowers wrote *The Complete Plain Words* – and the contagion spreads easily to the private sector. We have all seen its manifestations when receiving pompous communications from tradesmen or other parts of our service industries. The police, however, used to be considered the finest practitioners of verbosity. One assumes this was a tactic to make their officers seem impressive in court in the eyes of easily-intimidated jurors – no barrister or judge worth his salt would ever use such language. Why should an officer have been "proceeding in an easterly direction when I happened upon" the accused when he could as easily, and less long-windedly, have been "walking eastwards when I saw" him?

Another trait of pompous authority figures is to use the double negative: we had, in living memory, a prime minister who used phrases such as *not inconsiderably* with a frequency that increased as his credibility sank. It is also their habit, noted by Amis, to insert the redundant words *as to* before almost any question: here, too, we hear the voice of the policeman. "We want to know as to why you were in the vicinity on the evening in question" and "perhaps you could tell me as to whether you might be able to tell us your whereabouts last Tuesday night" give the flavour of the problem.

To compound its already numerous sins, the language of bureaucracy has a vocabulary that remains floating in the inkwell of a clerk in Edwardian England. Nowhere else would you hear such gems as "beyond peradventure", "whence he came", "in the event that" or "had the occasion to". These and others like them remain the stock phrases of the robotic bureaucrat who cannot bear – or considers himself paid insufficiently – to think about what he is writing and to communicate in plain English. At least certain phrases ("beyond peradventure", for example) do seem to have died, but others remain and, for so long as they do, are a gruesome temptation to the verbally weak-minded. Do not use a phrase where a word will do. Also, do not use an archaic phrase unless you wish your readers to laugh at you.

Mind your idioms

The dictionary defines an idiom as "the form of speech peculiar or proper to a people or country". It is, literally, the way we speak our language. Where in Chapter Five I described the differences between American English and the way English is spoken in the British Isles I was in essence referring to the two different idioms of the same language. That is what the word means in its broadest sense.

Yet there is a more specific sense, given as a subsidiary meaning in the dictionary as "a form of expression, grammatical construction, phrase, etc, peculiar to a language". Those who have learned a foreign tongue will know that these special phrases, or idioms, have to be learned separately, not least because if translated literally they fail to convey their exact meaning. For example: the French phrase *le petit coin* literally means "the little corner". This takes us only part of the way to its idiomatic meaning, the lavatory. A Frenchman, similarly, translating into his own language an English idiom such as *getting his leg over* or *kicking the bucket* would perhaps struggle to realise that the first meant sexual intercourse (usually with an overtone of illicitness) and the second meant dying. Idioms may be peculiar to a section of society and not easily understood by those not of that milieu, even if they technically speak the same language: *not safe in taxis* was a phrase once peculiar to the world of debutantes but eventually spread, perhaps as the taxi-taking classes expanded, to describe to anyone a man who could not be relied upon to keep his hands to himself when alone with a woman. Idioms are also generational; younger people may not know that *going deolali* (anglicised now, according to the dictionary, as *doolally*) was Indian Army slang for becoming insane, after the name of the town in India whose military hospital housed those of unsound mind until they could be sent back to *Blighty*; or that someone who is only *fifteen annas to the rupee* or *elevenpence ha'penny to the shilling* is *a couple of sandwiches short of a picnic*.

Idiomatic language is common in speech and in dialogue in novels and dramas. It should have little place, except for overtly comic effect, in the writing of serious non-fiction. As one can gather from *kicking the bucket* and *getting his leg over* many (but by no means all) idioms are slang and all except the rare, newly-minted ones are clichés. Since good style tries to avoid both vices, idioms are best reserved for the most informal speech or intimate communications, unless one is writing fiction. Like the use of any cliché, their use tends to suggest a paucity of thought by the writer.

In writing dialogue it is idiomatic to use the standard contractions of certain phrases such as *it's, can't, won't* and so on. It is a matter of taste and judgement about whether to use these in formal writing. Just one use of a contraction in, for example, a newspaper article can change its entire tone of voice from the formal to the casual. It is up to the writer to decide what effect he is seeking to achieve. In formal writing generally there should be no use of contractions. If suddenly one is used the writer should be conscious of the impact it will have on the reader, for whom it will come in the nature of a gear change.

Idiom is also a term used to describe the state of the language: it refers to what is accepted by convention rather than by strict grammatical rules. For example: the use of conjunctions in certain contexts has become a question of idiom. The Fowlers in 1906 saw it was happening, and the contagion has spread far since then. "Quite legitimate, but often unpleasant" was how they characterised it.[21] The examples they gave were "I presume you know" and "I assume you know", in both of which they would have liked to see a *that* before *you*. However, as I have observed elsewhere, a cluttering of *that*s may become tiresome and verbose. Conjunctions only really need be used where there is scope for ambiguity and confusion if they are not. "He drove the car he had hired earlier" makes perfect sense and requires no conjunction after *car*. "I knew he saw she understood" needs a conjunction somewhere to break up the staccato verbs and avoid any confusion: best after *saw*.

Keep metaphors fresh

The dictionary defines a metaphor as "a figure of speech in which a name or descriptive word or phrase is transferred to an object different from, but analogous to, that to which it is literally applicable". We may lapse into metaphor without realising it in our everyday speech. It is, essentially, an extended simile – which the dictionary defines as "a comparison of one thing with another, especially as an ornament in poetry or rhetoric". "My love is like a red, red rose" is a simile. "Shall I compare thee to a summer's day?" opens a sonnet that is a metaphor, and a detailed one at that. Metaphor has its place in the writing of non-fiction, journalism and even letters. The device is perhaps used most effectively, and frequently, by writers of fiction. Writers or speakers using metaphor require great mental agility. They must conceive, first, the idea that they wish to communicate, but then find a non-literal

21. *The King's English*, p367.

means of doing so. However, if the metaphor is to be successful it has to be original and logical. There is nothing wrong with using such figures of speech that fulfil this requirement.

Indeed, as the Fowlers pointed out in 1906, metaphor is the inevitable development of a language that contains only a primitive vocabulary to start with, but must find more sophisticated means of describing more profound concepts. They also pointed out how many words used in English commonly to describe everyday things began as metaphors: the example they give is the verb *explain*, which originally meant "to lay out flat".[22] I am not concerned with such etymological history here, fascinating though it be: my purpose in this section is to discuss metaphors that are not so established, and which are used self-consciously rather than unconsciously. As such, this section deals with metaphors that we mint, or think that we mint, ourselves rather than those that only the etymologist would recognise as having begun their lives as metaphors, but are now part of our everyday vocabulary. The Fowlers discriminated between "living" and "dead" metaphors in this way, the living ones being the fresh, obvious and active ones that we use consciously. Perhaps we need to be alert to a third division, which I would term "decaying".

Users of metaphor must beware of two dangers in particular. One is cliché. The other is the mixed metaphor. A **clichéd metaphor** is one that is decaying. It takes on the status of an old joke. It will usually be a phrase, not a word that once meant something concrete but has, through the acceptance of the validity of the metaphor, comes to mean something abstract. An example of a clichéd metaphor would be "several ministers have resigned: the rats are leaving the sinking ship". We all know that phrase. We know it so well that it is almost meaningless. If the writer seeks to convey a startling insight by its use he fails, because we have

22. *The King's English*, p210.

an automatic rather than fresh response to a form of words that seems to have been generated automatically, and is far from fresh itself. That is why I would presume to call it "decaying": it may never die, though.

Some words seem incapable of being uttered in contemporary English without a clichéd label being attached to them. One rarely hears of *wit* being anything other than *razor sharp*. People or traits are seldom described as English (unless for reasons of identification) unless they are *quintessentially* so. (*Quintessentially* is a metaphor, *quintessence* being a term from classical and mediaeval philosophy: "a fifth essence existing in addition to the four elements, supposed to be the substance of which the celestial bodies were composed and to be latent in all things".)

An example of a **mixed metaphor** (and, indeed, of the clichéd too) would be "after the death of his wife Smith was holed below the waterline, and feared that his goose would be cooked". In one sentence we move from the sea to the farmyard to the kitchen. We have to add confusion to our boredom. There is a danger of mixing our metaphors when we confuse the dead with the living: a dead metaphor has become a colourless abstract word and therefore is not susceptible to being mixed. Live or decaying ones retain too much of their original, concrete meaning and therefore are susceptible. People in officialdom, in their quest to try to be interesting to the general public without necessarily being informative, seem especially prone to the dodgy metaphor. During the bad winter of 2010 a Mr Grommet from the Meteorological Office was reported by *The Daily Telegraph* as having said: "We are in a situation where some of the advisories did not get picked up and were not presented strongly enough. In these circumstances we need to sit around a table and look at the thresholds to see if they should be made more flexible." Such a statement is not necessarily comprehensible even to those with a degree in physics.

The best fiction writers use metaphor sparingly, so that when they do use it it has an effect. Graham Greene, in *Brighton Rock*, wrote of the villain Pinkie encountering a group of blind people: "The Boy met the leader and pushed him out of the way, swearing at him softly, and the whole band hearing their leader move shifted uneasily a foot into the roadway and stood there stranded till the Boy was safely by, like barques becalmed on a huge and landless Atlantic. Then they edged back feeling for the landfall of the pavement."[23] By choosing that particular metaphor Greene is able to convey a sense of dangerous, perhaps even lethal, isolation: the elemental terror offered by the sea evokes the physical terror offered by Pinkie. However, because Greene's metaphors are as rare as islands in that ocean, they impress the reader and are packed with meaning.

Extensive use of metaphor in fiction or poetry is outmoded today. It irritates readers and causes them to think ill of the writer. Modern readers have a better sense of what it is for work to be over-written than was the case in the 19th century, or before. The plainness of most journalism – and journalism is much of what most people read today – has cleansed the palate and made the high-flown figure of speech seem laboured, pretentious and unnecessary. Should it occur other than sparingly in the writing of non-fiction it begins to look forced and becomes a distraction.

Understood in the setting of its time, however, it can still give pleasure to the reader; and some of the writers who use metaphor the most are valued highly because they use it so well. The opening of Book II of Milton's *Paradise Lost*, which we have already encountered in Chapter Four, proves the point:

> High on a throne of royal state, which far
> Outshone the wealth of Ormus and of Ind,
> Or where the gorgeous East with richest hand

23. *Brighton Rock*, by Graham Greene, (Heinemann, 1938), pp 185–6.

Showers on her kings barbaric pearl and gold,
Satan exalted sat, by merit raised
To that bad eminence.[24]

In some contexts – writing a business letter, a story for the news pages of a newspaper, or an official document – metaphor is out of place. Its use can only be rare, and in consequence its effect startling – provided it is freshly-minted. In other non-fictional contexts it can be used more freely – in letters designed to entertain and amuse or convey great emotion, in feature-writing, in documents or speeches that are designed to be arresting and persuasive. Look at the language of Churchill's great speeches from 1940, particularly these phrases from his "finest hour" speech after the Fall of France, to see metaphor used in its most powerful sense:

Hitler knows that he will have to break us in this island or lose the war. If we can stand up to him, all Europe may be free and the life of the world may move forward into broad, sunlit uplands. But if we fail, then the whole world, including the United States, including all that we have known and cared for, will sink into the abyss of a new dark age made more sinister, and perhaps more protracted, by the lights of perverted science.

He sustains the metaphor over two sentences. The first thought is light; the second darkness. At the end of a speech that had been mainly about matters of fact – and miserable fact at that – and a review of the terrible plight that Britain, alone, now faced, the use of a sonorous metaphor such as this was, and remains on the page 70 years later, exceptionally potent.

As ever in writing, logic remains important and the writer should not offend against it. Metaphorical nouns should always

24. *Paradise Lost*, Book II, lines 1–6, in *Poetical Works*, p232.

be allied with appropriate verbs. Take the noun *morass*, which still means a stretch of swampy ground. Its first metaphorical use, as a situation from which it is difficult to extricate oneself, dates from 1867, according to the dictionary. Because both the concrete and the abstract senses are current and familiar, care must be taken: the abstract must obey the logic of the concrete. During the financial crisis of 2008–09 pundits would often describe the problem of overwhelming public debt as having created a *morass*: it seemed a fair use of the term. However, what does one do with a morass? One can deal with it – by devising a plan of how to extricate oneself, if one has lacked the forethought to avoid entering it in the first place. One can, obviously, extricate oneself or, failing that, sink more deeply in. One can drown in it. One can slide in, and one can stagger out. However, one cannot grasp a morass. It seems geologically unlikely that one could clean it up either: if cleaning up is required, then *morass* had better be replaced by *mess*. One probably does not climb out, but is pulled out, or wades out. There will have to be similar restrictions of the use of certain verbs as applied to any nouns with similar properties: if your metaphor has a concrete use, be guided by it when you decide to use it in the abstract.

A persuasive tone

Directness in writing aids communication. However, there is a separate language of persuasion that has a tone different from that of the language of command; and it uses the subjunctive mood rather than the indicative. Instead of issuing orders such as "will you come here" one tries to obviate confrontation or resistance by writing, instead, "would you come here?" The use of this conditional tone suggests that the person at whom it is directed has a choice. Psychology dictates that such people are often more easily biddable than those backed into a corner. Other such gradations of tone are found in questions such as "shouldn't you drink less brandy in the evenings?", a more tactful version of "oughtn't you to drink less brandy?", and "could you find the money?" for "can you find the money?" Similarly, "you might like to take your muddy boots off" is a more polite way of saying "will you take your muddy boots off, please".

Tone is the obsession of the modern propaganda industry that seeks to influence how all of us feel about certain questions – be they political ones or those to do with advancing the reputation or visibility of a brand of car, a supermarket or a detergent. Orwell was here first, as his earlier sympathy for socialism was modified by his understanding of the totalitarian evil of communism. That was why he made the point about the political roots of verbosity, and the desire to dress up unpleasant concepts by avoiding a direct statement of them. Orwell argued that thinking more clearly is the key to political regeneration. It is certainly the key to not being taken in by the rubbish often written by others. It will warn writers against use of the passive voice – which, as Orwell hinted, people use to distance themselves from their acts.

Also under the heading of tone comes the question of **understatement**. It used to be one of the facets of the British national character that the strongest adjective of disapproval was *shocking*, and that for someone to say he was *unhappy* was a sign of perilous unease. In modern times, thanks partly to the sensationalism of some of the mass media and to the histrionics of both indigenous and imported television dramas, no point is considered adequately made unless it has been beaten home with adjectives, adverbs and prolixity. The overuse of *very* is another one of these sins, though one that applies more widely than just in expressions of obloquy, and helps writers and speakers surrender a sense of proportion in handling all manner of subjects. Such a tone is not the mark of a good communicator, who will convey disdain or disapproval with understatement and subtlety rather than by shouting and screaming.

Thank you, and goodnight

If one reads any of the 20th century works on good usage one always finds a section on **vogue words**: references to words that, at the time of writing, were much in fashion and being overused; or words whose legitimate meaning or usage was being abused at the time. The overused words of this age tend to have short lives, though some become distressingly persistent: an example is the use of the verb *to address*, which used to be restricted to the action of writing a destination on an envelope or talking to a public meeting, and is now used to describe someone giving his attention to almost anything. Such words tend to be imported to the minds of their users by the mass media. Since the mass media pursue novelty, the next wave of vogue words usually comes along before the old one has reached the shore. Nor is it only the media's exploitation of popular culture that brings these words into fashion. All-day news channels (or, to use the vogue term, *rolling news*) latch on to popular terms and exhaust them.

In Britain in the last decade or so we have heard time and again of *the target culture, best practice, prioritisation, vibrant communities, programmes* that are *rolled out* for the benefits of *stakeholders*, among other terms used by the propaganda arm of government. These terms are designed to convey an impression of action, purpose and (to use two other popular nouns) *inclusiveness* and *diversity*; but they soon wear out and intelligent people come to regard them with boredom or contempt. In response to the official propaganda the tribunes of the people in the press produce their own vogue terms: *feral children, hug-a-hoodie, the client state* and so on. It has also become popular for writers and officials alike to stop speaking of doing things in the future, and instead to plan to do them *going forward*. They are also agreed that any institution or service that has to be held to account or up for scrutiny must be shown whether or not it is *fit for purpose*. Almost everything a politician has to do is a *challenge* and it is *critical* that he or she should be able to *deliver* on it. No wonder people have such a poor estimate of politicians.

Not all such terms pass their sell-by date quickly. Richard Nixon was brought down in the Watergate scandal in 1974. Ever since, any scandal of almost any description seems to be denominated by having the suffix *-gate* applied to it. In the months while this book was being written a dispute over the use of scientific data in the global warming debate was called *climategate*, and the falsification of an injury in professional rugby became *bloodgate*. This usage ceased to be funny, let alone interesting, not long after it was first coined. Nor is this the only suffix to be so abused. The vogue for contests of endurance – be it dancing, reading aloud from Shakespeare or sitting in a bath full of baked beans – has led to an epidemic of nouns ending in *-athon* – such as *bikeathon*, *swimathon* and the ubiquitous *telethon*. Also, the coinage of *workaholic*, which borrowed from the addictive attributes of *alcoholic* and which the dictionary notes having started in America in 1968, then led to *chocoholic* or *chocaholic* (America, 1972), *shopaholic* (America, 1984), *sexaholic* (not yet in the dictionary), even *exercisaholic*, among other ludicrous neologisms. The rule is simple: if you spot a new coinage of any other sort, regard the joke as already over, and move on.

It is not only words, but also phrases, that offer themselves up for exhaustion. A popular film called *To Die For*, released in 1995, caused the phrase to become the (almost immediately tiresome) term of superlative approbation among a certain sort of people for some years. Many of us have been told that a friend has eaten a lobster cocktail *to die for*, or seen a set of watercolours of similarly lethal effect, and had to clench parts of our anatomy. It is a matter of taste whether the term *achingly* as in *achingly modern* or *achingly chic* is even more sickening.

These popular phrases vie with one another for the prize in idiocy. One well ahead of most of the field is exemplified in the phrase "he finished ahead of the next horse by a country mile". No authority that I can find specifies that the mile is any different in length in rural parts from what it is in urban ones. Presumably those who use this ludicrous term imagine they are being clever or funny, or possibly both. Their audience knows better. Only marginally less offensive is a phrase weather forecasters use to impart some sense of homeliness and affection to their work when they have to describe some unpleasant aspect of the climate: that we are going to have "a wet old day", "a strong old wind", "a cold old night" or a "foggy old morning". The absurdity of this term requires no amplification beyond its very expression.

It is easy for the intelligent, thoughtful writer to avoid such lapses. Yet one needs when writing to weigh every word, so that the less obvious, but still irritating, words and clichés are omitted too.

I have dealt with political correctness and its effect on language in detail in Chapter Six, but one word that has become one of the foremost weapons of the movement is *appropriate*. Its antonym, *inappropriate*, is if anything used with even more severity. Political correctness is about prescription and proscription, and its puritanical considerations are regularly applied with the threat that an act or a form of words is *inappropriate*, or a deviation from *appropriate* behaviour. This usage is part vogue word, part sinister euphemism. It euphemises not so much the act under criticism as the action of the critic. A man who steals a kiss from a female colleague at the office Christmas party will find himself condemned for *inappropriate* conduct. It is deemed not to be *appropriate* for a public figure to make irate remarks about the Welsh, for example. We are seldom given a standard, however, against which ideals of appropriateness can be measured.

No shock horror

No-one, least of all a journalist, can discount the effect of the tabloid press (and its televisual equivalent) on the language. It is the fuel that feeds the vice of exaggeration that I have referred to above in the section on tone. There are certain words and phrases that are staples of tabloid journalism, an honourable trade whose customers require its products to be not merely direct and comprehensible – so should all journalism be – but to speak their language. Those of us who are not employed by the tabloid press, and who do not have to abide by the formulas that cause it to be profitable, have a choice in this matter. We can use its language, and have our thoughts interpreted as being rooted in the same clichéd and apparently superficial ground from which tabloidism grows, or we can choose to avoid the formulaic and the sensational in our own speech and writing and seek to convey a more measured and original voice.

The language of tabloid exaggeration is apparent on every page of what the trade calls the "red-top" newspapers. Prices *soar*, and then they *crash*. In politics, *rows* about *issues* are always *erupting*, and they are inevitably *furious*. The *key* participants in them *clash*, and they evince *rage*. The consequence of an *outrage* is that there will be a *probe*, leading up to a *damning report*. Its *shock findings* will be followed by a *clampdown* (or a *crackdown*). The opponents of the transgressors will *slam* their behaviour and seek to *topple* them.

Any death, especially of a *teen*, is a *tragedy*, and if more than one person dies it is a *catastrophe*. It leaves grieving *loved ones gutted*. Should the victim be a young girl, she was *bubbly*, especially if blonde. Young men, unless proven criminals, had in their lives had *huge respect* from their *mates*.

On the sports pages, managers of soccer teams *vow* that their sides will do better, knowing they risk being *axed* if they do not.

Should a team suddenly become *brilliant* it will be because a *star* player has shown he is a *hero*, and can expect a *hike* in his wages. He may then *launch* a new career as a fashion *icon*. Should the team *crash* to defeat in a cup final, all its *fans* would be *devastated*.

Celebs will usually have *amazing lifestyles* that are *revealed* by the tabloid press as a series of *stunning events*. These will often be *fuelled* by champagne and sometimes by drugs. They entail living in a million-pound *home*, but also possibly sharing a *love nest* with a *stunner* and, as the paper will *reveal*, a *love child* as a result of extensive *cheating* on a spouse. The wronged woman (for it usually is a woman) will be *brave* during her *ordeal*: until it *emerges* that she has had a *toyboy* too, with whom there have been nights of *nookie*. This tale may well also be a *nightmare* for those concerned where they endure a *frenzy* and possibly even a media *hell*. Women in such stories never wear dresses during their *glamorous* nights out, only *gowns*. And *gowns*, like *mansions* or *homes*, come with an obligatory adjectival price-tag, usually the product of guesswork rather than of research, and often therefore "a £1,000 gown". Anyone in public life who is in trouble – a judge, an MP or an Army officer – is usually *top* (or, in more thoughtful articles, *senior*) and his predicament is one of *shame* that leaves him *disgraced*.

Anyone who has been educated at a public school is a *toff*. He lives in a *mansion* (as may some grammar-school or comprehensive-school types who have become *fat cats*, particularly if they also own a *Roller* and the women of the family go *horse riding*). Such pursuits are *posh*, and none is *posher* than a *blood sport*. Sometimes such people have made their *dosh* thanks to a *scam*. They are also often members of *exclusive* clubs.

Some of the italicised words are pure slang and have no place in respectable writing – *celebs, nookie, posh, dosh* and *scam*, for example. Others come under the heading of coy or vulgar euphemism – *toyboy, love child, love nest, cheating* and *stunner* are what might more directly be called *gigolo, illegitimate child, flat, committing adultery* and *mistress*. Some are simply failures of terminology: those who ride horses go *riding*, not *horse riding*; and those who shoot or hunt practise *field sports*. *Blood sports* is a politically-loaded term popularised by opponents of field sports, and often used unwittingly by newspapers that have no editorial objection to them.

The main objection to most of the tabloid language highlighted above is that it devalues the currency. If somebody is *devastated* because his football team has lost a match, how does he feel when he gets home and finds his wife and children have been killed in a fire? If a woman is *brave* because of her reaction to the way in which her philandering husband embarrasses her publicly, how are we to describe her if she endures with courage and fortitude a horrible and potentially fatal illness? How can the ordeal of one experience compare with that of the other? If one death, however sad for those concerned, is a *tragedy*, how does one describe the moral effect of a plane crash in which 400 people are killed? If a man who scores a goal is a *hero*, what term do we reserve to describe one who wins the Victoria Cross? If an MP suffers *shame* because he claims for a food-mixer improperly on his expenses, what does he suffer if he is convicted of a criminal offence? If he is *disgraced* for being found in bed with someone else's wife, what adjective do we use of him if he is found to have perpetrated a systematic fraud, or is convicted of paedophilia? Above all, if unexceptional facts (often supplied to the newspaper by a celebrity's public relations adviser) are described as having been *revealed* when, in fact, all they have been is *disclosed*, what verb is to be used for something that is a genuine revelation?

Other words have become clichés and are therefore meaningless. Little weight is carried now by the metaphorical use of verbs such as *soar, crash, launch, emerge, fuel* and *clash*. Nouns like *toff, fat cat, clampdown* and *icon* are just lazy labels for people or for abstract activities; so too are phrases such as *damning report* and *shock finding*. *Respect* (huge or otherwise) in this context is an absurdity. It has become a word used in urban argot to describe not a feeling of reverence by one for another, but what a self-regarding person who has watched too many gangster films imagines is the estimation in which he should be held by others.

Brilliant is an adjective that should now only be used to describe a bright light: some newspapers apply it to so many columnists, series, special offers or free gifts that it is remarkable that their readers have not been blinded. I have given warning throughout this book of the dangers of promiscuity with adjectives. Their usage reaches its nadir in tabloidism, as *top, senior, furious* and *amazing* all show. People who buy the sort of newspapers in which this language is routine do so with certain expectations. People who read publications with a reputation for being more measured have expectations too, but they are likely to be different. Such readers are bemused, or may even feel insulted or patronised, when the writing they read is laced with sensationalism. It is a cheap effect easily obtained by what for a tabloid writer is likely to be a deliberate choice of language, but which for any other writer may be like a disease picked up by an unfortunate chance. It is therefore well to take precautions.

It is not only words that become clichéd in journalistic overuse; it is also formulas and constructions when they are overused in writing. One of these is the habit – reviled by Fowler in the early 20th century but still current today – of a writer's attempting to be interesting by giving much information about a subject before disclosing who the subject is. A news story in a tabloid newspaper in January 2010 began: "Eyes bulging with fury, cheeks purple and moustache bristling, the sergeant major draws himself to his full height...." In formal writing it is better to declare whom or what one is writing about before engaging in a detailed description of the subject. The sensation it creates is cheap and can mislead the reader. It is akin to the effect, itself rarely welcome, of using a pronoun in a sentence before its technical antecedent. Unless one is performing in the more routine parts of the tabloid press, or self-consciously writing parody, this sort of thing is to be avoided.

Time for a laugh

In any piece of writing, a moment of humour is as the proverbial ray of sunlight: if it is original and subtle, that is. Fashions in humour change rapidly. The Fowlers found it necessary in 1906 to lecture their readers about the dangers of "polysyllabic humour" (writing *olfactory organ* rather than *nose* was manifestly a side-splitter in late Victorian England), of "playful repetition" (using the same phrase several times) and what they call "the well-worn 'flood-of-tears-and-sedan-chair' pleasantry". This last example is from Chapter 35 of *The Pickwick Papers* ("Miss Bolo rose from the table considerably agitated, and went straight home, in a flood of tears, and a sedan chair"). Most would regard it as zeugma, or where the same verb is used with two disparate objects: a contemporary example would be "he drove a BMW, and his wife mad". However, more precise rhetoricians would call it syllepsis, because the nature of the verb has to change according to the nouns: one is literal (the sedan chair) and the other figurative (the flood of tears). The Fowlers also objected to "worn-out phrases of humorous tendency" of the sort one repeatedly encounters today in certain writers: such as when describing drunks as men "who have dined not wisely but too well".

Much humour today seems based on the random use of profanities, which leaves the person writing for a sensitive audience somewhat at a loss. However, the pursuit of the original moment of humour is valuable, for its success, if achieved, is a rare prize. There are few things at which the British excel today, but leavening prose with the occasional joke is one of them. American newspapers are going out of business far more quickly than

English ones, and the unremitting earnestness of the writing of most American journalists may be one of the reasons. When one stops reading a newspaper for news – because that is all available on the internet or on television – one can, in Britain at least, read it for entertainment and even, now and again, for the experience of fine writing. This is not usually the case in America.

I have occasionally touched upon the value of understatement in writing, notably in making my case for the sparing use of adjectives. It is also invaluable in humour, since the best jokes are often those whose full meaning may occur to the reader only several paragraphs after he has first encountered them. Another device is use of the unexpected, the paradoxical and the simply ironic. In perhaps the most darkly amusing novel of the 19th century, *The Way of All Flesh*, Butler has Alethea think: "He likes the best music…and he hates Dr Skinner. This is a very fair beginning."[25] Should anyone seek practical instruction in the subtle but extended use of irony, Butler's novel provides it and repays careful attention by both educating and entertaining its reader.

And finally…

If you have managed to absorb the contents of this book you will have grasped the essential points of what is required to communicate well and to create a good style: accurate and logical grammar, precise choice of words and concise and original expression. Not everything one writes needs to be couched within the formal structure of an argument, as I describe in the next chapter. However, everything should logically have a beginning, a middle and an end. The hardest part is then finding something original to say – with a beginning, a middle and an end.

25. *The Way of All Flesh*, p164.

Nothing helps hone a good style more than practice; and, apart from practice, nothing helps hone a good style more than reading those who have mastered it themselves. Some of the writers I have cited in this book – Orwell, Huxley, Greene, Butler and Dickens, for example – are perfect in this regard. Such writers hardly ever use a redundant word, or the wrong word. Most of our quality newspapers and periodicals are well-written. Contemporary fiction and non-fiction are less predictable in their precision of expression. If those who wish to write better become critical readers then their own writing will improve, because they will be more alert to the potential pitfalls. The best way to write better is to write more, but in this spirit of self-criticism. The goal of writing well is, as a result, one that cannot possibly become boring.

CHAPTER NINE

Three saints

As some readers may have gathered, I have reached my own conclusion about the finest writer of English prose: George Orwell.
He seems to have had an instinctive ability to communicate, condi-
tioned by extensive reading and refined by prolific practice. Orwell
was the best sort of journalist: he wrote for an educated audience
to whom he made no concessions. He invited their respect not
merely by the originality of his subject matter and the penetra-
tion of his insights, but through the courtesy he did his readers of
making himself clear. It is an almost impossible task to choose one
extract of Orwell's to exemplify his ability with the language. After
much deliberation, here is part of the celebrated (and scandalising)
account of his prep school days, *Such, Such were the Joys*:

> Love, the spontaneous, unqualified emotion of love, was some-
> thing I could only feel for people who were young. Towards people
> who were old – and remember that "old" to a child means over
> thirty, or even over twenty-five – I could feel reverence, respect,
> admiration or compunction, but I seemed cut off from them by
> a veil of fear and shyness mixed up with physical distaste. People
> are too ready to forget the child's physical shrinking from the
> adult. The enormous size of grownups, their ungainly, rigid bod-
> ies, their coarse wrinkled skins, their great relaxed eyelids, their
> yellow teeth, and the whiffs of musty clothes and beer and sweat
> and tobacco that disengage from them at every movement! Part
> of the reason for the ugliness of adults, in a child's eyes, is that the

child is usually looking upwards, and few faces are at their best when seen from below. Besides, being fresh and unmarked itself, the child has impossibly high standards in the matter of skin and teeth and complexion. But the greatest barrier of all is the child's misconception about age. A child can hardly envisage life beyond thirty, and in judging people's ages it will make fantastic mistakes. It will think that a person of twenty-five is forty, that a person of forty is sixty-five, and so on. Thus, when I fell in love with Elsie I took her to be grown up. I met her again, when I was thirteen and she, I think, must have been twenty-three; she now seemed to me a middle-aged woman, somewhat past her best. And the child thinks of growing old as an almost obscene calamity, which for some mysterious reason will never happen to itself. All who have passed the age of thirty are joyless grotesques, endlessly fussing about things of no importance and staying alive without, so far as the child can see, having anything to live for. Only child life is real life. The schoolmaster who imagines he is loved and trusted by his boys is in fact mimicked and laughed at behind his back. An adult who does not seem dangerous nearly always seems ridiculous.[1]

What strikes one at once about this writing is its astonishing clarity. It is grammatically perfect. Its syntax is smooth and regular. Its vocabulary is simple. Its adjectives are mainly objective rather than subjective. Above all, its sentences are short. All these factors help mitigate what many would consider the weakness of the structure, the exceptionally long paragraph. Orwell has one idea in this extract – half of a very long paragraph. It comes near the end of his long essay, and he is trying to convey the essentials of the child's attitude towards authority as embodied in the person of the adult. He saw no reason to divide the argument up into

1. *Such, Such were the Joys*, in *George Orwell* (Secker & Warburg/Octopus, 1980), pp828–9.

shorter paragraphs. He could have done so easily had he wished, and it was a matter of taste that he did not. A matter of taste, that is, except in one particular: the momentum caused by his short sentences within the paragraph drives the reader on, and any break within the paragraph to divide it into smaller ones would be an interruption to the flow at this important point. There is a sound reason for what he has done, and it is to do with his reaching the culmination of his argument after a long piece of writing that is mainly descriptive.

Terseness of the sort that characterises the tone of this passage is the only suitable vehicle for the apophthegm, and the example of this that ends the extract is the perfect climax to the passage and a seal on the argument he is making. As well as having clarity, it has momentum: that is the effect, principally, of the rhythm obtained by the frequency of short, simple words. Anyone who wishes to improve his ability to write English should, beyond a manual such as this, read as much Orwell as he can. It is the epitome of educated modern English style.

The post-war period in English fiction has produced some superb prose writers. One of the more underestimated – though her fame has risen in the years since her death – is Barbara Pym. This is from *No Fond Return of Love*:

> "I'm Dulcie Mainwaring," said the fair-haired woman. "My room seems to be next to yours. I wondered if we might go down to dinner together?"
>
> "If you like," said Viola rather ungraciously. "My name's Viola Dace, by the way. What does one do and wear?"
>
> "I suppose nobody really knows," said Dulcie. "It might be like the first night on board ship when nobody changes for dinner. I believe it's the first time a conference of this sort has been held here. I know they have 'religious bodies', and writers, too, I believe. I suppose we're writers, in a way."

"Yes, we might call ourselves that." Viola had taken out her lipstick and was applying it almost savagely, as if she were determined to make herself look as unlike somebody who worked on the dustier fringes of the academic world as possible.

Dulcie gazed fascinated at the result, but the brilliant coral-coloured mouth in the sallow face certainly looked bizarre and striking, and made her slightly dissatisfied with her own careful "natural" make-up.

"It's an unusual idea having a conference of people like us," said Dulcie. "Do we all correct proofs, make bibliographies and indexes, and do all the rather humdrum thankless tasks for people more brilliant than ourselves?"

She seemed to dwell on the words almost with relish, Viola thought, as if she were determined to create an impression of the utmost dreariness.

"Oh, my life isn't at all like that," she said quickly. "I've been doing research of my own and I've already started a novel. I've really come here because I know one of the lecturers and . . ."

She hesitated, the feeling of dismay rising up in her again, for surely it had been a mistake to come. This worthy Miss Mainwaring, whom one could just imagine doing all the dreary things she had described, was not, however, the kind of person in whom she would dream of confiding.

"I just do odd jobs and make indexes," said Dulcie cheerfully. "I found it better to work at home when my mother was ill, and I haven't really thought of taking a full-time job since she died."

A bell began to toll, which seemed to Viola to add to the gloomy feeling Dulcie had given her.

"That must be dinner," she said. "Shall we go down?" It would surely be possible to shake her off some time during the evening.[2]

---

2. *No Fond Return of Love,* by Barbara Pym (Virago Books, 2009), pp3–4.

If anything, Pym's prose is terser than Orwell's. It has even fewer adjectives, and every one that is used adds something significant to the description. Viola's mouth is "coral-coloured" and her face "sallow": the originality of the first adjective contrasts with the familiarity of the second and creates a vivid paradox in the mind of the reader. The understatement of the prose lends it a tension that would be hard to achieve by overstatement or hyperbole. Nothing distracts the attention of the reader from the intentions of the writer in conveying the sense of a scene. The paragraphing is logical and perfectly structured. Sentences, again, are short. The dialogue is natural and in keeping with the concision of the narrative. In its clarity, the prose quickly reveals much about the two women. It is a model piece of novel-writing. There is a consistent pace to the story. Pym uses devices such as paradox and meiosis to create interest and vividness. Tone, rather than adjectives, creates an impression. The apparent ordinariness of the context in which the women meet – at an academic conference in a Derbyshire boarding school – is offset by the excellence of the style, ensuring the involvement of the reader in the story.

My final saint is Enoch Powell. Whatever the occasional controversy of Powell's politics, he was a superb stylist. A former classics professor and a first-class textual critic, he understood the need to judge every word not just in terms of its meaning, but in terms of its utility. Powell's skill with words made him a natural journalist, and he plied that trade in publications of a similar quality to those in which Orwell wrote: and to similar effect. In this extract, Powell is not (as Orwell was in his) being descriptive; he is being polemical.

If one's object in composing a piece of prose is to persuade the reader of the truth of a contention, the structure of the argument one uses in advancing one's case will be crucial to one's ability to succeed. My practical criticism tutor at Cambridge, Sidney Bolt, gave a master class in this to me and a handful of fellow undergraduates 30 years ago that remains perhaps the most memorable piece of teaching I ever experienced. He used as his text not a speech by Demosthenes or Cicero, but an article by Powell (of whom, coincidentally, I would nearly 20 years later write the biography), published in *The Times* in 1974, shortly after Powell had refused to contest the first election of that year. Bolt showed us how Powell, drawing on his experience as a formidable classicist, had used the established form of classical argument to justify his actions in this magazine article.

Bolt showed how the piece was divided into nine sections, each of which adopted a different approach to the subject matter, and by incremental stages developed the main points Powell wished to make. This was not simply to explain himself to his large constituency of supporters throughout Britain who had been unable to grasp his reasons for standing down from the Commons. It was also to warn that democracy itself was under threat if political leaders did not improve their attitude towards those who gave them their mandate. One lesson, not only of good rhetoric but also of good journalism and indeed of persuasive writing in any form, is to do more than state the obvious. In Powell's argument, this sting in the tail is but one of the ways that he uses the structure of his piece to give more evidence, or more rhetorical force, to his contentions in each of the separate sections of that structure.

I reprint the piece in full below: not as it appeared in *The Times* but broken up in Bolt's scheme, with the title and nature of each section explained. Most analyses of classical argument admit to only five parts in the structure, not the nine that Bolt outlined: the introduction, the narration, the confirmation, the refutation and the conclusion. As will be seen from Bolt's structure, he subdivides some of these.

For anyone trying to write a powerful argument, the dissection of the structure may be helpful in pointing a writer towards a structure of his own. It is not enough to ensure the argument is successful: that will depend on its logic, its evidence and the excellence of the style of the writer or speaker. Also, it may be of interest to those who read polemics to see how far, if at all, the polemicist has chosen to proceed according to the map drawn up by Greek rhetoricians two and a half millennia ago.

The article begins with the **Exordium,** or formal introduction. As well as introducing the subject matter to the reader, it also enables the writer to convey something of his own personality and tone of voice. Powell does this with a quotation from Horace and a dash of humour at the expense of the profession he himself had followed for the preceding quarter-century. The introduction is about first impressions: it is the writer's opportunity to get his readers on his side from the first few words, before sharing with them his basic thesis – in this case, that Parliament and the democratic process of which it stands as the pinnacle have been undermined by recent events:

> According to the poet Horace, the mark of a wise man is "not to be surprised by anything". If there is any class of person who should aim at that qualification, it is the politician. At least, he should endeavour not to be seen to be surprised at anything. I suppose I ought not, therefore, to admit to having been taken aback by certain features of the late election. Still, they seem to me to be so disquieting in themselves that one's surprise is better not concealed.
>
> Public scepticism about parties, politics and politicians is neither new nor necessarily unhealthy, but the assumption so widely, even unquestioningly prevalent now, that any correspondence between the proclaimed intentions and policies of political parties and their actions in office cannot, and perhaps even should not, be expected, is certainly unhealthy; for, if accepted, it reduces elections and Parliament to a charade.

Then comes the **Narratio.** This is where the polemicist provides the initial evidence supporting his contention. Powell tells the story of how the government of which he had been a notional supporter at the 1970 election had, in 1972, effected a U-turn on one of its most fundamental policies, namely its opposition to the statutory control of wages and salaries. He reminds his readers how he had questioned the Prime Minister responsible, Edward Heath, about this, and how he had been given short shrift in response:

> In November 1972, when the Conservative government introduced that very policy of statutory control of wages which at the 1970 election it renounced and repudiated in the most thorough manner, I asked the then Prime Minister in the House of Commons: "Does my right honourable friend not know that it is fatal for any government or party or person to seek to govern in direct opposition to the principles on which they were entrusted with the right to govern?" I was immediately told by both low and high that this is just what governments do do, and good luck to them if it works out.

This statement of facts then leads into Powell's main point, the **Propositio,** which he precedes with an arresting paradox:

> As it happened, the predictable and predicted contradictions of statutory wage control were precisely the occasion and cause of Mr Heath's downfall. But that is not my point. My point is that the reversal, despite having proved manifestly disastrous, was not called into question.

This requires further discussion. Powell recalls the further paradox of his having been attacked for protesting at this breach of faith, and how his own motives were impugned. He develops the factual background in an **Amplificatio** after which he proceeds to give the reader a foretaste of the main conclusion that he will reach. By the end of this section, which is by way of the confirmation section described by standard rhetoricians, Powell has presented further evidence for his thesis.

So little surprising or reprehensible was it considered to reverse diametrically the most specific of commitments, that for a Conservative member of Parliament who had shared in that commitment to draw attention to the reversal, and to attack and denounce it, was treated as something that could only be accounted for in terms of personal rancour and vindictiveness.

What is more, it was universally expected (so far as I could tell) that, come an election, the same member would find no problem in presenting himself to the electors as the official candidate of a party seeking support and approval for the actual policies he had consistently denounced. To decline to do so was found so paradoxical and quixotic that it had to be supposed a subtle and tortuous machination for self-advancement.

As somebody once inquired in a different context, "What sort of people do they think we are?" If the public really expects parties to invert without shame or apology the principles on which they have gained power, and politicians to seek re-election on the opposite arguments to those on which they have spoken and voted in the last House, then obviously neither Parliament nor political party can provide the electors with the means to guide and judge the government of their country; for unless a broad correspondence is assumed and enforced between profession and performance, all links in the chain of democratic responsibility are snapped.

This argument has a further aspect, and Powell develops it briefly in a **Divisio**:

This is something much deadlier than the time-worn aphorism that all parties are the same under the skin. No doubt impartial circumstance, and the natural desire to carry as broad a measure of public support as possible, do cause, and always will cause, a tendency for parties to move in office towards their opponents rather than away from them. That does not deprive the electorate of an effective voice; but the assumption that policies not merely can, but usually will, be inverted does do so. At this last election it produced an alarming consequence.

Powell is already trying to anticipate the arguments of his opponents, and this leads quite naturally into the **Refutatio**. In this section he looks further at views that his opponents hold, but seeks to show that his way is the correct way:

I am not concerned here with the merits of the question of Britain and the EEC, but I take it as a fact that a large number of electors regard the present British membership of the Community as an issue either more important than all others, or one of the most important. That is a view with which those who favour membership must agree no less strongly than those who oppose it.

At this election nobody reading the manifestos of the Conservative and Labour parties, even disregarding the speeches and votes of the last Parliament, could doubt that the issue was being placed before the electors, and in the only form in which they can decide it, namely, a choice between parties. Any elector, therefore, whose opinion in that issue conflicted with the professions of the party he would otherwise support, faced a painful, but real, decision: what matters most? The right and the opportunity to take that decision were effectively removed from the electorate by the assumption that no credence could be given to any assertion, however emphatic and explicit, of any party at a General Election. "They do not mean it", said the electors, "therefore we have no choice."

Powell's **Confirmatio,** the clinching evidence of his thesis, comes after his refutation rather than before it:

> The consequent divorce of party from policy reduces party to faction. Support of a political party becomes equivalent to support of a favourite football team. This explains the paradoxical accusation of "disloyalty" against anyone who invites the electorate to vote on policies, and the cries of angry or agonized astonishment when a member of Parliament, personally elected upon a certain policy, who has maintained it by voice and vote in the House of Commons, proclaiming it to be in his opinion (right or wrong) of overriding importance, advises those electors who agree with him to vote accordingly when their first opportunity comes at a General Election.

Powell's conclusion is structured in two short but distinct parts. The first is his **Peroratio,** where he strives for a rousing end by use of a colourful classical allusion, and one laced with paradox:

> In the sanguinary riots of Byzantium, no doubt "loyalty" to the Greens or Blues was the highest virtue. The issue, however, was not the government of the country but the outcome of a chariot race, nor was the process parliamentary democracy.

He then ends with an **Apophthegm**, which may be regarded as the intellectual version of the extended sound bite: it is the perfect conclusion, because it sums the argument up by linking back to the problem outlined in the introduction, and does so in a self-contained statement of opinion that seems made for a dictionary of quotations:

> When the connection of policy with party is assumed to be spurious or reversible, parliamentary politics sink to the level of triviality, and

men will begin to look for other ways to influence or control the nation's affairs.[3]

The conclusion, as well as summing up the consistent theme of the piece, will also leave the reader with something to think about: in this case, Powell's unspoken fear that the British people would find a means other than the ballot box to change their governments, since the governments themselves had shown democracy such disrespect. Powell himself told me, some years later, that when writing a piece such as this he believed the mark of a sound conclusion was that it could serve almost as well as the introduction. This article is no exception.

3. J Enoch Powell, *The Times*, 11 March 1974.

Appendix I
The right address

If you are writing about people of what the Victorians used to call rank, or about anyone in the Armed Forces, the church or academia, it is not a matter of snobbery to use their correct titles. It is good manners, and it shows an intelligent understanding of the importance of being accurate in use of nomenclature. Old countries and old cultures such as ours, like several others in Europe, have these feudal relics as an inevitable part of their history. This chapter will deal briskly with how to write to and about the royal family, aristocracy, baronetage and knightage; the clergy; the Army, Royal Navy and Royal Air Force; and academic titles. Any piece of prose writing that includes a reference to any such people is immediately devalued if that reference is wrong: so knowing the correct way to refer to them is every bit as important as mastering grammar and the true meaning of words.

The greatest problem that people seem to encounter when having to use a title is with forenames. We say Mr John Smith, or Miss Mary Smith, so why shouldn't we say Lord John Smith, or Lady Mary Smith, if they have these titles and these forenames? Convention dictates that there are very good reasons why we should not. The conventions may appear to be confusing but they are, rather like English grammar, entirely logical and designed to avoid ambiguities.

Lords and Ladies

The problem often arises when writing about politicians who have been ennobled. John Smith may have been in the public eye for decades as a prominent back-bencher, then as a junior minister, and finally in the cabinet. All through that time he was plain John Smith. However, when the time comes for him to be sacked, and the grateful nation he has served shows its thanks by having him ennobled, the problems begin. Journalists who have written about him for years will find it hard to call him Lord Smith. Who is Lord Smith? They feel that if they call him Lord John Smith everybody will know that he is the politician formerly known as John Smith who, having received a peerage, is now a Lord. So calling him Lord John Smith makes the point that (a) he is the man we all knew as John Smith and (b) he is a Lord. Maybe it does; but it is wrong.

The use of the title *Lord* with a Christian name and surname is correct only if it refers to the younger son of a duke or a marquess. The heir to the dukedom or marquessate – the only, elder or eldest son – will usually use his father's second title by courtesy as his own. For example: the Duke of Wellington's heir is the Marquess of Douro. Younger sons take the family name (in the case of the Duke of Wellington, Wellesley) and precede it with the title *Lord* and their forename – for example, Lord John Wellesley. So Lord John Smith is correct only if Lord John is the younger son of a duke or marquess whose family name is Smith. If, as in the case of most ennoblements, John Smith's father was Mr Smith, and his mother was not a duchess or a marchioness in her own right, when he takes his peerage his style becomes Lord Smith. Smith being a common name, there may be three or four of them alive. To differentiate the Lords Smith from each other the College of Arms will have insisted, at the creation of the second and any subsequent Smith peerage, on each having a territorial suffix that must be used to avoid confusion. So there may be Lord Smith of Brighton, Lord Smith of Blackpool and Lord Smith of Bournemouth. If writing about them, the full title need be used only in the first instance; unless one is writing about two or three of them in the same piece of prose, in which case their territorial suffixes must be retained in order to avoid confusion.

The five ranks in the English, Scottish, Irish and United Kingdom peerages are (in descending order) duke, marquess, earl, viscount and baron. The Duke of Anywhere is always called by that title. In writing about a marquess, earl or viscount, use his rank first – for example, the Earl of Anywhere, or Viscount Anywhere – and then in any subsequent mention call him Lord Anywhere. Barons are only called that if they happen to be foreigners. A man may be raised to the peerage as Baron Smith of Brighton, but he will be called Lord Smith of Brighton.

Women operate in a similar, but not identical, fashion. Any daughter of a duke, marquess or (here is a difference) an earl styles herself Lady Mary Smith, for example. If she marries Mr John Brown she may call herself Lady Mary Brown. She may do likewise if she marries Sir John Brown, or she may choose to call herself Lady Brown. If she marries into the peerage she is likely to use her husband's rank and become Lady Brown (if her husband is a baron), Viscountess Brown, the Countess of Margate, the Marchioness of Margate or the Duchess of Margate. If she is a marchioness, a countess or a viscountess, use her title in full the first time – as with her husband – and subsequently call her Lady Anywhere. The Duchess of Anywhere is at a second mention "the Duchess". Lord Smith's wife is Lady Smith, unless she is the daughter of a duke, marquess or earl, in which case she may correctly choose to style herself Lady Mary Smith. If Mary Smith marries Lord John Brown, the younger son of a duke or a marquess, she becomes Lady John Brown, or Lady John at subsequent mentions.

Life peeresses are always baronesses (though that is not compulsory; there is nothing in law to prevent a life peeress, or a life peer for that matter, being given any other rank in the peerage). Unlike lords who are barons but are not referred to as such, baronesses are. So if Mary Smith, after a lifetime of devoted public service, receives a life peerage and becomes Baroness Smith of Brighton, that is how we would refer to her in the first instance. Subsequently she would be Lady Smith. She is never Lady Mary Smith.

The children of a peer or of a peeress in her own right who do not have a title by courtesy may style themselves "the Honourable". This should be used, however, only when addressing envelopes to such people, or on the front cover of the order of service for their wedding or funeral, and then abbreviated to "Hon".

The widow of a peer may style herself "the Dowager Duchess of Anywhere" or "the Dowager Countess" to avoid confusion with her daughter-in-law, who will on the death of the Dowager's husband have become the Duchess or the Countess. Sometimes she may choose to be known as "Mary, Duchess of Anywhere", though this is a style often preferred by divorced peeresses who wish to keep using their ex-husband's title.

European titles obey few of these rules, and are best treated with circumspection. Continental aristocracies include barons, counts, margraves and grand dukes, and one or two surviving archdukes. None of those titles is ever used as the form of address of a British peer.

Baronets and knights

Baronets are not knights, even though they share the same title of *Sir*. Baronets are baronets, and their titles are heritable. Sir John Smith, 4th Bt., on his death may be succeeded by his son Charles, who becomes Sir Charles Smith, 5th Bt. His wife is Lady Smith, unless she is the daughter of a duke, a marquess or an earl, in which case she may choose to be styled Lady Mary Smith. There are many orders of knighthood in Britain (the Garter, the Thistle, St Michael and St George, the Royal Victorian Order, the Order of the British Empire and plain old Knights Bachelor) but what they all have in common is that the title dies with the holder. The wife of a knight is Lady Smith, with the exceptions already noted for the wife of a baronet.

The judiciary

A Justice of the Supreme Court (formed in 2009 to replace the House of Lords as the highest court in the land) is a life peer and is styled Lord Smith. An appeal court judge is usually a knight or a dame. Therefore he or she will be styled Lord Justice Smith or Lady Justice Smith and will be Sir John Smith or Dame Mary Smith. A high court judge is a knight or a dame. He or she will be styled Mr Justice Smith or Mrs Justice Smith (irrespective of whether she is married). Should there be more than one high court judge with the name of Smith, the forename will also be used to distinguish them: so there may be Mr Justice John Smith and Mr Justice George Smith (this applies to Lords Justices of Appeal too, who would be known as Lord Justice John Smith, etc). A judge of the Crown Court is His Honour Judge Smith, or Her Honour Judge Smith. They will not usually be knighted or given a damehood. If they are Queen's Counsel they may use the letters *QC* after their names: higher judges do not do this.

Justices of the Supreme Court and Lords Justices of Appeal are also Privy Counsellors: their title of *Rt Hon* would be used only in formal documents or when addressing them on envelopes. Note that the plural of Lord Justice is Lords Justices.

The Armed Forces

Service ranks are self-explanatory and seem to cause trouble only when interfered with by other titles. Officers reaching the rank of Lieutenant-General are usually knighted, at which point Major-General John Smith becomes Lieutenant-General Sir John Smith. Some senior generals receive peerages, at which point General Sir John Smith becomes General Lord Smith. The same applies to the two other services – Air Marshal Sir John Smith, Admiral Lord Smith and so on. Chaplains and padres would be styled Major the Reverend John Smith, or Squadron Leader the Reverend John Smith. In civilian life only officers of field rank or above would normally continue to use their military titles – though it is rare these days for anyone below the very highest ranks, who technically never retire, to do so. Field rank begins with majors, though captains holding an adjutant's appointment qualify. Should you be asked to address, or to write to, any civilian as Lieutenant Smith he is certainly an impostor of some sort, and you would be well advised to call the police.

Other titles

There are relatively few pitfalls when it comes to using titles connected with religion, the Armed Forces or academia. One of the most common is when referring to clergymen (or, increasingly these days, clergywomen). The Reverend John Smith or the Reverend Mary Smith is correct. The Reverend Smith is not. His or her Christian name, or rank, is required: so the Reverend Mr Smith, or the Reverend Miss Smith, or the Reverend Dr Smith will do. The Reverend Smith is the product of that most God-fearing of countries, America, but it is an abomination here. We should no more write Reverend Smith than we should Sir Smith. Most members of the episcopate are doctors of divinity, and it is quite correct to refer to the Archbishop of Canterbury or the Bishop of Bath and Wells in the first instance, but to call them Dr Smith subsequently.

The title *Dr* itself can bring all sorts of difficulties. Not all medical practitioners are so termed. Members of the Royal College of Surgeons and certain other specialists style themselves *Mr*. In teaching hospitals some of the more senior medical men may be neither *Dr* nor *Mr* but *Professor*. Should their distinction have been marked also by a knighthood, or even a peerage, their title of chivalry or nobility immediately precedes their name: so it would be Dr Sir John Smith, or Professor Lord Smith. A surgeon who was knighted or ennobled would, obviously, stop using the honorific *Mr*. Most people who hold doctorates of philosophy, science, music, letters, laws or divinity would use the title only in a relevant context: when in a university or some similar academic position or, in the case of doctors of divinity, while in the cloth. Composers or conductors with doctorates of music used to style themselves Dr Vaughan Williams or Dr Sargent, but this has fallen out of fashion. Those who hold only honorary doctorates of any description would never normally use the title. In America anyone with a doctorate of almost any description and of any value will inevitably style himself *Dr*. This is not necessarily a mark of charlatanry so much as a sign of that society's regard for the benefits of erudition.

Writing letters

Should you find in a second-hand bookshop an etiquette guide from the period before 1939 you will find in it elaborate instructions on how to write a letter to a person of rank. Obsequiousness both in the form of address and in the valediction was the fundamental rule. Letters to the Sovereign were supposed to begin "May it please Your Majesty" and to end with the confirmation that the writer remained "Your Majesty's most humble and obedient servant", something unlikely to be true and even less likely to be proved true. As one went further down the social scale the degree of deference decreased, but not too markedly. Letters to peers below the rank of duke and to bishops would begin "My Lord". At the very bottom of the scale, a letter to an untitled man (other than a tradesman) with whom one was unacquainted would begin "Dear Sir", to a woman "Dear Madam". The envelope for the former would be addressed to John Smith Esq (irrespective of whether Mr Smith met the criteria for the appellation *esquire*); the envelope addressed to a married woman at her home (as opposed to her business) address would say "Mrs John Smith". A few people cling to these vestiges of formality today, and they are not wrong to do so. For most people, however, this is an age of greater informality, with deference in decline, and a woman no longer identified principally by the name of her husband; and the way we write letters often reflects that.

To start with the Sovereign: she should be addressed simply as "Madam" at the start of any letter, which should conclude with the equally simple "Yours faithfully". Her sons should be addressed as "Sir" and her daughter as "Madam"; this rule holds good for all those bearing the style and title of Royal Highness. A non-royal duke can be addressed as "Dear Duke"; all other peers, from marquess downwards, as "Dear Lord Smith"; and these letters should end "Yours sincerely". Write to the younger son of a duke or a marquess as "Dear Lord John", to his wife as "Dear Lady John", and to the daughter of earls and above as "Dear Lady Jane". Baronets, knights and their wives should be addressed as "Dear Sir John" or "Dear Lady Smith", the letters ending "Yours sincerely". Write to "Dear Archbishop", "Dear Bishop" or "Dear

Dean", or to "Dear Dr Smith" as you choose. Military ranks and academic titles must always take a surname, so write "Dear General Smith", "Dear Admiral Smith", "Dear Professor Smith" or "Dear Dr Smith".

With the abbreviation *Esq*, be sure not to use it with any other title. One occasionally sees the solecism "Mr John Smith Esq"; and anyone who is a knight, baronet, peer or clergyman, or holds any rank in the Armed Forces or any academic distinction that confers the title of doctor or professor, is not by definition an esquire. The abbreviation *Esq* must precede any letters following the surname: so it is John Smith Esq, FRCO, not John Smith FRCO, Esq. On the question of envelopes, they are the only places where the honorific "the Honourable" (abbreviated to *Hon*) should be used for the son of an earl (if he is not the elder son with a courtesy title) and the children of viscounts and barons, as in "Hon John Smith" or "Hon Mary Smith". As the late Hugh Massingberd, the distinguished genealogist, used to put it, the title *Hon* was something about which "only the postman knows".

Appendix II
Editorial matters

Dear Sir

Addressing letters, which I have dealt with in Appendix I, is but one part of the art of writing letters: what goes in the body of the text will depend on what sort of letter it is, what sort of person is going to receive it, and what sort of message it needs to convey. The points about good style that I have outlined here hold good for any letter-writing. Indeed, in his lapidary *The Complete Plain Words*, Sir Ernest Gowers made many of the same points: brevity, short sentences and an effect of clarity were all highly desirable. Gowers's work was directed to civil servants or those communicating with others predominantly on business; and there are clearly differences in approach to be noted in conducting private correspondence. One is likely to find oneself sending four sorts of communication these days: the business letter on behalf of one's employer, the business letter on behalf of oneself, the private letter to a friend or relation and the informal business email such as to a colleague. The first three categories may well also be emails these days.

Clearly, private correspondence can be highly informal depending upon the degree of intimacy and familiarity between the correspondents; this should not, though, be an excuse for bad grammar or obscurity caused by choice of words. Business letters demand strict formality: when sent on behalf of a company they create a distinct impression of what sort of company it is, and individuals too can do themselves no favours by sending a badly-crafted letter to a government agency or a private business with whom they are having dealings. This is especially true if applying for jobs, or making some other request whose likelihood of being granted depends to some extent on the character of the applicant.

As well as making the usual points that I have already rehearsed, Gowers makes some further points specific to business letter-writing that I must acknowledge here. If you are replying to a query, make sure you understand exactly what you are being asked (this in itself will be a safeguard against verbosity). "Begin by answering his question" is also good advice, as is "confine yourself to the facts of the case".[1] Gowers also warns his readers against formality, but he means what we would probably better term now "impersonality"; he urges officials in particular to be "friendly" towards their correspondents. He would not have countenanced any informality in the sense of slang or sloppy grammar, and neither should the rest of us.

Dealing with numbers

In writing prose one often has to deal with numbers, dates and statistics. It is important to be consistent, and following simple rules will help to do this. In newspapers, numbers from one to nine are usually written as words, but 10 and above are given as numbers. In books as opposed to newspapers it is often the case that numbers up to ninety-nine are written out in full, with numbers used for 100 and above. In both cases words are used again for round figures such as one million, two million, 27 million, one billion, 16 billion, 40 trillion. A billion used to be a million million; it is now 1,000 million. A trillion is 1,000 billion. As the national

1. *The Complete Plain Words*, pp29–30.

debt rises, it is important to have a grasp of these stratospheric terms. For unround numbers, only figures will do – so one has to write 3,978,665 rather than three million, nine hundred and seventy-eight thousand, six hundred and sixty-five. At the lower end, make a rule and stick to it about where to stop using words and start using numbers.

When it comes to writing dates I prefer to write 3 September 1939 rather than 3rd September 1939, because the abbreviation seems unnecessary. And I prefer either form to September 3 1939, because it seems better to separate the two numbers by the word. In describing a period between two dates, use the following formula: "from 1939 to 1945" or "from 4 August to 19 September" rather than put a dash between the two dates.

Proper names

There are English conventions for the spelling of foreign words, but that is the problem: there is usually more than one convention. When writing geographical names it used to be the case that one simply took an authoritative atlas, such as *The Times*'s, and copied its spelling. However, some today would question even that. There still are many accepted English spellings for European cities that the locals call something completely different: no English writer would dream of writing *Firenze* or *Wien* for *Florence* or *Vienna*. However, the spelling of some French towns has become gallicised in recent years – we now write *Lyon* and *Marseille* whereas it used to be *Lyons* and *Marseilles*. This must be attributable to greater familiarity with that culture, both through travel and language; I start to hear Italophiles talk of *Torino*, but I doubt *Turin* will be displaced just yet.

There are also political considerations when it comes to using names. Where a place name has changed by general consent it becomes absurd or even offensive to use the old style: no-one would call Zimbabwe *Rhodesia* now, or Sri Lanka *Ceylon*. However, where the name change has not occurred by consent a political point may just as easily be made by sticking to the old style: many people still say *Burma* and not *Myanmar* to signal their disapproval of the tyrannical regime there. Indian place names are a particular problem: the politically-correct world likes to say *Mumbai*, which is found patronising by tens of millions of Indians who are quite happy still calling it *Bombay*; *Bollywood* has yet to become *Mullywood*. Such usages must for the moment be matters of taste, but preferably of informed taste.

If there is doubt about a proper name, the *Oxford English Dictionary* or its *Concise* version often has a ruling, and I tend to follow those. The alternative is to look on Google and see which spelling of a particular word has the greater currency: *Habsburg* (at time of writing) has 1,800,000 entries, *Hapsburg* just 361,000 (with the helpful question "did you mean *Habsburg*?" as a superscription). One may then draw one's own conclusions.

Capitalisation

The Victorians used to capitalise almost every name they could find, almost to the extent of German practice (every German noun begins with a capital letter). We are now moving towards the French practice, in which so few words begin with capital letters that it comes as rather a shock to find one, other than at the beginning of a sentence, that does. Individual publications and publishers make their own rules about this. It is probably best, if one has to make up one's own mind about it, to make a logical rule and stick to it. Of choice, I would capitalise according to the following scheme.

In one's own country it should be the Queen, the President,

the Prime Minister, the Chancellor of the Exchequer. Abroad it should be the Queen of Spain and the President of the United States as heads of state: but the French prime minister, the German finance minister, and so on. This means no disrespect, but simply avoids clutter. Similarly, do not bother to capitalise titles such as the shadow secretary of state, the chief executive of Tesco, the chairman of Lloyd's – unless you happen to be working for any of those institutions and house style dictates it.

For other titles, I would say in the first instance the Earl of Essex and thereafter the Earl, and the Archbishop of Canterbury and thereafter the Archbishop; but it would be an earl, an archbishop, and so on. Capitalise institutions at home and abroad because they are proper names.

Abbreviations

Full points between the letters of abbreviations are typographically ugly and should be avoided: so write BBC, ITV, the MCC and the NHS. If an abbreviation is as well known as any of those four you probably don't need to write it out in full the first time you use it. If there is any doubt that your reader or readers might not know what the abbreviation means, write it out in full the first time and use the abbreviation subsequently: so the International Monetary Fund, and then the IMF.

Acronyms are abbreviations that appear to be a word of their own. Most of them are capitalised by their initial letter only – Aids, Unesco, Nato and so on. Some are now so familiar that they have lost their initial capital and become ordinary nouns – such as radar, for example. Some writers capitalise all the letters of acronyms, but this can look cluttered.

Italics

I have dealt with the question of italicisation earlier, but for the avoidance of doubt: italicise the titles of books, films, newspapers, magazines, paintings and poems known by their titles; poems known by their first lines may be given in single quotation marks. So it would be *Paradise Lost* but 'Say not the struggle naught availeth'. Also italicise foreign words and phrases that have not passed into common English usage (and, if they are German nouns, give them an initial capital letter): so write *mauvais quart d'heure* but panache, or *Weltanschauung* but angst or blitzkrieg.

Glossary

Alliteration is where words that follow each other begin with the same letter or sound: "Peter Piper picked a peck of pickled pepper" is an extreme example, "sweet sessions of silent thought" is less so.

Allusion used to mean wordplay or a pun. It is now the term given to an indirect reference in one piece of writing to another, often in the form of disguised quotation. When someone says, on going to bed, that he is going "to the land of Nod", he is alluding to the Bible – whether he knows it or not.

Anacoluthon is the use of two or more inconsistent constructions in the same sentence. Shakespeare used this from time to time as a stylistic device, such as in King Lear's remark that "I will have such revenges on you both, That all the world shall – I will do such things...". Others perpetrate anacolutha by accident, through ignorance, creating a sense of grammatical incoherence.

Anaphora is the repetition of the same word or phrase in successive clauses: "We shall fight on the beaches, we shall fight on the landing grounds, we shall fight in the fields and in the streets...".

Antithesis is an opposition or contrast of ideas presented in successive clauses or sentences: "as I became richer, my brother became poorer".

Antonym is a word that is the exact opposite of another: *dead* is the antonym of *alive*; *antonym* is the antonym of *synonym*.

Apophthegm is a pithy saying that embodies an important truth in a few words, and which may often be used to clinch an argument; examples are "the wages of sin is death", Carlyle's "speech is silvern: silence is golden" or the same author's "the history of the world is but the biography of great men".

Aposiopesis is from the Greek for "falling silent": it is when something is deliberately left unsaid, either because the speaker is so overcome with emotion, or because he wishes to create an effect by leaving the interpretation or completion of a thought to the reader or listener. It is often represented in writing by the punctuation … .

Apostrophe has a rhetorical meaning that is unrelated to the use of the term for a punctuation mark. It means an exclamatory remark addressed to some specific persons, whether present or not. Ozymandias's "Look on my works, ye Mighty, and despair!" is apostrophic.

Asyndeton means an absence of conjunctions: such as in "wee, sleekit, cow'rin, tim'rous beastie!"

Bathos is anti-climax. "He came; he saw; he had a cup of tea" is bathetic.

Catachresis is an improper use of words, notably the application of a term to something to which it does not properly apply; it is well-used to describe the perversion of a metaphor. To describe someone as *prevaricating* when in fact he is *procrastinating* is catachrestic.

Epigram is a pointed saying, usually witty, and often but not exclusively uttered in memoriam. Milton's "they shall read this clearly in thy charge:/New presbyter is but old priest writ large" is epigrammatic.

Hyperbaton is a phrase in which the normal order of words is inverted, for the sake of emphasis: "Much have I travelled in the realms of gold/And many goodly states and kingdoms seen…".

Hyperbole is an exaggerated statement, designed for effect and not to be taken literally: "I shall kill that boy when I find him".

Irony uses words to mean something opposite to what they appear to express. If a child does something stupid and is told what a clever boy he is, that is irony: its relations with ridicule and sarcasm are often, but not inevitably, close.

Litotes is a device by which a quality is expressed by negating its opposite: "it was not a pretty sight".

Meiosis is understatement, or the representation of something as less than it really is. It is sometimes confused with litotes. "Shakespeare was a competent playwright" is meiotic.

Metaphor is the means by which a word or phrase that literally means something specific is applied to a thing, person or concept to which it does not literally relate. "We are faced by a sea of troubles" is metaphorical.

Metonym is a word used as a symbol for an idea, institution or concept: *Whitehall* is a metonym for the apparatus of government in Britain; *Fleet Street* a metonym for the press; *Carey Street* for bankruptcy.

Neologism is the minting of new words: all words were neologistic once.

Onomatopoeia is when a word sounds like the sound it represents: *tweet*, *bang*, *cuckoo* and *woof* are all onomatopoeic.

Orthography means the correct spelling.

Oxymoron is a concise contradiction. *Bitter-sweet* is the most famous example, but also the French *jolie-laide*, to describe a woman who is both pretty and plain.

Paradox describes a statement that has an apparently contradictory conclusion, but which turns out to be true. "He swam every day; went for a run before dinner; ate only organic foods; neither smoked nor drank; but died before he was 50" is paradoxical.

Parody is the humorous imitation of another work, usually for satirical purposes. In *Ulysses*, for example, Joyce parodies the language of advertising in one of the episodes: and much else in other parts of the book.

Pleonasm is one of the enemies of good writing that this book seeks to defeat. It is the use of more words in an expression than are needed to convey its meaning.

Polemic is a controversial argument couched in strong terms, often taking the form of a verbal attack on a person, an institution or a doctrine.

Polysyndeton is the use of many conjunctions, or perhaps the same conjunction many times, to create an effect: "And Adam gave names to all cattle, and to the fowl of the air, and to every beast of the field…".

Satire is the process of holding up people, institutions, customs, follies or vices to ridicule, often by use of some of the other devices in this list – notably parody, hyperbole, meiosis, catachresis and paradox.

Simile is the comparison of one thing with another: "My love is like a red, red rose…'.

Solecism is another enemy that this book sets out to defeat: it is a violation of the rules of grammar or syntax. "He gave the present to my wife and I" is not the worst imaginable example.

Synecdoche is the representation of a whole by a part, or a part by a whole: "all *hands* on deck", or "the *guns* will number from the right".

Synonym is a word that has a similar meaning to another word: *vast* and *big*, for example, or *little* and *small*.

Syntax, according to the dictionary, is "the arrangement of words (in their appropriate forms) by which their connection and relation in a sentence are shown". This could be taken to mean the simple structure of a sentence. It also means "the department of grammar which deals with the established usages of grammatical construction and the rules deduced therefrom". *Syntax* seems synonymous with what many people call *grammar*. It is a term to be used carefully because of its being susceptible of more than one meaning.

Tautology is a stylistic fault that causes the same idea to be repeated within a single statement: "it was the only unique example in the world".

Tmesis is the separation of parts of a word, or compound word, by another word or words. In British English it is often found in slang, in usages such as *abso-bloody-lutely*, and rarely in formal writing.

Zeugma is where, typically, one verb has two objects without its being repeated; it sometimes is deployed with humorous effect, the verb being used in one instance abstractly and in the other concretely. "He lost his nerve, and then his money" or "she packed a change of clothes and a hell of a punch" exemplify this. In strict rhetorical terms, however, the use of the verb to govern in one sense a concrete and in another an abstract object is called **syllepsis**.

Bibliography

Anyone interested in language, and determined to use it correctly, should begin with a decent dictionary. The authoritative one for British English is the *Oxford English Dictionary* (2nd edition, 1989, with various supplements). It is now available through most public libraries online, or by private subscription. It has been metaphorically by my side – or literally as a window on the screen of my Macintosh – throughout writing this book.

Scarcely less important have been the standard texts of English prescriptive grammar, which were published either as a by-product of the great work on the *OED* in the early part of the last century, or as part of the surge of interest in academic philology and grammar that arose not entirely coincidentally at around the same time, or shortly thereafter. These begin with *The King's English*, by HW and FG Fowler (Oxford University Press, 1906) and HW Fowler's *A Dictionary of Modern English Usage* (OUP, 1926). Charles Talbut Onions worked with them on the *OED* and produced his *Advanced English Syntax* in 1904, which dealt with the technicalities of grammar to a far more specialised level than the Fowlers would two years later; their book is more discursive and corrective, highlighting errors and advising on how to avoid them. Onions's work is the philological equivalent of the Laws of Cricket. I have used the revision of his work by BDH Miller, published in 1971 by Routledge and Kegan Paul as *Modern English Syntax*, in which Miller incorporated notes made by Onions for a revision that had not been accomplished by the time of Onions's death in 1965. I have also consulted *Usage and Abusage* by Eric Partridge, in the 1973 Penguin edition, being a revision of a work originally published in 1947. It was nearly contemporaneous with Sir Ernest Gowers's *Plain Words: A Guide to the Use of English* (HMSO, 1948), which itself was followed by the *ABC of Plain Words* (HMSO, 1951). These were combined in 1954 as *The Complete Plain Words*, and then published by HMSO in an edition revised by Gowers's fellow mandarin Sir Bruce Fraser in 1973: I have worked from the Pelican edition of the same year. I also scoured *An ABC of English Usage*, by H A Treble and G H Vallins (Oxford, 1936).

At the more technical end of philology I consulted three books by Otto Jespersen: *Language, its Development, Nature and Origin* (George Allen and Unwin, 1922); *The Philosophy of Grammar* (George Allen and Unwin, 1924); and *Essentials of English Grammar* (George Allen and Unwin, 1933). A valuable modern perspective is to be found in *Language Change: Progress or Decay?* by Jean Aitchison (Fontana, 1981). William Empson's *Seven Types of Ambiguity* (3rd edition, Chatto and Windus, 1977) and *The Structure of Complex Words* (3rd edition, Rowman and Littlefield, 1977) help refresh the memory and the senses about the range of meaning that even the simplest of expressions may have, and why precision in choice of words is important.

To clear my thoughts on general matters pertaining to the history of the language I consulted *A Short History of English*, by Henry Cecil Wyld (John Murray, 1914); *Our Mother Tongue: A Grammar and History of the English Language*, by H M Hewitt and George Beach (University Tutorial Press, 1904); *Outlines of the History of the English Language*, by T N Toller (Cambridge University Press, 1900); *A History of the English Language*, by Albert C Baugh and Thomas Cable (Routledge and Kegan Paul, 3rd edition, 1978); and *The English Language*, by Robert Burchfield (Oxford, 1985).

Finally, three books of different degrees of pungency by men of letters about aspects of English, and how to write it: George Orwell's seminal essay *Politics and the English Language* in the collection *Why I Write* (Penguin, 2004); CS Lewis's *Studies in Words* (Cambridge University Press, 2nd edition, 1967); and Kingsley Amis's rather insolently titled *The King's English* (HarperCollins, 1997): though of the cockiness of borrowing the Fowlers' brand we must acquit Sir Kingsley, who was dead at the time, and presumably convict some marketing man.

Throughout the book I have, as readers will have noticed, cited works by various writers in using examples of their work for illustrative purposes. Where I have made exact quotations, the details of the books are to be found in the footnotes.

Index

Index